emotional memory across the adult lifespan

ESSAYS IN COGNITIVE PSYCHOLOGY

North American Editors:
Henry L. Roediger, III, *Washington University in St. Louis*
James R. Pomerantz, *Rice University*

European Editors:
Alan D. Baddeley, *University of York*
Vicki Bruce, *University of Edinburgh*
Jonathan Grainger, *Université de Provence*

Essays in Cognition is designed to meet the need for rapid publication of brief volumes in cognitive psychology. Primary topics will include perception, movement and action, attention, memory, mental representation, language and problem solving. Furthermore, the series seeks to define cognitive psychology in its broadest sense, encompassing all topics either informed by, or informing, the study of mental processes. As such, it covers a wide range of subjects including computational approaches to cognition, cognitive neuroscience, social cognition, and cognitive development, as well as areas more traditionally defined as cognitive psychology. Each volume in the series will make a conceptual contribution to the topic by reviewing and synthesizing the existing research literature, by advancing theory in the area, or by some combination of these missions. The principal aim is that authors will provide an overview of their own highly successful research program in an area. It is also expected that volumes will, to some extent, include an assessment of current knowledge and identification of possible future trends in research. Each book will be a self-contained unit supplying the advanced reader with a well-structured review of the work described and evaluated.

FORTHCOMING

Mulligan: *Implicit Memory*
Surprenant & Neath: *Principles of Memory*
Brown: *Tip-of-the-tongue Phenomenon*
Lampinen, Neuschatz, & Cling: *Psychology of Eyewitness Identification*
Worthen & Hunt: *Mnemonics for the 21st Century*

PUBLISHED

Kensinger: *Emotional Memory Across the Lifespan*
Millar: *Space and Sense*
Evans: *Hypothetical Thinking*
Gallo: *Associative Illusions of Memory*
Cowan: *Working Memory Capacity*
McNamara: *Semantic Priming*
Brown: *The Déjà Vu Experience*
Coventry & Garrod: *Saying, Seeing and Acting*
Robertson: *Space, Objects, Minds and Brains*
Cornoldi & Vecchi: *Visuo-spatial Working Memory and Individual Differences*
Sternberg, et al.: *The Creativity Conundrum*
Poletiek: *Hypothesis-testing Behaviour*
Garnham: *Mental Models and the Interpretations of Anaphora*
Evans & Over: *Rationality and Reasoning*
Engelkamp: *Memory for Actions*

For updated information about published and forthcoming titles in the *Essays in Cognition* series, please visit: **www.psypress.com/essays**

emotional memory across the adult lifespan

ELIZABETH A. KENSINGER

Psychology Press
Taylor & Francis Group

New York   London

Psychology Press
Taylor & Francis Group
270 Madison Avenue
New York, NY 10016

Psychology Press
Taylor & Francis Group
27 Church Road
Hove, East Sussex BN3 2FA

© 2009 by Taylor & Francis Group, LLC

Printed in the United States of America on acid-free paper
10 9 8 7 6 5 4 3 2 1

International Standard Book Number-13: 978-1-84169-483-2 (Hardcover)

Library of Congress Cataloging-in-Publication Data

Kensinger, Elizabeth A.
Emotional memory across the adult lifespan / Elizabeth A. Kensinger.
p. cm. -- (Essays in cognitive psychology)
Includes bibliographical references (p.   ) and indexes.
ISBN 978-1-84169-483-2 (alk. paper)
1. Memory. I. Title.

BF371.K49 2009
153.1'3--dc22   2008041019

Visit the Taylor & Francis Web site at
http://www.taylorandfrancis.com

and the Psychology Press Web site at
http://www.psypress.com

To my parents, Dale and Jeannette, and to Jon.
For all of the joyous memories.

CONTENTS

SECTION III   EMOTIONAL MEMORY IN OLDER ADULTS

PREFACE

The Greeks worshiped the goddess Mnemosyne (from whom the term *mnemonics* originated), praying to her for retention of experiences that were particularly important to them. Thus, it seems that since ancient time people have understood that not all experienced events are equally likely to be remembered. Although many factors can influence which experiences we remember and which we forget, one critical determinant is whether the experience is infused with emotion. We are much more likely to remember events with emotional importance and personal significance than we are to remember the more mundane of life's experiences. Over the past couple of decades, there has been increasing interest in understanding how emotion influences memory formation and retrieval, both at the level of behavior and at the level of the brain.

My own interest in the topic began when I was working with Alzheimer's disease patients. One woman explained how her husband had forgotten about attending the first birthday party of his granddaughter within weeks of the party's occurrence. The son of another patient expressed dismay that his mother was unable to remember that he recently had gotten married. These anecdotes spurred my desire to understand emotion's effects on healthy individuals' memories and in those with an age-related disease. At that time, there was little research examining how emotional memory changes as adults age. Over the past few years, however, research on emotional memory in older adulthood and in age-related disease has increased dramatically. This book provides a review of the recent advances in understanding emotion–memory interactions across the adult lifespan, integrating studies using behavioral, neuropsychological, and neuroimaging approaches. We are still far from having a complete picture of how emotion influences human memory, and there are many questions that remain to be answered. I hope that by pointing out some inconsistencies and gaps in the literature, this book will inspire further research into the intricacies of emotion's modulation of memory.

I have benefited from phenomenal mentors and colleagues throughout my research career. I am particularly indebted to Suzanne Corkin,

Daniel Schacter, and Anthony Wagner; each of them has played an instrumental role in guiding my thinking on the topics reviewed in this book. I owe a debt of gratitude to the members (past and present) of the Corkin, Schacter, and Wagner laboratories and to my colleagues at Boston College for creating stimulating intellectual environments in which to study emotion's modulation of memory. I thank the members of my laboratory; their scientific curiosity is a source of intellectual rejuvenation, and their excitement about emotion–memory interactions reminds me of why I started down this research path nearly a decade ago. I am particularly grateful to Jennifer Dimase, Alisha Holland, Christina Leclerc, Mara Mather, Katherine Mickley, Keely Muscatell, and Jill Waring for their feedback on earlier drafts of this book, to Donna Addis, Lisa Feldman Barrett, David Gallo, Angela Gutchess, Jessica Payne, Benton Pierce, Maya Tamir, and Robert Waldinger for helpful discussion, and to Paul Dukes, Roddy Roediger, and Lee Transue for their editorial guidance. I also thank the National Institute of Mental Health, the National Science Foundation, the American Federation for Aging Research, the Searle Scholars Program, and the Dana Foundation for supporting my research.

Elizabeth A. Kensinger
Boston College

Introduction and Background

1

Emotion, Memory, and Their Interactions

☐ Historical Perspective on Emotion– Cognition Interactions

For centuries, scholars assumed that cognition and emotion were separable. Although cognition could trigger emotional responses and emotional processing could influence cognitive thought, the two types of processes were considered to be non-overlapping and distinct (Aristotle, trans. 1991; Plato, trans. 1992). Moreover, in the instances where interactions between emotion and cognition were thought to occur, the effects were assumed to be opposing. Emotional processes were thought to hijack cognitive ones, making individuals prone to irrationality. Conversely, rational thought was believed to curtail emotional processing.

Over the past two decades, empirical evidence has forced a re-examination of these assumptions. Counter to the notion that emotion processes will always impede cognitive ones, many studies have revealed instances in which emotional engagement results in cognitive enhancement rather than cognitive decline. For example, having an emotional (or affective) response to a stimulus often aides in decision making; individuals who lack emotional reactions perform more poorly on a range of decision-making tasks than do individuals who show intact affective processing (e.g., Bechara, Damasio, & Damasio, 2000). Individuals also are better at detecting and maintaining focus on stimuli with emotional meaning (e.g., Dolan & Vuilleumier, 2003) and, as is the focus of this book, individuals often show mnemonic benefits for stimuli that are emotionally relevant.

3

Although there continues to be significant debate about how best to conceptualize emotion and cognition (e.g., Lazarus & Folkman, 1984; Neisser, 1976; Zajonc, 1984), researchers no longer can ignore the robust interactions between these processes or treat them as opposite ends of a continuum.

Indeed, interest in emotion–cognition interactions has exploded in the last few years. A literature search conducted using the National Library of Medicine's search engine revealed just over 8500 articles that included the keywords "emotion and cognition." Over half of these articles had been written in the last decade. Interest in the intersection between emotion and cognition has been far-reaching. Behavioral economics, which assumes the premise that markets operate within a framework influenced by human limitations in rationality, has forced an evaluation of how human cognition acts within an emotionally vibrant context. Affective computing within artificial intelligence and computer science has led to re-examinations of the links between intelligent thought and affective response. The examination of emotion–cognition interactions has spurred a host of cross-disciplinary fields of research (e.g., affective neuroscience, social cognitive neuroscience, neuroeconomics), yielding new insights into the behavioral and neural intersection between emotional and cognitive processes.

This book explores the influence of emotion within the cognitive domain of memory. Despite many metaphors of memory as a storage cabinet, containing files of every past event, in reality we remember only a fraction of life's experiences. A multitude of factors can influence what we remember and what we are doomed to forget, but one critical contributor is the emotional salience of the event. Events that evoke emotional reactions are more likely to be remembered than events that lack emotional importance. In this book, we examine the cognitive (thought-level) and neural (brain-level) processes that lead to effects of emotion on memory.

This book is organized in three parts. The first part (which you are now reading) presents a broad overview of emotion and memory. In order to understand the myriad interactions between emotion and memory, first it is necessary to describe how emotion and memory may be broken down into core components. Neither the term *emotion* nor the term *memory* describes a single entity. Both are umbrella terms used to describe a host of related, but distinct, processes. Thus, there is no single effect of "an emotion" on "a memory." Rather, the interactions between emotion and memory vary depending on the type of emotion assessed (e.g., whether pleasurable or aversive) and on the type of memory assessed (e.g., whether measuring short-term storage or long-term retention of information).

The second section of this book describes the effects of emotion on young adults' memories, focusing on the effects of emotion on the transient storage of information, and on the retention of information over the long term. I discuss the effects of emotion on the memory processes that we use consciously, and on the processes that guide our actions even when we are unaware of their influence. Occasionally, I describe effects of emotion on other types of cognitive processes (e.g., attention, perception) that have downstream effects on memory. For example, emotion exerts strong influences on attentive and pre-attentive processes, biasing the likelihood that individuals will detect, and will remain focused on, emotional information in the environment (reviewed by Dolan & Vuilleumier, 2003; Pessoa, 2005). Although not direct effects of emotion on memory, these influences of emotion nevertheless have significant consequences for memory performance. Information to which we attend, or about which we think deeply, will tend to be remembered better than information that grabs our attention only transiently. Throughout the chapters of Section II, I put particular emphasis on examining the extent to which memory for emotional information is supported by distinct cognitive or neural processes from those that support memory for non-emotional information. That is, does emotion enhance memory by boosting the same processes that help us to remember non-emotional information? Alternatively, is information with emotional relevance better remembered because of the engagement of entirely different processes that we do not use when remembering non-emotional information? Although it may seem contradictory, the answer to both questions may be "yes." I present evidence that individuals recruit emotion-processing regions when learning or retrieving emotional information, and that activity in these regions seems to correspond with improved memories for these experiences. However, these regions seem to exert their effect, at least in part, through modulation of the same types of processes as are recruited when individuals remember non-emotional information.

The third segment of this book discusses the interactions between emotion and memory that occur in older adults, examining how advancing age changes the processing and retention of emotional information. An influential framework for understanding age-related changes in emotional memory has described the aging process as one in which people become more focused on emotional goals and on situations that elicit feelings of well-being (Carstensen, Isaacowitz, & Charles, 1999). This section examines the extent to which the focus of older adults on emotional goals influences the types of experiences to which they attend and about which they remember. Interestingly, older adults sometimes seem to attend to positive information in the environment at the exclusion of negative information, and they often remember more positive information than younger adults (a "positivity effect" as described by Mather & Carstensen, 2005). However, there appear to be limits on this positivity effect. I describe instances in which older adults are just as likely as young adults, or even more likely, to focus on negative information in the environment and to remember negative experiences. I also present evidence that, in both young and older adults, negative information can be remembered with more detail than positive information. I pay particular attention to the cognitive processes that may lead to age-related preservation or change in emotional processing and emotional memory, with particular consideration to differences between relatively automatic processing of emotional information (which may remain fairly stable with aging) and more controlled and deliberative processing of emotional information (which may be altered with aging). See Mather (2006) for more discussion of this intriguing dissociation.

☐ What Is Emotion?

Before we proceed to examine the effects of emotion on memory, first it is necessary to talk a bit about what is meant by emotion. In 1884, William James posed the question, "What is an emotion?" Although there has been extensive discussion regarding how best to answer that question, there still is no clear consensus. *Emotion* is a term that has been used widely to connote a variety of feeling states. There is no single agreed upon definition of emotion, most likely because the term refers not to a single, discrete entity, but rather to a set of processes that include subjective feelings, cognitive appraisals, physiological reactions, and expressive actions. There continue to be significant debates about how best to characterize emotion (see Barrett, 2006; Barrett et al., 2007; Izard, 2007; Frijda & Sundararajan, 2007; and Panksepp, 2007 for recent debates regarding the construct of emotion). At the heart of these debates is the question of whether emotional experience is fractionated into discrete entities (e.g., fear, happiness) or whether emotion is better described by changes along dimensions of experience. An influential framework, and the one that I adopt throughout this book, describes emotional experiences within a two-dimensional space with axes of valence (how pleasant or unpleasant) and arousal (how excited/agitated or soothed/placated; Lang, Greenwald, Bradley, & Hamm, 1993; Lang, Bradley, & Cuthbert, 1998a, 1998b; Reisenzein, 1994; Russell, 1980; Russell & Barrett, 1999; Schlosberg, 1954). Although a lot of research examining the effects of emotion has been restricted to examining how people remember high-arousal versus low-arousal information, I describe a number of studies that have focused on understanding to what extent the effects of emotion on memory depend upon the combination of valence and arousal experienced.

Beyond how we conceptualize the fragmentation of emotional space, however, what is meant by emotion will differ depending on how it is elicited or measured. For example, if we use self-report to measure emotion, then we are examining the subjective feelings or cognitive appraisals associated with emotion. If, in contrast, we rely on physiological measurements, then we are measuring emotion as a change in the biological (but not necessarily psychological) state of the organism. Because of the influences that they can have on the meaning of emotion, it is important to describe briefly the types of research methods used to elicit and assess emotion.

Eliciting and Assessing Emotions

For quite a while, the study of emotion seemed to be an intractable topic. How could one systematically study a construct that, at its core, seemed tied to an introspective state unique to each individual? Although it is impossible to assure that, for example, my state of fear is equivalent to yours, over the past few years great strides have been made in developing standardized methods for eliciting and assessing emotions.

Often emotions are elicited through presentation of external stimuli, such as narrated film slides, colored photographs, or verbal or auditory stimuli. Researchers have compiled extensive databases of stimuli that have been rated for their emotional content as well as along other dimensions (e.g., Bradley & Lang, 1999; Lang, Bradley, & Cuthbert, 1999), making it easier for researchers to select stimuli matched on a host of variables (e.g., verbal frequency, object familiarity), thus reducing the concern that effects attributed to emotion may actually be due to differences in other non-emotion dimensions. In other cases, emotions can be elicited through internal generation of information, such as remembering emotional events, imagining emotional situations, or enacting emotional actions or postures.

Sometimes, researchers present these stimuli in close proximity to one another, with the intended result being that participants fluctuate relatively rapidly between emotional states. For example, an individual may feel pleasure upon seeing a picture of a smiling baby but may soon feel displeasure if the following picture is of an injured child. This methodology allows researchers to examine the effects of short-term fluctuations of emotional state on, for example, memory performance. In other words, are individuals better able to remember the injured child, which elicited a feeling of displeasure, than to remember the smiling baby linked with a feeling of pleasure?

In other instances, researchers are interested in how less transient changes in emotional state influence cognitive ability or they wish to investigate the effect of emotions not easily elicited by single stimuli presented in the laboratory (e.g., embarrassment, stress, anger). "Mood induction procedures" often are used to achieve these goals. These procedures range in their design. Participants may listen to music that evokes feelings of excitement or melancholy; they may be exposed to other primary reinforcers or punishers (e.g., money or food may be given or taken away from participants); they may interact with another individual (usually a confederate of the experimenter) who behaves in a way that is likely to trigger an emotional reaction; they may read a series of statements describing changes in mood while imagining the described feeling state (e.g., Velten mood induction; Velten, 1968); or they may recall prior experiences that caused them to feel a particular way. In contrast to the transient emotions that often are elicited by single stimuli, these mood induction procedures often elicit changes in affective state that last for minutes to hours, allowing researchers to examine the effects of longer-term, sustained emotional states on cognitive performance (e.g., Blaney, 1986; Isen, 1993; Niedenthal, Halberstadt, & Setterlund, 1997; Park & Banaji, 2000).

Just as there are a range of methods that are used to elicit emotion, so too are there a variety of techniques used to assess the presence or the quality of the emotion. Broadly speaking, emotions can be measured at the level of behavior (e.g., asking people to report their subjective feelings, or examining the time that it takes them to detect or classify different types of emotional stimuli) or at the level of physiology (e.g., examining people's biological responses to a stimulus or situation). Within each of these subdivisions, there are many variations in assessment, each with its own assumptions about the nature of emotion, emotion's time course, and the extent to which one's emotional state is privy to conscious awareness. For example, for behavioral assessments of emotional states, participants may be asked to rate their affective state along a scale with verbal labels (e.g., rating how much pleasure or displeasure they are feeling or how excited or calmed they are) or with visual depictions of affective states (e.g., a "Self Assessment Manikin"; Lang, 1985); they may be asked to turn a dial to indicate moment-to-moment fluctuations in their emotional state; or they may be asked to indicate how frequently they have experienced particular types of emotions within some prior time frame (e.g., Watson, Clark, & Tellegen, 1988; Feldman, 1995). Each of these measurements relies on the participant's introspection. Although that often is exactly what researchers wish to measure, at other times it may be problematic to rely on a method susceptible to biases or subjective interpretation. In these instances, researchers often have relied on participants' perception or classification of affective stimuli as a more objective way to gauge their emotional state. These studies have taken advantage of the fact that changes in affective state tend to be associated with changes in the types of information most likely to be perceived and attended. For example, individuals who are in an anxious state will be more likely to perceive negative stimuli and will show greater interference from irrelevant negative information than will individuals in a non-anxious state (Hermans, Vansteenwegen, & Eelen, 1999; Mogg, Millar, & Bradley, 2000; Ohman, Flykt, & Esteves, 2001; Ohman & Soares, 1994). These effects of emotion on information processing occur relatively automatically and without the awareness of participants (reviewed by Mathews & MacLeod, 1994; MacLeod & Mathews, 2004) and therefore can be used to deduce the degree to which individuals are experiencing a particular type of emotional state. A range of information processing tasks has been used to this end. Emotional Stroop tasks (measuring the speed and accuracy with which participants can name the color of font in which emotional and non-emotional words are written), probe reaction time tasks (assessing the time it takes participants to respond to a stimulus), implicit association tasks (determining the speed and accuracy with which participants can group items from a pleasant category together with items from a racial, gender, or age group), and affective priming tasks (measuring participants' responses to a target as a function of the concordance of the preceding prime) are among the most common (see reviews by MacLeod, 1991; Robinson, 1998; Wells & Matthews, 1994).

Although it is often the behavior of the individual that a researcher is most interested in measuring, in other instances the biology of that individual is of equal or greater interest. In these cases, researchers often turn to physiological measurements or to brain imaging. Many physiological signatures change with fluctuations in emotional state: galvanic skin conductance, heart rate, blood pressure, blood volume, and blood flow all can be altered. By measuring these fluctuations, researchers can gain an objective measure of the change in one's emotional state (see Bradley & Lang, 2000). Neural activity also changes as a function of emotional state, and examining the neural activity within particular brain regions can provide leverage for understanding individual or group differences in affective state. A couple of cautions are worth noting, however. First, although for practical reasons researchers often limit themselves to an examination of a single physiological measure, or to an examination of neural changes isolated from other behavioral or physiological measures of emotion, these measurements are best used in concert with one another. No single method is likely to capture the range of biological responses of an organism during an affective state. Results revealed from a single measure may mask or accentuate the actual changes in affective state. Moreover, physiological and neural changes need not correlate strongly with the behavioral expression of emotion. For example, as will be discussed in Section III of this book, young and older adults often give very similar ratings regarding their emotional responses to stimuli (e.g., Denburg, Buchanan, Tranel, & Adolphs, 2003; Kensinger, Brierley, Medford, Growdon, & Corkin, 2002; Kensinger, Anderson, Growdon, & Corkin, 2004). Yet, the two age groups can differ markedly in their physiological responses to those stimuli (Levenson, Carstensen, & Gottman, 1994; Levenson, Friesen, Ekman, & Carstensen, 1991; Tsai, Levenson, & Carstensen, 2000; Denburg et al., 2003). In these instances, researchers must carefully consider which measure is most relevant to their question of interest and must consider the implications of low correlations between their different measures of emotional state. Second, within the neuroimaging literature it is important to distinguish neural *correlates* of emotion (i.e., regions that tend to be active at the time that an emotion is experienced) from neural *substrates* of emotion (i.e., those processes that mediate the expression of an emotion; see Davidson [2004] and Cacioppo [2007] for further discussion). It often is assumed that if regions show changed activity based on emotional state, then those regions must be critically involved in that affective modulation. However, those two facts need not logically follow one another. Furthermore, as noted by Barrett and Wager (2006), there may be important differences between examining the probability that a brain area is active when a person is experiencing an emotion (e.g., that the amygdala is engaged when a person is afraid) and the probability that a region's activity is associated with the experience of an emotion (e.g., that a person is afraid when the amygdala is activated). Thus, there may be regions where activity *corresponds* with an emotion but does not *cause* the emotion.

By recognizing the inherent limitations of each method, research combining behavioral and physiological investigations of emotion has made great strides in understanding the affective experience. By combining neuroimaging approaches with investigations of individuals with lesions to discrete brain regions, researchers are beginning to distinguish the neural correlates of emotion from the neural substrates. Unlike neural correlates, not only should neural substrates be active during an emotional experience, but also damage to the regions should disrupt the emotional experience. Researchers also are beginning to take caution in interpreting neural activity as evidence of emotional states (e.g., there is an increasing appreciation that amygdala activity may be elicited even in situations in which no psychological feeling of emotion is present; see Anderson, Yamaguchi, Grabski, & Lacka, 2006 for further discussion).

As this section has emphasized, emotion is not a single entity, and not every researcher uses the word emotion to mean the same thing. Even within the body of research that has described emotion as an affective space created by axes of valence and arousal, there has not been consensus regarding how to examine where a person is located within this space (i.e., how positive or negative a person is feeling, and how calm or excited he or she feels). Some have relied exclusively on behavioral testing. Others have used physiological measurements such as changes in skin conductance, heart rate, or blood volume. Still others have used neuroimaging approaches. There also has not been agreement with regard as to how best to examine the effects of emotion on memory. Some researchers have focused primarily on valence differences (comparing things that are positive to things that are negative) without regard to differences in arousal. Others have focused exclusively on arousal and have ignored effects of valence (i.e., collapsing together positive and negative events into "arousing" events). It is important to keep in mind these different methods when trying to resolve controversies within the literature and when trying to assemble a big picture view of how emotion influences memory.

☐ Introduction to Emotion's Influence on Memory

The concept of memory has existed for millennia. Like emotion, however, the study of memory initially was considered to be intractable to scientists: How could a person gain access to the contents of another's mind? The German philosopher, Hermann Ebbinghaus, began the systematic investigation of memory. He realized not only that human memory was worthy of study, but also that its capacity could be objectively measured. Through a number of careful assessments of his own memory, Ebbinghaus (1964) revealed the first learning curve (the amount of time that it takes to memorize information) and the first forgetting curve (the decay of that learned knowledge over time).

Ebbinghaus believed that to understand memory processes, one should study the retention of information void of meaning or personal importance. Thus, his own investigations were conducted on his memorization of nonsense syllables. This abandonment of information with personal relevance may have helped to convince naysayers of the objectivity with which human memory could be studied, but it also seemed to lead the field away from investigations of personally relevant memory. For nearly a century, memory researchers seemed to embrace the view that memory was best understood in contexts stripped of emotional meaning or reference to the self. Slowly this assumption has begun to fade, and over the past two decades there has been an increased emphasis placed on understanding how memory processes differ when information is personally important or when it evokes emotional reactions.

The vast majority of this research has examined the effects of emotion on declarative, long-term memory—our ability to consciously retrieve information from prior experiences. This research has revealed that emotion can influence the quantity of information remembered, the quality with which it is remembered (e.g., the memory's vividness), and the types of details that one can remember about a prior event (Kensinger & Schacter, 2008). Although long-term, declarative memories are what most of us think about when we hear the term *memory*, in fact memory refers to a much broader set of processes. When we look up a number in the phone book (or on an Internet database) and then rehearse that number as we walk to the phone, we are using working memory (the active updating and manipulation of information over the short term). We also are using working memory every time we link words together to form a sentence or follow a discourse on television. Emotion can have pervasive effects on our working memory, influencing the types of information that we hold in mind over the short term, and affecting how well we can turn our attention from one aspect of our environment to another.

The effects of emotion also pervade domains of memory about which we have no conscious awareness; our prior experiences can influence how rapidly or adaptively we respond to information in the environment even if we have no memory of our prior encounters with that type of information. For example, if a person tries a new food and becomes ill soon after eating it, he or she often will develop an instant "taste aversion." The person will now avoid that new food (see Bahar, Samuel, Hazvi, & Dudai, 2003 for a recent study of taste aversion). Critically, this type of taste aversion can exist even if the person does not consciously remember the event that triggered the aversion. This is only one example of the myriad ways in which our prior experiences can shape our current behavior without our awareness. Every time we ride a bicycle or use a computer keyboard, our actions are guided by our prior uses of those items. As we will discuss, emotion can affect the likelihood that prior experiences influence our current behavior.

Thus, like emotion, memory is not a single construct. Rather, memory encompasses a host of processes that together allow our prior experiences to mold our current thoughts and behavior. The goal of this book is to give the reader an overview of how these different mnemonic processes are influenced by our affective state and how those emotion–memory interactions change as an adult ages.

The Neurobiology of Emotion and Memory

The quest to find the neurobiological root of emotions has been ongoing for millennia—since the ancient Greeks' attribution of emotional states to imbalances among blood, yellow bile, black bile, and phlegm. Although emotional states are now placed squarely within the domain of the mind and brain, a precise understanding of how emotions arise has yet to be determined. If you ask most students of psychology or neuroscience to tell you about the neural basis of emotion processing, they will likely mention the limbic system. Indeed, the limbic system was originally proposed to be this center for emotional processing. As will be described in the following, the conception of the limbic system has turned out to be at least as useful for understanding mnemonic function as it has been for understanding emotional processes. Although many of the key players involved in emotion processing are within the limbic system, how those regions interact with one another, and with other cortical and subcortical regions, remains an active topic of investigation.

☐ Neuroanatomy of the Limbic System

The term *limbic* is a derivation from the Latin term *limbus*, which means border or margin. The phrase "limbic lobe" was coined in the late 1870s by the French neurologist Paul Broca, referring primarily to the cingulate and parahippocampal gyri, structures that form a rim or *limb* around the brain stem and diencephalons (thalamus and hypothalamus structures; black regions in Figure 2.1). The concept of the limbic lobe was popularized in

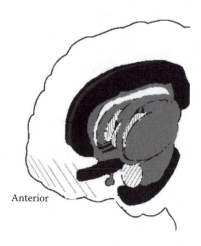

Anterior

FIGURE 2.1 Schematic of the regions that make up the limbic lobe as originally proposed by Paul Broca (regions outlined in black) and regions that make up the limbic system as revised by James Papez (grey regions) and Paul MacLean (striped regions).

1937 when James Papez (1937), a neuroanatomist at Cornell University, suggested that the limbic lobe played a critical role in emotion processing. In his definition of the limbic lobe, which Papez determined by injecting the rabies virus into the hippocampus of a cat and tracking the virus's spread throughout the brain, the limbic lobe included not only the cingulate and parahippocampal gyri but also the hippocampus, fornix, thalamus, and mammilary bodies (grey regions in Figure 2.1). This definition of the limbic lobe was later refined by Paul MacLean to include the amygdala, the septal area, the nucleus accumbens (a part of the striatum), and the orbitofrontal cortex (striped regions in Figure 2.1). Often, this larger collection of regions is referred to as the "limbic system," whereas the term *limbic lobe* is used to connote the regions defined by Broca and Papez (see reviews by Barbas, 2000; Parent, 1996; Swanson, 2003).

In broad terms, the limbic system can be divided into two subsystems. The first is centered on the hippocampus and is critical for declarative, long-term memory. The second is centered on the amygdala and plays an essential role in affective processing. The output of each of these subsystems includes the hypothalamus, which, as we will discuss, plays a critical role in regulating the body's response to emotional arousal and stress. Thus, emotion–memory interactions occur via direct interactions between the hippocampal memory system and the amygdalar affective system and through effects on hypothalamic function.

☐ Hippocampal Memory System

The importance of the hippocampal memory system became apparent in 1953, when the neurosurgeon William Scoville performed an experimental brain operation to relieve the epileptic symptoms of a man now known by his initials, H.M. (Scoville & Milner, 1957). The focus of H.M.'s seizures was in the medial temporal lobe, and so these structures were removed bilaterally. The surgery achieved its goal of lessening the severity and frequency of H.M.'s epileptic seizures; however, it left him with a profound amnesia. H.M. cannot consciously recall from long-term memory any event that he has experienced after 1953, and he also does not appear to be able to relive his past experiences in the same way as individuals with intact medial temporal lobe structures (reviewed by Corkin, 2002; Kensinger & Corkin, 2008). In marked contrast to his dramatic deficit in the formation of declarative (explicit, conscious) memories, H.M.'s performance in other perceptual and cognitive domains has remained intact, and he has retained the ability to show implicit or unconscious effects of his prior experiences. Thus, he is not shocked to see a computer or a cellular phone, and he has acquired a host of new skills, ranging from learning to trace designs seen only in a mirror to learning how to operate a wheelchair. H.M.'s pattern of spared and impaired abilities led to the realization that declarative memory is separable from other forms of memory (e.g., nondeclarative, implicit memory), with the hippocampal system playing an essential role in the formation of new declarative memories but not in the acquisition of nondeclarative ones (see reviews by Corkin, 1984, 2002).

The hippocampal memory system usually is considered to include the hippocampal formation (composed of dentate gyrus, hippocampus proper [Cornu Ammonis or CA fields], and subicular complex) the entorhinal cortex, the perirhinal cortex, and the parahippocampal cortex (Suzuki & Amaral, 2003, 2004; upper panel of Figure 2.2). As we process information in our environment, it feeds through sensory areas and into the hippocampal system via the perirhinal and parahippocampal cortices. These regions send strong projections to the entorhinal cortex, which serves as the primary source of input into the hippocampus (see Amaral & Insausti, 1990; Amaral, Insausti, & Cowan, 1984; lower panel of Figure 2.2).

Although there is debate about the exact division of labor within these distinct medial temporal lobe regions (see Kensinger & Corkin, 2008, for review), there is evidence that not all regions of the hippocampal memory system perform the same set of functions. For example, it appears that the hippocampus proper plays a particularly important role in the formation of memories that require novel associations to be formed between different items (i.e., relational or associative memory; see Aggleton & Brown, 1999; Eichenbaum, 2000; Kensinger & Corkin, 2008 for reviews). In

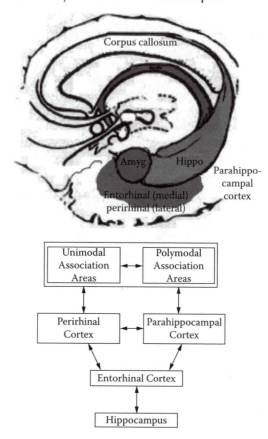

FIGURE 2.2   Regions included within the hippocampal memory system (upper panel) and the information flow through those regions (lower panel). Figure adapted from Lavency & Amaral, 2000. Note: corpus callosum is labelled for landmark purposes only and is not a part of the hippocampal memory system.

contrast, the surrounding medial temporal lobe cortices (e.g., entorhinal and perirhinal cortex) may play a dominant role in memory for intra-item features (i.e., features intrinsic to an item, such as its color) rather than for inter-item associations (i.e., how one item relates to another—which came first, how close in space the two items were to one another, etc.—Brown, Wilson, & Riches, 1987; Davachi, Mitchell, & Wagner, 2003).

☐ Amygdalar Affective System

The second subdivision of the limbic system consists of the amygdala and its related structures, including the cingulate gyrus, orbitofrontal cortex, and medial prefrontal cortex. These structures play a critical role in our subjective feeling of emotion (i.e., feeling states). They also mediate our physiological expression of emotion (see Kober et al., 2008; Pessoa, 2008 for recent reviews of emotion–cognition interactions in the brain as they relate to conceptions of the limbic system).

The idea that the amygdala might play a role in emotion began when Kluver and Bucy (1937) discovered that monkeys with lesions to the medial temporal lobes displayed unusual behaviors. They showed blunted emotional reactions to threats, to social actions of other animals, or to objects that they would usually avoid; they became hypersexual and were unable to distinguish appropriate sexual partners (i.e., opposite-sex members of the same species) from inappropriate ones (e.g., same-sex individuals or inanimate objects); and they explored any stimulus in their environment, regardless of its novelty, by sniffing it or trying to eat it. The lesions made by Kluver and Bucy were quite large, and so the researchers were unable to isolate which regions within the medial temporal lobe were responsible for these behavioral changes. However, later studies by Weiskrantz and William (1957) and Geschwind (1965) demonstrated that amygdala damage could bring about many of these behavioral changes. Without the amygdala, the affective significance of sensory information could not be recognized. Since that time, the amygdala has been a primary focus of research on the neural basis of emotion processing.

The amygdala does not act in isolation, of course. The affective significance of sensory information is thought to be computed via reciprocal interactions between the amygdala and the medial prefrontal and orbitofrontal cortices (Elliott, Friston, & Dolan, 2000; Dolan & Morris, 2000; Kringelbach, 2005; Kringelbach & Rolls, 2004). These interactions allow establishment of a representation that includes both the sensory features needed to recognize an object and the affective value of the object (Craig, 2002; Holland & Gallagher, 2004).

The amygdala is known to play a role both in the physiological expression of emotion and in the subjective feeling of emotion. For example, amygdala stimulation in humans often leads to a feeling of fear, accompanied by autonomic reactions such as dilation of pupils, release of adrenalin, and increased heart rate (see Parent, 1996 for review). Conversely, humans with amygdala damage demonstrate a fearless state. Although they may be cognitively aware of dangers in the environment, they do not report feeling fear, nor do they display physiological responses to stimuli that typically would elicit fear (Adolphs, Tranel, Damasio, & Damasio, 1995; Adolphs, Tranel, Bechara, Damasio, & Damasio, 1996; Broks et al., 1998; Scott et al., 1997).

For quite a long time it was thought that the amygdala played a selective role in the processing of fearful information. Recent research, however, has suggested that the amygdala is likely to play a broader role in the processing of emotional information (see Baxter & Murray, 2000; Davidson & Irwin, 1999; Baas & Kahn, 2004 for reviews). Patients with amygdala damage often are impaired at recognizing or displaying a variety of emotions, including disgust and surprise as well as fear. Neuroimaging studies have frequently shown that the amount of amygdala activity tends to be related primarily to the level of arousal elicited by the stimuli rather than by the particular type of emotion elicited (Garavan, Pendergrass, Ross, Stein, & Risinger, 2001; Hamann, Ely, Grafton, & Kilts, 2002; Hamann & Mao, 2002; Kensinger & Schacter, 2006c).

Different regions of the amygdala may respond to different ranges of emotional stimuli. Just as the hippocampal system actually is comprised of many distinct structures which perform specialized functions, so too is it misleading to refer to the amygdala as a single entity. "Amygdaloid complex" is a more accurate term, reflecting the fact that the structure is comprised of a collection of nuclei that lie at the anterior end of the hippocampus. The amygdaloid complex is divided into three main subdivisions: the corticomedial group, the basolateral group, and the central nucleus. Regions of the bed nucleus of the stria terminalis and of the substantia innominata sometimes are also considered to be included in the "extended amygdala," an anatomic concept based on evidence that these cells are of the same type as those in the central nuclei of the amygdaloid complex (Cassell, Freedman, & Shi, 1999; Johnston, 1923).

Although there is extensive evidence that these different subdivisions of the amygdala serve distinct functions in most animals (Swanson & Petrovich, 1998), and there is good reason to believe that these dissociations hold in humans as well, the vast majority of the research reviewed in this book will refer to the amygdala as if it were a single structure. This simplification is a reflection of the limitations of localization currently available in research on the function of the human amygdala. For example, in the typical neuroimaging studies conducted in humans, function can be resolved to a region that approximates a 3-mm cube; this relatively large size prevents strong conclusions regarding the functioning of distinct subdivisions of the amygdala. However, methodological developments are occurring that will allow researchers to begin to address the functionality of distinct regions of the amygdala. A challenge for future research will be to move away from investigating interactions between the amygdala and the hippocampal memory system and instead to examine how interactions may differ depending on the particular subdivisions of each of these regions. As will be discussed in Chapter 7, new research findings are emphasizing that some of the apparently contradictory effects of emotion on memory can be understood by considering that not all regions of the amygdala must play the same modulatory role and by appreciating that amygdalar interactions need not be equivalently strong with all medial temporal lobe structures.

☐ The Hypothalamic–Pituitary–Adrenal (HPA) Axis

The outputs of both the hippocampal memory system and the amygdalar affective system proceed through the hypothalamus, the control center for most of the body's hormonal systems. The hypothalamus releases many hormones that can act on remote sites throughout the brain and body to increase or decrease the secretion of other hormones. Of most relevance to the discussion of affect–memory interactions is the pathway through which the hypothalamus modulates release of cortisol, a hormone that is emitted when an organism is under stress. Under conditions of stress, the hypothalamus releases corticotropin-releasing hormone. This hormone acts on the pituitary gland, which in turn releases adrenocorticotrophic hormone. Adrenocorticotrophic hormone causes the adrenal glands, located on top of the kidneys, to increase their secretion of cortisol. Positive and negative feedback occurs at various sites along this hypothalamic–pituitary–adrenal (HPA) axis in order to ensure that cortisol production stays within a certain range, and that cortisol release is terminated after the stressor has dissipated.

The amygdala often acts as a modulator of hypothalamic activity. Almost any physiological response (e.g., cardiovascular or respiratory change) that can be elicited by stimulating the hypothalamus also can arise through amygdalar stimulation (reviewed by Kaada, 1972; Zolovick, 1972). Direct connections between the amygdala and the hypothalamus serve to modulate the release of both epinephrine (adrenaline) and glucocorticoids during emotionally arousing events (see Davis, 1997). These hormones then exert actions throughout the central nervous system, including back in the amygdala. At least in animals, it appears that these stress hormones affect the release of noradrenaline in the basolateral nucleus of the amygdala (Quirarte, Roozendaal, & McGaugh, 1997), a nucleus that has direct connections with the hippocampal memory system. Chronic release of these hormones (as may happen with chronic stress) may fundamentally alter the nature of noradrenaline release in the basolateral amygdala (Braga, Aroniadou-Anderjaska, Manion, Hough, & Li, 2004), perhaps leading to long-term changes in amygdala–hippocampal connectivity.

Thus, it is important to note that not only can the amygdala have direct modulatory effects on the hippocampal memory system, but amygdalar activity also can have indirect influences on memory performance by influencing the hormonal release triggered by the hypothalamus. Direct versus indirect effects of the amygdala on the functioning of the hippocampal memory system will be an important issue to consider when we discuss the neuroimaging evidence for amygdala–hippocampal interactions. Although articles often imply that such interactions stem from direct connections between these regions, it is plausible that correlations between activity in the amygdala and in the hippocampus result from indirect influences as well as direct ones.

CHAPTER

Methods for Investigating Emotion–Memory Interactions

The prior chapters have emphasized the complexities inherent in examining emotion–memory interactions. How, then, can researchers begin to gain traction on the question of how different types of affective experience influence different mnemonic functions? This chapter outlines the three main approaches that researchers have used to study the effects of emotion on human memory: (1) behavioral assessments, (2) studies of patients with brain damage, and (3) neuroimaging investigations of healthy and abnormal brain function. These methods are complimentary, each providing a window through which we can see how emotion modulates memory. By integrating findings from these different approaches, we can begin to assemble a fuller picture of emotion–memory interactions.

Behavioral assessments of emotional memory allow us to see how the effects of emotion on memory are manifest. In what types of situations do emotions help versus hinder memory? What types of information are better remembered for emotional events than for non-emotional ones? Does the effect of emotion on memory intensify or dissipate over time? Cleverly designed behavioral experiments also can help us to understand whether emotion influences the types of cognitive processes used to remember information. For example, if emotion enhances memory through engagement of attention-demanding processes, then asking people to perform a secondary task (which draws attentional resources) at the same time as they are asked to remember an emotional event should weaken the beneficial effects of emotion on memory. In contrast, if emotion enhances memory through relatively automatic processes that do not rely heavily on attentional resources, then dividing participants' attention by giving them a second task to perform should have little effect on memory for emotional information (see Kensinger & Corkin, 2004c; Mather & Knight, 2005 for use of such methods).

Behavioral investigations in healthy individuals, therefore, are essential for establishing a framework in which to explore the effects of emotion on memory. These investigations often tell us what the interesting questions are and where controversy or contradictions exist. What they cannot easily distinguish, however, are behavioral differences that arise from additional use of the same sorts of processes versus differences that arise because of recruitment of novel types of processes. For example, if a behavioral study reveals that people are more likely to remember negative items than neutral ones, it is hard to determine whether this enhancement results because of increased engagement of the same types of processes (e.g., elaboration, rehearsal) that help individuals to remember neutral items, or whether it is because of engagement of distinct types of processes (see Talmi, Luk, McGarry, & Moscovitch, 2007 for further discussion).

Neuropsychological and neuroimaging approaches are excellent for determining whether it is increased engagement of the same types of processes or engagement of novel processes that leads to behavioral effects. As noted in Chapter 2 in the discussion of the amnesic patient H.M., the study of patients with brain damage has been instrumental in determining which types of cognitive abilities are reliant on distinct types of processes and which sets of cognitive processes depend on shared neural substrates. Neuroimaging studies also do an excellent job of highlighting whether two behavioral effects rely on recruitment of the same network of regions or on distinct networks.

Although neuropsychological and neuroimaging approaches are similar in their ability to detect dissociations of function, they are not redundant methods. Neuropsychological research has been instrumental in informing us about which neural structures are *necessary* for a particular cognitive or affective process. However, these behavioral studies of patients cannot inform us as to the entire network of regions that are recruited; nor can they always tell us about precise localization of function (lesions often are large and extend across functional boundaries), or about the connectivity between brain regions that occurs in healthy individuals (due to the plasticity of the brain, connections in an injured brain may not always be the same as connections in a healthy brain). In contrast, although neuroimaging methods cannot isolate only those regions that are *needed* for a process, they can identify the neural networks that are *recruited* during a particular process and can allow conclusions to be drawn about the connectivity between those regions. Neuroimaging also is effective at examining the *processing stage* during which a particular region plays a role, whereas studies of patients with brain damage can draw limited conclusions about the stage during which a region is necessary. For example, with the amnesic patient H.M., it is impossible to determine whether his memory deficits arise during the encoding of information into long-term memory, during the consolidation phase, or during the retrieval phase.

In contrast, neuroimaging can pinpoint regions whose encoding-related activity (or retrieval-related activity) corresponds with accurate memory, thereby elucidating the phases during which regions come online during mnemonic processing. Thus, in order to fully understand emotion–memory interactions, the most effective approach often is to identify a behavioral effect of interest, and then to combine neuropsychological and neuroimaging approaches to clarify the neural mechanisms through which emotion exerts a particular effect on memory.

☐ Behavioral Assessments of Emotional Memory

Researchers have used a variety of behavioral assessments to investigate interactions between emotion and memory. Some of the first studies of emotional memory took advantage of the fact that, on occasion, highly surprising and emotional events are shared by many individuals. Researchers have assessed participants' memories for events such as the assassination of John F. Kennedy or the terrorist attacks of September 11, 2001 to examine how the emotional salience of a memory affects what is remembered about the event itself (e.g., when the event occurred, the sequence of events that transpired) and about the personal context in which the event was experienced (e.g., where people were or who they were with at the time when they learned about the event's occurrence; see Bohannon & Symons, 1992; Christianson, 1992; Keenan & Baillet, 1980; Neisser, 1982 for reviews).

As will be discussed in Chapter 7, these investigations have provided a number of insights into how the emotional content of information influences the mechanisms that we use to remember information. However, highly emotional public events occur rarely, and it is nearly impossible to find control events that, while lacking emotional meaning, share the other features of the emotional public events (e.g., events that received media coverage and unfolded over the same duration of time). Because of these limitations, it has been necessary to find ways to examine the effects of emotion on memory in a more controlled, laboratory setting, in which experimenters can choose the particular stimuli that will be shown to participants.

In these studies, the goal is to match the emotional and non-emotional stimuli on the dimensions, aside from emotion, that might be likely to influence memory. For example, we know that factors such as information's novelty, semantic relatedness, or visual complexity can influence memory, and so it is important to control for these factors when examining the effects of emotion on memory. One clever way in which researchers have gone about doing this is through the creation of narrated slide shows, in which the images shown to participants are held constant, but parts of the narration are changed to create either an emotional slide show or a non-emotional one. For example, Cahill and McGaugh (1995) adapted a slide show used by Heuer and Reisburg (1990) that depicted a mother and son going into a hospital. In one version of the slide show (the neutral version), participants heard a narrative about how the boy was traveling to the hospital to visit his father who worked there. In another version (the emotional version), participants instead heard that the boy had been hit by a car as he and his mother were walking, and that the boy had to undergo surgery. The critical finding was that participants who listened to the emotional narrative remembered more about the slides, particularly those that had been associated with the arousing information (e.g., the boy having surgery), than did the participants who listened to the neutral narrative. This finding has now been demonstrated in a large number of studies and across a number of different languages.

A number of other methodologies also have been used to examine the effects of emotional content on memory in the laboratory. As described in Chapter 1, there now are a variety of standardized databases with pictorial, verbal, or auditory stimuli that evoke a range of emotional responses. Many researchers have used these stimuli in their experiments, and by equating emotional and non-emotional items on a number of features (e.g., familiarity, category membership, semantic relatedness, visual complexity), they have gone to great lengths to assure that purported effects of emotion on memory are not confounded by other dimensions of difference.

Although many studies have focused on how the emotional *content* of information influences memory, often these effects are intertwined with the effects of emotional *state* on memory. If we learn that a young boy is having surgery after being in a car wreck, not only are we encoding information with emotional content, but we also are likely to be induced into a particular mood by that information. Many researchers have been interested in examining the effects of emotional state on memory. There are likely to be at least a couple of ways in which a person's emotional state can influence his or her memory. First, there are mood-congruency effects. That is, when a person is in a particular mood, he or she is likely to remember information that is consistent with that mood. Second, there are mood-dependent effects. Information learned in one mood state may be more likely to be remembered when an individual is returned to that mood state (reviewed by Ellis & Asbrook, 1991; Blancy, 1986). Each of these effects is explained by the principle of encoding specificity, which states that memory is best when there is overlap between the types of processes used at encoding and those used during retrieval, and when one's physiological state is similar during encoding and retrieval (see Tulving, 1982). If we consider a person who is sad when he or she is recalling past experiences, the principle of encoding specificity would predict that the person would remember more sad events than happy ones. The sad events are consistent with the person's current mood (a mood-congruency effect), and the person's sad mood during retrieval likely matches the mood experienced during the initial encoding of the sad event (a mood-dependency effect).

Mood-congruency and mood-dependency describe the ways in which emotional state can influence memory for affectively charged information. Emotional state, however, can also influence memory for non-emotional information. It is thought to do so by altering the resources available for processing incoming information (e.g., Christianson, 1986; Eysenck & Calvo, 1992; Loftus & Burns, 1982), by influencing which stimuli are selected for processing (e.g., MacLeod & Mathews, 2004), and by affecting how the information is encoded. For example, positive emotional states tend to be associated with more heuristic (rule-of-thumb) processing and with reliance on schemas (general knowledge structures) or stereotypes (e.g., Bless et al., 1996). In contrast, negative emotional states tend to be associated with more analytical processing and with attention to detail (see Martin & Clore, 2001; Simon, 1967).

In order to examine the effect of emotional state on memory, researchers often induce participants into a particular mood state (as described in Chapter 1). After being induced into these mood states, researchers can then examine the efficiency or accuracy with which participants can encode or retrieve information. For example, participants may be asked to watch a movie or to listen to music that induces a particular mood (e.g., sadness). Once induced into this mood, participants may be asked to encode a series of words, or to retrieve a series of words that they have learned previously. By comparing the memory performance of participants induced into the sad mood to the performance of participants in a control condition (with no mood induction), researchers can examine the effect of mood on memory performance (e.g., Yeung, Dalgleish, Golden, & Schartau, 2006; see also Payne, Nadel, Allen, Thomas, & Jacobs, 2002 for use of similar methods to examine the effects of stress on memory).

Another way that researchers have examined the effects of emotional state on memory has been to use neuropharmacological manipulations to simulate moods (I use the word *simulate* here because it is not clear that neuropharmacological manipulations always lead to feelings akin to those that arise through mood induction procedures). For example, some participants may be given the stress hormone cortisol while others may be given a placebo. Researchers can then compare the mnemonic performance of the two groups to deduce the effects of stress or anxiety on memory performance (see Buchanan & Tranel, 2008 for a recent example).

☐ Neuropsychological Examinations of Emotional Memory

As outlined in the introduction to this chapter, although behavioral assessments can reveal effects of emotion on memory, they cannot determine whether those effects arise from additional (or lesser) use of the same sorts of processes typically engaged during mnemonic processing or whether the effects arise from a change in the types of recruited processes. To examine these questions, researchers have turned to neuropsychological and neuroimaging approaches.

It is important to note that almost all human neuropsychological research is grounded in animal research. Although this book focuses exclusively on investigations in human memory for emotional information, studies in rats and nonhuman primates first provided evidence that the amygdala does not play a critical role in memory for non-emotional information (i.e., amnesia did not result from its removal), but that it does play a fundamental role in modulating memory for emotional information (see Baxter & Murray, 2000; Davis, 1997; LeDoux, 2000; Phelps & LeDoux, 2005; McGaugh, 2004 for reviews).

Amygdala Damage and Emotional Memory

Some of the first human evidence that there were distinct processes for remembering emotional information compared to non-emotional information came from studies of patients with lesions in the amygdala. Some of these lesions resulted from genetic disorders (e.g., Urbach-Wiethe disease, which can result in mineralization of the amygdala bilaterally) and others arose from stroke or from herpes simplex encephalitis (an inflammation of brain tissue following viral infection). Occasionally the amygdala also is resected unilaterally to surgically treat epilepsy that has not responded to other treatments.

Neuropsychological evaluations of patients with bilateral amygdala damage typically have revealed normal motor function, language ability, and short-term memory. The patients often show somewhat reduced long-term memory performance, particularly for information with emotional content. Most notably, in contrast to healthy individuals who often will be more likely to remember emotional information than non-emotional information, patients with bilateral amygdala damage receive no such mnemonic benefit for emotional information (reviewed by Buchanan & Adolphs, 2002). Patients with unilateral amygdala damage also tend to show reduced memory for emotional information, although debates are ongoing regarding whether the deficits that arise from left and right amygdala damage are equivalent (see Adolphs, Tranel, & Denburg, 2000; Brierley, Medford, Shaw, & David, 2004; Buchanan, Tranel, Denburg, & Adolphs, 2001; Phelps, LaBar, & Spencer,1997; LaBar & Phelps, 1998).

Emotional Memory in Neurodegenerative Disease

A similar blunting of the emotional memory enhancement has been demonstrated in patients with Alzheimer's disease, a form of dementia characterized by the accumulation of intracellular neuritic plaques and extracellular neurofibrillary tangles. By the later stages of the disease, these cellular abnormalities are widespread; however, early in the course of the disease, the concentration of plaques and tangles is particularly dense in the medial temporal lobe. The hippocampal formation shows marked atrophy quite early in the disease, and a volumetric reduction in the entorhinal cortex (which provides much of the input into the hippocampus) is one of the best indicators that an individual has early Alzheimer's disease. Given the essential role of the hippocampus for memory formation and retrieval (as discussed in Chapter 2), it makes sense that patients with mild Alzheimer's disease would be best identified by their difficulties remembering recently learned information. Indeed, the clinical profile of Alzheimer's disease requires memory impairment along with decline in one other area of cognition (language, motor function, attention, executive function, personality, or object recognition; see Knopman et al., 2001). Deficits in episodic memory tend to be the best way of distinguishing people with Alzheimer's disease from healthy older adults (see Kensinger & Corkin, 2003a, 2003d for a review of cognitive deficits in Alzheimer's disease).

However, in addition to changes in the hippocampal memory system, the amygdala also undergoes substantial volumetric and cellular changes. Plaques and tangles accumulate in the amygdala just as in other medial temporal lobe structures, and the volume of the amygdala undergoes decline as well. Thus, studies of patients with Alzheimer's disease provide a way to examine the effects of amygdala damage on emotional memory. Although the changes in emotional memory with Alzheimer's disease are not as pronounced as those that follow complete ablasion of the amygdala, a number of studies have suggested that patients with Alzheimer's disease do not show a normal memory advantage for emotional information (e.g., Abrisqueta-Gomez et al., 2002; Kensinger et al., 2002; see Chapter 16 for more discussion).

☐ Neuroimaging Investigations of Emotional Memory

This patient research has clearly implicated the amygdala in emotional memory. But, of course, the amygdala is not acting in isolation. In order to elucidate the network of regions that subserve memory for emotional memory, researchers have turned to neuroimaging methods. The three most commonly used neuroimaging methods are positron emission tomography (PET), functional magnetic resonance imaging (fMRI), and event-related potentials (ERP). This book focuses primarily on fMRI investigations of emotional memory; however, findings from PET and ERP will be mentioned where relevant.

Positron Emission Tomography

PET is a neuroimaging method that uses radiotracers labeled with short-lived positron emitting isotopes to track chemical transmission or blood flow in the human brain. When used to identify neural correlates of cognitive processes, the radiotracer is radioactively labeled glucose, fluro-2-deoxy-D-glucose (FDG). Because glucose is utilized more readily by active neurons, neuronal activity can be deduced by detecting the regional update of the radiolabeled glucose.

The temporal resolution of PET is quite low, however. PET can only detect changes in glucose uptake that occur over many seconds or minutes. Thus, PET requires that analyses compare glucose uptake during one "block" of items to glucose uptake during another block (with a block usually lasting upwards of 30 sec). For example, in order to examine the processes involved during retrieval of studied information, researchers typically will compare glucose uptake during a block that includes mostly "old" studied items (with a few catch trials to make sure that participants are paying attention and are not mindlessly saying "old") as compared to a block that includes mostly "new" nonstudied items. Although much useful knowledge can be gained from these types of analyses, the blocked-design approach is limited in the types of questions that it can answer. Perhaps most importantly, blocked designs do not allow state effects to be distinguished from item effects. That is, if a region is more active (i.e., utilizes more glucose) during the blocks with mostly old items than during the blocks with mostly new items, it is impossible to know whether that is because the region is involved in some type of retrieval orientation (i.e., with the process of determining the "oldness" of an item), or whether that region shows a correspondence with memory accuracy (i.e., with the ability to accurately recognize an item from a prior encounter). With regard to memory for emotional and neutral information, the interpretations can get even murkier. If a region is more active during the encoding or retrieval of a block of emotional items compared to a block of neutral items, how do we know whether that region is involved in *memory* for the emotional items or, more broadly, in the *processing* of the emotional items?

Functional Magnetic Resonance Imaging

fMRI methodology allows for the measurement of blood flow changes in the brain as individuals process information. Because changes in blood flow are closely tied to changes in neural activity in the brain, fMRI allows for an indirect measurement of activity in discrete brain regions. fMRI allows the online measurement of activity changes even to fairly short events (e.g., those that last only a few milliseconds), and it allows localization of those activity changes to precise brain regions (e.g., within a 3-mm cubic volume).

A significant advantage of fMRI (and ERP) over PET is that signals related to a single item's presentation can be isolated. Thus, items can be sorted based on, for example, whether the person correctly remembered an item or incorrectly believed that the item was a nonstudied one. This type of item-based ("event-related") analysis has made it possible to distinguish regions that are active during all retrieval attempts (regardless of whether they are correct or incorrect) from regions that are more active during accurate recognition than during inaccurate retrieval attempts. These designs also have made it possible to distinguish regions recruited for emotional processing (e.g., regions that are more active during the presentation of emotional compared to non-emotional items) from those implicated in emotional memory (e.g., regions that are more active when emotional information is correctly recognized than when it is forgotten).

Another critical advance made possible by the event-related analysis stream is referred to as a "subsequent memory" paradigm (reviewed by Paller & Wagner, 2002). In a subsequent memory paradigm, participants encode a list of items while they undergo a neuroimaging scan. Later, participants are given a memory test for the items studied in the neuroimaging environment. Data from the memory test are then used, on a post-hoc basis, to sort the items that participants studied during the neuroimaging session into those that participants later remembered and those that participants later forgot. If a brain region shows greater activity during the encoding of items that are subsequently remembered than during the encoding of items that are subsequently forgotten, researchers can infer that the region plays a role in the successful encoding of those types of items.

Although the vast majority of fMRI research has focused on clarifying the discrete regions that subserve cognition, it is likely that many behavioral changes arise not through the activity of functionally segregated brain regions but rather through integrated and distributed changes among many regions. Thus, investigators have recently begun to combine standard fMRI analysis techniques with functional connectivity analyses (i.e., determination of the correlations between spatially remote cellular activities) and effective connectivity analyses (i.e., modeling of the influence that one cellular system exerts on another; Greicus et al., 2003; McIntosh & Gonzalez-Lima, 1994). These combinations are proving useful in understanding not only the regions that are "key players" in emotional memory, but also how these regions interact with one another during memory formation and retrieval.

Event-Related Potentials

In contrast to fMRI and PET which measure changes in blood flow to active regions of the brain, other neuroimaging techniques such as electroencephalography (EEG) and magnetoencephalography (MEG) measure the electrical and magnetic signals that result from cell-to-cell communication. These techniques are superior to fMRI in their temporal resolution, resolving temporal signals with millisecond accuracy. However, the methods do not provide the high spatial resolution of fMRI. Because these methods measure signals from the scalp, a person may be able to infer general information about the location from which signals emanates, but it is difficult to achieve more precise spatial localization. Recent studies have begun to integrate fMRI with MEG or EEG to create maps with millimeter spatial resolution and millisecond temporal resolution. This type of multi-modal imaging is likely to be influential in understanding both the location and timing of neural activity.

Emotional Memory in Young Adults

CHAPTER 4

Emotion's Modulation of Implicit Memory

Although the term *memory* is colloquially used to refer to our conscious ability to remember past experiences, within psychology and neuroscience the term is used more broadly to incorporate unconscious influences of our past on our current perceptions and actions. In some instances, we are not aware of (and thus cannot report) the influences of some of our prior experiences, even though our behavior can provide evidence of those prior experiences. For example, if you tried to explain to someone how to successfully hit a tennis ball, or how to drive a stick-shift car, you likely would not do a very good job of consciously constructing the chain of sequences that you carry out to succeed at these tasks. Similarly, you may realize that you are very afraid of dogs but not remember that there was a particular event that triggered this fear (whereas perhaps your parents would remember that you were bitten by a neighbor's dog as a small child). Even though you might not be able to consciously remember the sequence used to hit a tennis ball, or the reason for your fear of dogs, your behavior provides a clear indication of your training in tennis and of your earlier encounter with a vicious dog. These unconscious influences of our past experiences on our current behavior are typically referred to as *implicit* or *nondeclarative* memories, reflecting the fact that they are *implicit* in our behavior rather than being *declared* in an *explicit* fashion. Unlike most forms of long-term memory, which rely on the hippocampal formation (see Chapter 2), implicit memory can exist even in individuals with damage to the hippocampal memory system. Although the majority of human research has focused on examining emotion's influence on explicit memory, there also are far-reaching effects of emotion on implicit learning. It is likely that at least as much, if not more, of our behavior is molded through unconscious influences of past experiences than through our conscious recollection of prior events. Therefore, it is critical to understand how emotion may influence our behavior at this implicit level.

Some of the first evidence for a modulatory role of emotion in implicit memory came from studies of fear conditioning. Fear conditioning refers to the ability to learn, across a number of trials, that a particular type of stimulus (e.g., a blue square) will predict the occurrence of a negative event (e.g., a loud noise). Although initially the blue square will elicit no response from a participant, if the presentation of the blue square usually precedes the occurrence of a loud noise, then over time the participant will begin to have a physiological response to the blue square (e.g., their skin conductance, heart rate, or blood volume may change). The presence of this physiological response to the blue square is an indication of learning. The person is showing the response because he or she has learned that the square predicts the occurrence of the negative event. Critically, this type of learning can occur even when individuals are unaware of the relation between the blue square and the loud noise, highlighting the implicit nature of this learning. There has been extensive evidence from humans and animals suggesting a critical role of the amygdala in fear conditioning. When the amygdala is damaged, this contingency learning is prevented (see reviews by Lavond, Kim, & Thompson, 1993; LeDoux, 2000; Maren, 2001). By contrast, damage to declarative memory networks (e.g., regions of the hippocampus) does not impair the formation of these associations.

These conditioning studies have elucidated an important mechanism through which we can attach affective meaning to items in the world around us. Through conditioning, stimuli that at first were neutral (i.e., a blue square) can come to take on affective qualities (i.e., signaling danger). Although most studies have focused on the acquisition of aversive associations, it is likely that conditioning underlies many of the affective associations that we make, including about the appetitive or rewarding nature of information (reviewed by Martin-Soelch, Linthicum, & Ernst, 2006).

Although conditioning is arguably the most well-studied case of the effects of emotion on implicit learning, implicit memory can take many forms (see Figure 4.1). In this chapter, we focus on the effects of emotion on two other forms of implicit memory: a person's perception or response to a stimulus due to his or her prior exposure (*repetition priming*) and a person's ability to acquire new skills over time (*procedural memory*).

☐ Effects of Repetition on Preference

A tremendous amount of research has focused on how prior processing of information can influence a person's preference for a particular type of stimulus. In the typical study, participants are shown a series of items

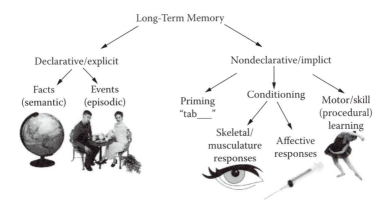

FIGURE 4.1   Varieties of long-term memory.

(e.g., abstract drawings) and then later are asked to indicate how much they like a series of drawings. Unknown to the participants, some of the items are those that they studied previously, and others are those that were never studied. The usual finding is that participants will have a preference for the items that they have studied previously, despite their lack of awareness that they have previously encountered those stimuli (the "mere exposure effect"; see Bornstein, 1989; Harrison, 1977; Zajonc, 2001 for reviews). The (unconscious) familiarity with the drawings leads people to find them more appealing, whereas the novel drawings are viewed less positively. This finding may be linked to the fact that novelty is often associated with arousal (i.e., we tend to find novel states arousing) and with amygdala responsivity (Williams et al., 2007; Wright et al., 2003), whereas familiarity is more likely to be linked with feelings of safety. Although the specific underpinnings of the mere exposure effect, as well as the conditions under which it will occur, continue to be discussed (see Bornstein, 1989; Cutting, 2006; Gordon & Holyoak, 1983; Rhodes, Halberstadt, & Brajkovich, 2001), the existence of the mere exposure effect highlights that repetition of non-emotional information can influence one's affective response to that information.

□ Effects of Emotional Content on Repetition Priming

Although it is well established that repetition can change our affective response to information, what happens if we repeat information that initially had emotional salience? Will our responses to emotional information be different the second time around, even if we are unaware that we have

FIGURE 4.2 If presented with the figure on the left, participants will tend to have a hard time identifying the object. If, however, the participants have recently seen the picture on the right, they will be faster at identifying the object on the left as an umbrella. The effect of the earlier exposure to the umbrella is evident in people's behavior even when the people do not consciously remember that they have previously seen the umbrella image. This effect is an example of repetition priming.

encountered the emotional information previously? Although there has been less research focusing on these questions, recent research has begun to examine whether the emotional content of information will influence the change in behavior that occurs with the information's repetition. We know from extensive research that if I show you a series of non-emotional objects, you will make a decision about an object (e.g., whether it would fit inside of a shoebox) faster if it is the second time you have seen the object as compared to the first time. This is the phenomenon of *repetition priming*: prior exposure to a stimulus facilitates or biases a response to a perceptually or conceptually identical stimulus (see Figure 4.2; Gabrieli & Bergerbest, 2003 for review). This priming reflects implicit learning because it can occur even when participants are unaware that they have recently seen the object, and the priming effect occurs as robustly in amnesic patients with damage to the medial temporal lobe as it does in healthy individuals.

Conceptually, there are reasons to believe that emotion could enhance these types of repetition priming effects. There is evidence that the amygdala can modulate the function of sensory-processing regions. The amygdala has extensive connections with visual processing regions (Amaral, Price, Pitkanen, & Carmichael, 1992), and there often is a correlation between the amount of activity in the amygdala and the amount of activity in visual-processing regions. Perhaps because of these connections, individuals tend to be faster and more accurate at detecting emotional information in their environment compared to non-emotional information (Davis & Whalen, 2001; Ohman, Flykt, & Esteves, 2001; Tabert et al., 2001; Vuilleumier, Richardson, Armony, Driver, & Dolan, 2004). It is plausible that emotion's modulation of sensory processing would lead to increased efficiency of processing for repeated emotional items as compared to repeated neutral items (i.e., to a greater repetition priming effect for emotional items than for non-emotional items). From an evolutionary perspective, an exaggerated increase in efficiency of processing for emotional items would make a great deal of sense.

Indeed, the few studies that have examined the effects of emotion on repetition priming have found that emotion enhances the priming effect (Burton et al., 2004; Collins & Cooke, 2005; LaBar et al., 2005; Luo et al., 2004; Michael, Ehlers, & Halligan, 2005). For example, LaBar et al. (2005) asked participants to study a series of negative and neutral pictures. After a delay, participants were asked to rate whether briefly presented pictures were negative or neutral. In general, there was a priming effect, whereby participants required less exposure time to determine whether a previously presented picture was negative or neutral than to determine whether a novel picture was negative or neutral. However, the magnitude of the priming effect was greater for the negative items than for the neutral items. This finding suggests that repetition of emotional items leads to an even greater increase in processing efficiency than the repetition of neutral items.

As outlined previously, it would make sense if these changes occurred because of emotion's modulation of perceptual-processing regions. Indeed, neuroimaging studies have provided evidence that this priming enhancement arises from differences in the responsiveness of perceptual regions to the emotional stimuli. Ishai, Pessoa, Bikle, and Ungerleider (2004) examined the neural responses within the visual cortex as participants viewed repetitions of faces displaying fearful and neutral expressions. Prior research had shown that there often were reductions in the neural responses to repeated as compared to novel stimuli (see Schacter, Dobbins, & Schnyer, 2004 for a review on priming). One plausible hypothesis for these reductions is that, with priming, the processing in the regions becomes more efficient, thereby requiring less neural activity for the same level of processing. Using event-related fMRI, Ishai and colleagues demonstrated that a number of regions within the ventral visual processing stream showed larger reductions in activity for repeated fearful faces than for repeated neutral faces. In other words, the magnitude of activity reduction was greater for the fearful faces than for the neutral faces. These findings suggest that repeated fearful faces may be associated with more efficient processing than repeated neutral faces, consistent with the behavioral enhancements in repetition priming for emotional information. Thus, emotion can facilitate the benefits of repetition, leading to large enhancements in the efficiency with which the information is processed.

Not all types of emotional stimuli show exaggerated priming, however. In particular, the effects of emotion on perceptual priming appear to vary depending on the arousal level elicited by the stimuli. Thomas and LaBar

(2005) showed participants taboo, negative nonarousing, and neutral words and asked participants to decide whether the words were concrete. Later, they asked participants to view a series of words (some that had just been studied) mixed in with pseudowords. Participants' task was to indicate whether each was a word or a nonword. Priming was measured as a reduction in the time that it took participants to make an accurate decision about the studied words as compared to the nonstudied ones. Participants showed robust priming effects for all item types; they were faster to make an accurate decision about studied words as compared to nonstudied words. But, importantly, they showed exaggerated priming for the taboo words (which elicited arousal) relative to the neutral words. In other words, the repetition benefit was greater for the taboo words than for the other types of words. There was no difference in the magnitude of priming for the negative nonarousing words and the neutral words.

These results suggest that items that elicit arousal may be processed differently from items that do not elicit arousal, with arousing (but not nonarousing) items leading to increased modulation of sensory processing. These findings are consistent with evidence suggesting that amygdala modulation of visual processing occurs primarily when information is arousing (e.g., Anderson, 2005; Keil & Ihssen, 2004; Morris, Friston, & Dolan, 1997) and not when information is nonarousing. These results also fit nicely with the findings from studies on the effects of valence and arousal on declarative long-term memory, suggesting that items that are arousing are remembered due to amygdalar modulation of memory processes; whereas items that are nonarousing are remembered due to processes that occur independently of amygdala modulation (see Chapter 9 for further discussion).

These studies emphasize that the processing of emotional items is especially likely to be facilitated by repetition, particularly if the emotional items elicit arousal. If with every repetition the processing of emotional information enjoys exaggerated benefits from those received for non-emotional information, it would make sense that over time we could respond to emotional information in a particularly rapid fashion. Thus, repetition-priming effects could be one important mechanism through which we come to respond in a relatively automatic and prioritized fashion to the emotional information in our environment.

☐ Effects of Emotional State on Repetition Priming

Although links between repetition priming and prioritized processing of affective material have not been discussed widely when examining the effects of emotional content on healthy individuals' processing, many have argued that repetition-priming effects should provide a window into understanding the response biases that occur with affective disorders. There has been a tremendous amount of research examining the effect of one's mood or anxiety level on repetition priming. This research, however, has not provided a clear picture regarding the effects of mood or anxiety on priming. Many studies have demonstrated that participants who are anxious will show enhanced priming for threat-related stimuli as compared to individuals who are not anxious. However, a number of studies have revealed no effects of anxiety on priming for threat-related information (reviewed by McNally, 1997).

One reason for these contradictory findings has been proposed to relate to differences in the types of processes supporting performance on repetition priming tasks (see McNally, 1997). In particular, repetition priming is thought to be separated into perceptual and conceptual domains (Keane, Gabrieli, Growdon, & Corkin, 1994; Keane, Gabrieli, Fennema, Growdon, & Corkin, 1991). Perceptual repetition priming refers to the facilitated processing of a perceptually identical item due to its prior presentation. For example, participants might be shown a series of words (e.g., table, ankle). After a brief delay, they will be asked to perform what is presented as an unrelated task. They might be shown a series of words flashed briefly on a computer screen and asked to read the words aloud. The critical finding is that participants will be able to read the previously studied words even when they are presented at a very fast speed. In contrast, participants will require a longer presentation time in order to read the nonstudied words. This reduction in response latency (i.e., the speed of response) to identify the previously presented words is the perceptual repetition priming effect.

A few lines of evidence point to a perceptual basis for these priming effects. The effects can occur for newly formed representations (e.g., pseudowords) that have no pre-existing representations, suggesting that the effect is not reliant on conceptual knowledge (Gabrieli, Milberg, Keane, & Corkin, 1990; Keane, Gabrieli, Growdon, & Corkin, 1994; Schacter, Cooper, & Delaney, 1990). The effects are unaffected by whether participants initially study items with a "deep" processing task that draws attention to the meaning of the items or with a "shallow" task that only focuses on the perceptual qualities of the items, again suggesting that the effects are not influenced by attention toward conceptual features. However, the effects are greatly influenced by perceptual overlap at study and at test. Perceptual-priming effects are greatest when stimulus characteristics such as font, size, and format remain constant across multiple repetitions of an item. If those stimulus characteristics are changed, the priming effects are drastically reduced (reviewed by Wagner & Koutstaal, 2002; Wiggs & Martin, 1998). Thus, if participants study the word "table" and later are asked to identify the word "**TABLE**" they will not show the same benefit as if they were asked to identify the word "table" written in the same font.

In contrast to the types of effects just described, some repetition-priming tasks seem to rely on access to the meaning of an item rather than to its perceptual features only. For example, after studying a list of words that included the word "angle," participants will be more likely to complete the word stem "ang___" with the previously studied word "angle" than with other alternatives, such as "angel" or "anger." Importantly, this priming occurs even when the words are studied aurally and are completed as visual stems (reviewed by Wagner & Koutstaal, 2002; Roediger & McDermott, 1993). Thus, these types of priming effects cannot rely on perceptual similarity because the stimuli at study and at test use different formats.

Neuropsychological and neuroimaging studies have supported the dissociation of perceptual and conceptual priming. For example, Alzheimer's disease results in impaired performance on conceptual priming tasks such as the just-described word-stem completion priming task (Burke, Knight, & Partridge, 1994; Gabrieli et al., 1994; Heindel, Cahn, & Salmon, 1997), but these patients show preserved performance on perceptually based repetition priming tasks using pseudowords (Keane et al., 1994; Keane et al., 1991) or novel visual stimuli (Gabrieli et al., 1994). Conversely, damage to the temporo-occipital regions impairs repetition priming on perceptually based tasks (Keane et al., 1994), but not on conceptually based ones (Keane et al., 1995). Consistent with these patient data, neuroimaging studies have found that perceptual priming often is associated with changes in posterior visual regions, whereas conceptual priming-related changes often arise in temporo-occipital regions including the superior temporal gyri and inferior temporal regions (reviewed by Schacter & Buckner, 1998).

Interestingly, effects of mood or anxiety on conceptually oriented priming tasks tend to be much greater than effects on perceptually oriented tasks (see McNally, 1997). These results are intriguing in suggesting that the biases that occur in affective disorders may arise due to relatively higher-level, conceptual processing changes rather than to changes in how low-level incoming information is processed. Future research is needed to examine the extent to which the effects of emotion are similar on perceptually driven and conceptually driven priming tasks and to examine the neural processes that mediate the effects of emotion on these forms of priming.

☐ Effects of Emotion on Skill Learning (Procedural Memory)

Skill learning refers to practice-related facilitation of task performance. As we learn to perform a task, we tend to make fewer errors, to perform the task more quickly, and to perform it in a more automatic fashion. With practice, we move from a more deliberative or "cognitive" stage of task performance, keeping in mind the steps required to perform the task, to a more autonomous stage, performing the task without much cognitive control (see Anderson, 1983; Fitts, 1964).

There has been increasing evidence to suggest that emotion may influence the speed with which new skills are learned. This modulation of skill learning appears to occur for a variety of skill types (motor, perceptual, and cognitive) and to result from interactions between the amygdala and the striatum, a portion of the basal ganglia often associated with the coordination of motor commands (Doya, 2000), and with the ability to acquire new skills (Knowlton, Squire, & Gluck, 1994; Poldrack, Selco, Field, & Cohen, 1999). For example, Packard and colleagues (Packard, Cahill, & McGaugh, 1994; Packard & Cahill, 2001) trained rats on two versions of a water maze task. In both versions, rats completed a number of training trials in which they swam (from the same starting position each time) to a platform hidden in opaque water (always in the same location). Because rats find it aversive to be submersed in the water, they are motivated to find the platform as quickly as possible. After training, two types of test sessions occurred. In one version, rats were tested from a different starting location from the trained location. Therefore, the rats had to maintain a spatial map of the water maze in order to find the platform (a hippocampal-dependent task). In the other version, the rats started from the same location as in all prior trials. Thus, the rats could simply carry out the set of actions used previously to find the platform (a striatum-dependent task) and did not need to have a spatial map of the water maze in order to succeed. Performance on each version of this task was found to be modulated by the amygdala. Injections of a *d*-amphetamine agonist into the amygdala—which causes an increase in norepinephrine release—enhanced performance on both tasks (see McGaugh, 2004 for review). Thus, at least in animal models, the amygdala appears to modulate both hippocampal-dependent and striatal-based learning.

The amygdala appears to modulate striatal-based skill learning in humans as well. Steidl, Mohi-Uddin, and Anderson (2006) trained participants on a striatal-dependent weather prediction task (Knowlton et al., 1994). In this task, participants were presented with a series of cards and were asked, based on the depictions on those cards, to predict the weather. Successful performance on this task required implicit learning of the contingencies between the cue (card pattern) and the outcome (weather). Participants became more accurate at predicting the weather with additional practice on the task, but usually they could not verbalize the strategies that they were using to guide their performance. Critically, Steidl et al. (2006) showed participants negative arousing, positive arousing, or neutral pictures either after completion of the first phase of the weather prediction task or during the task itself. After one week, and again after three months, participants returned to the laboratory to perform the task.

Participants who viewed the arousing pictures during the initial task performance showed better retention of learning over the 3-month interval than participants who did not view the arousing pictures.

These data provide intriguing evidence that emotion can modulate procedural learning just as it influences other forms of implicit memory. Whether such effects always will be beneficial, or whether mood states may sometimes impair skill-learning remains to be seen. The time frame over which emotion exerts its influence also needs to be explored further. For example, Steidl et al. (2006) presented evidence that although emotion enhanced retention over a 3-month delay, it had no effect on retention over a 1-week delay. Thus, the effects of emotion may be slower acting for skill learning than for other forms of memory.

☐ Concluding Remarks

Although the bulk of research has examined emotion's modulation of declarative memory, many effects of our past are manifest not in our explicit retrieval of those experiences but rather in implicit changes in our behavior. The existing data make clear that emotion can have widespread effects on implicit learning, ranging from conditioning to priming to skill learning. Though much still needs to be learned about the conditions in which emotion exerts its influences, these studies have been critical in emphasizing that emotion's modulation of memory is not limited to interactions with the hippocampal memory system. Rather, emotion seems to play a broader modulatory role, influencing many branches of the long-term memory system.

Emotion's Influence
on Working Memory

In Chapter 4, we examined the effects of emotion on the unconscious effects of prior experience. The majority of research on the effects of emotion on human memory, however, has focused on understanding how emotion influences memories for information about which people are consciously aware. Often, a distinction is made between information that we hold in mind over short periods of time ("working memory") and information that is stored over the long term ("long-term memory"). In this chapter, we focus on the effects of emotion on working memory, whereas in later chapters (Chapter 6 through Chapter 9) we discuss the effects of emotion on long-term memory.

Working memory refers to a limited-capacity system used to store and manipulate information "online" over a short period (usually a few seconds). This active storage is essential for performance of a variety of cognitive tasks. For example, if I ask you whether it is cheaper to buy a 6-pack of soda for $6.40 or to buy six single cans that each cost $1.05, in order to answer the question, you must hold in mind the relevant numbers, perform the proper calculations, and then make your selection. You are using your working memory to reach your decision.

The specifics of the working memory system continue to be debated and expanded upon (see Baddeley & Hitch, 1974; Cowan, 1988; Jonides & Smith, 1997; Engle & Oransky, 1999; Engle, Kane, & Tuholski, 1999; Cowan, 1995). However, many have adopted an influential model, proposed by Baddeley and Hitch, in which working memory is described as consisting of two "buffers" that hold verbal (the phonological loop) and non-verbal (the visuospatial sketchpad) information online for short periods of time. The coordination of these buffers is supported by a "central executive" (modeled after the Supervisory Attentional System; Norman & Shallice,

1980), a limited-capacity attentional system that selects goal-relevant behavior by focusing and switching attention. Since the original model of Baddeley and Hitch, it has been suggested that no single "central executive" exists; rather there are likely a host of attentional processes that allow one to process task-relevant details and to ignore task-irrelevant information (e.g., Baddeley, 1998).

In contrast to the model of Baddeley and colleagues, others conceptualize working memory as the activated components of long-term memory stores (Engle & Oransky, 1999; Engle et al., 1999; Cowan, 1995). Thus, working memory is an active store for the information that we are thinking about in the here-and-now, whereas long-term memory is a more passive store of our previous experiences. In these models of working memory, attentional processes are once again critical for the operation of the system. It is through attentional filtering or selection that a subset of information stored in long-term memory reaches the working memory system, allowing that information to be worked with and updated.

☐ Effects of Emotional State on Working Memory

The vast majority of studies examining the link between emotion and working memory have focused on how one's emotional state influences the efficiency of the working memory system. In these studies, participants typically have been induced into a positive or a negative mood and then administered the experimental task following this mood induction procedure. Most of these studies have revealed that negative mood is associated with poorer performance on tasks requiring working memory ability. Individuals in a negative mood tend to do poorly on tasks requiring updating of information, problem solving, or flexible deployment of attention (e.g., Spies, Hesse, & Hummitzsch, 1996; Cheng & Holyoak, 1985; Mathews, May, Mogg, & Eysenck, 1990; but see Bolmont, Thullier, & Abraini, 2000 for a beneficial effect of anxiety). Thus, negative mood appears to hinder working memory performance, reducing its efficiency and effectiveness.

Although it is not entirely clear what leads to these adverse effects of negative emotion, one likely contributor is that an individual's intrusive thoughts or worries may distract the individual from the task-relevant information (Eysenck & Calvo, 1992; Seibert & Ellis, 1991). Consistent with this hypothesis, there is some evidence that negative mood states can have a disproportionate effect on verbal working memory as compared to visuospatial working memory (Ikeda, Iwanga, & Seiwa, 1996; Gray, 2001). Because verbalization of one's worries would be likely to interfere with the phonological loop more than with the visuospatial sketchpad, this hypothesis fits with the finding that verbal working memory can be impaired by negative mood to a greater degree than nonverbal working memory (see Nitschke, Heller, Palmieri, & Miller, 1999 for further discussion).

The effects of positive mood states on working memory performance are not as consistent as the effects of negative mood. While some studies have found enhancing effects of positive mood on working memory performance (Oaksford, Morris, Grainger, Williams, & Mark, 1996), other studies have found detrimental effects of positive emotion (Isen & Daubman, 1984; Isen, 1999). There is evidence that individuals in positive moods tend to rely more on heuristic processing and on general schematics than do individuals in neutral or negative moods (see Chapter 9 for further discussion). One possible contributor to these contrary findings, therefore, is that positive emotion assists performance on tasks that benefit from the use of heuristics but impairs performance on tasks that require attention to detail or analytical processing (see Ashby, Valentin, & Turken, 2002 for a review of the influence of a positive affect on working memory).

Neuroanatomically, the effects of emotional state on working memory are likely mediated, in large part, by interactions among prefrontal regions. The prefrontal cortex—and particularly its dorsolateral regions—is critical for information manipulation and updating, the processes that are the hallmark of working memory (Miller & Cohen, 2001; Smith & Jonides, 1999). Neuronal activity within these regions can be modulated by motivational state and by stress level, causing changes in the efficiency with which the working memory system operates (Hikosaka & Watanabe, 2000; Watanabe, 1996; see also Watanabe, 1998). For example, negative states such as anxiety and stress can impede the dopaminergic response in the prefrontal cortex and could disrupt working memory performance due to this alteration (Arnsten & Goldman-Rakic, 1998). By contrast, positive states can enhance dopaminergic neurotransmission, boosting working memory efficiency (reviewed by Ashby, Valentin, & Turken, 2002).

More generally, there is evidence that the orbitofrontal cortex, believed to be critical for processing emotional information (see Rolls, 2000; O'Doherty, Kringelbach, Rolls, Hornak, & Andrews, 2001), can interact with ventral and dorsolateral prefrontal regions critical for semantic elaboration, phonological rehearsal, and information manipulation. A number of neuroimaging studies have indicated that activation in orbitofrontal cortex is inversely related to activity in dorsolateral prefrontal regions (Perlstein, Elbert, & Stenger, 2002; Mayberg et al, 1999; Northoff et al., 2000; Drevets & Raichle, 1998). Although the directionality of these connections remains to be clarified, orbitofrontal activation during mood states could correspond with downregulation of dorsolateral prefrontal activity. Because the dorsolateral prefrontal cortex is essential for working memory performance, this downregulation could have an impairing effect on working memory.

☐ Effects of Emotional Content on Working Memory

Although these studies suggest that emotional *state* can influence working memory performance, fewer studies have examined whether the affective *content* of information maintained in working memory can also influence performance. Additional factors, such as intrusive thoughts (Seibert & Ellis, 1991), attention focus on internal stimuli (Ingram, 1990; Carver, Peterson, Follansbee, & Scheier, 1983), and emotional load (Mackie & Worth, 1989) may occur with mood induction procedures but not with tasks that manipulate emotional content. Thus, the effects of emotional content on working memory might be expected to be less robust than the effects of emotional mood states.

Indeed, Suzanne Corkin and I found that across a range of working memory tasks, manipulations of emotional content had no significant effect on memory accuracy (Kensinger & Corkin, 2003b). Importantly, however, we did find some indication that emotional content can have an impairing effect on working memory performance in terms of slowing reaction time. We asked participants to perform an *n* back task in which they were asked to indicate whether the stimulus that they were viewing matched the stimulus that had been presented *n* items previously. (On a 2-back version, the stimulus would need to match the one presented two prior, with one intervening item; on a 3-back version, the stimulus would need to match the one three prior, with two intervening items.) The results revealed that participants were slower in making their decisions when fearful faces were the target than when neutral faces were the target (see also Perlstein, Elbert, & Stenger, 2002 for evidence of hindering effects of emotional content on working memory). Moreover, the slowing was particularly pronounced when two fearful targets appeared one right after the other. We interpreted these results as reflecting the fact that, when participants are processing fearful faces, there are additional dimensions of information that must be inhibited in order to allow for processing of only the task-relevant (stimulus identity) information. This increased demand on inhibition may slow the response times to those fearful-face target items. This explanation also fits with the finding that the preceding item type influenced speed of responding on the task. When two fearful faces were presented back-to-back, emotional processing was likely much higher, perhaps requiring participants to engage in more inhibitory processing in order to ignore the fearful facial expression and instead to make the identity match required for successful task performance. Thus, it would follow that individuals would be slowest in the fear-fear instances and fastest in the neutral-neutral conditions (with reaction times to fear-neutral and neutral-fear sequences falling somewhere in between).

One ambiguous aspect of this task design related to the fact that matching stimuli always matched on both facial expression and facial identity. Thus, participants could plausibly use either (or both) of these dimensions to make their decision. Muscatell and Kensinger (2007) reasoned that if the emotional aspects of a stimulus "grab" attention and gain prioritized processing (e.g., Bargh, Chaiken, Govender, & Pratto, 1992; Pratto & John, 1991; Reimann & McNally, 1995; Williams, Mathews, & MacLeod, 1996), then this biasing of attention toward emotional stimuli could result in an enhanced likelihood that the emotion-relevant aspects of information are maintained within the working memory system while the emotion-irrelevant aspects of information are filtered out of the working memory system. To address this hypothesis, we asked participants to perform two versions of an *n* back task. In each version, participants saw a series of individuals displaying emotional (fear, anger, happiness, sadness, surprise) or neutral facial expressions. In an identity-matching version of the task, participants had to indicate whether the person was the same as the person presented two prior, regardless of whether the facial expression also matched. In an expression-matching version of the task, participants had to ignore the identity of the face and to indicate whether the facial expression displayed matched the expression displayed two faces earlier (i.e., with one different intervening face). In the identity-matching condition, participants were slower to make their decisions when the target expression was fearful than when it was neutral. In contrast, in the expression-matching condition, participants were much faster and more accurate at making their decisions when the target expression was fearful than when it was neutral (Muscatell & Kensinger, 2007).

Thus, just by changing the nature of the *n* back task (from identity matching to expression matching) we were able to change the effects of emotion on working memory performance from being inhibitory to being facilitative. This pattern of results is consistent with the hypothesis that the effects of emotion on working memory arise from attentional biasing toward emotional content (Williams et al., 1996). This biasing of attention appears to be beneficial to some tasks but detrimental to others, depending on task requirements. In particular, it appears that attention is focused on stimulus dimensions that convey the emotional salience and diverted from other stimulus dimensions less related to the source of the emotion, thus leading to performance benefits in tasks in which participants are asked to attend to the emotion-relevant dimensions (e.g., to facial expressions) but to performance impairments on tasks in which participants are asked to ignore the emotion-relevant dimensions.

Consistent with this hypothesis, many studies have found that if participants are asked to read aloud the color of ink in which a word is written, they will have greater interference (i.e., will be slower to name the color) if the printed word is emotional than if it is neutral (the emotional Stroop task; Gotlib & McCann, 1984). The explanation for this effect is that because the processing of the emotional words is prioritized, participants are worse at inhibiting their processing of those verbal stimuli than of non-emotional words. In other words, participants must use more cognitive resources in order to inhibit their processing of the emotional words than of the non-emotional words (reviewed by Williams et al., 1996).

In addition to these relatively automatic effects of emotion on attention, the emotional content of stimuli may also influence controlled processing of the information. Individuals may be more likely to elaborate on emotional information because of its personal relevance (Heuer & Reisberg, 1990; Doerksen & Shimamura, 2001) or its distinctiveness (Christianson & Engelberg, 1999; Pesta, Murphy, & Sanders, 2001; see Chapter 9 for further discussion). These controlled processes could also affect working memory performance, although, as with the more automatic processes discussed previously, the direction of the modulation is likely to differ depending on the specific task characteristics. If the additional processing for the emotional stimuli was focused on task-relevant information, then this should facilitate performance. If, in contrast, task-irrelevant details were processed because of the elaboration, then this could impair working memory performance because the limited-capacity system would become full of task-irrelevant details, leaving fewer resources available for the processing of task-relevant information.

From a neurobiological perspective, changes in prefrontal activity may underlie the effects of emotional content on working memory just as prefrontal interactions seem critical to the influences of emotional state on the working memory. Perlstein, Elbert, and Stenger (2002) provided evidence that working-memory related activity is reduced when individuals are retaining negative pictures over a delay as compared to neutral pictures. Future studies are required to clarify whether these effects occur across a variety of working memory tasks, and whether the impairing effects of negative emotional content on working memory operate via the same mechanisms as the impairing effects of negative mood on working memory. Nevertheless, the currently existing data suggest that not only can negative emotional *state* impede working memory performance (as described in the prior section) so too can maintenance of negative emotional *content*.

☐ Concluding Remarks—Comparing Effects of Emotion on Working Memory and Long-Term Memory Performance

As we will discuss in the next chapter, emotion often enhances the long-term retention of information. Indeed, Kensinger and Corkin (2003b) found that even in instances in which emotion had no effect on working memory accuracy, or slowed participants' performance on a working memory task, there were long-term memory benefits for the emotional information. These results indicate that emotional content can have distinct effects on working memory performance and on long-term memory performance. At a cognitive level, the differential effects may arise because the same processes that benefit long-term memory (e.g., orienting toward emotional aspects of stimuli, elaboration of emotional information) may have no benefit on working memory performance, and in fact may distract attention away from task-relevant information. At a neurobiological level, the divergent effects may arise because of differences in the systems that support working memory (prefrontal and parietal processes) and those that support long-term memory (hippocampal mechanisms). However, research that directly compares the effects of emotion on working and long-term memory is sparse, so further research will be required to enhance our understanding of the interplay between the influences of emotion on these different memory systems.

6

Emotion and Long-Term Memory Enhancements

Thus far, we have discussed the effects of emotion on nondeclarative memory (Chapter 4) and on memory for information retained over the short term (Chapter 5). However, emotion also has robust effects on long-term declarative memory, our ability to consciously remember experiences that occurred more than a few seconds ago. In fact, the vast majority of research that has examined the effects of emotion on human memory has focused on the influence of emotion on declarative long-term memory. In the next few chapters, we examine the effects of emotion on our ability to consciously remember prior experiences from our lives. We discuss the mechanisms through which emotion enhances the likelihood of remembering information (Chapter 6), the extent to which emotion influences the subjective vividness or the objective accuracy of a memory (Chapter 7), the types of information that are more, versus less, likely to be remembered when an event contains emotional relevance (Chapter 8), and the effects that stimulus characteristics (Chapter 9) or participant characteristics (Chapter 10) can have on the effects of emotion on declarative memory ability.

☐ Behavioral Evidence for the Emotional Memory Enhancement Effect

Emotion can have robust effects on the likelihood that information is remembered over the long term. If you ask a friend to tell you a memory from his or her life that had to do with a tree, it is likely that you will be told a story of an emotional event. Perhaps your friend once fell out of a tree and broke her arm or spent a particularly happy afternoon decorating a tree for the holidays. It is much less likely that your friend would recount a mundane memory about walking past a tree on her way to work. More systematic investigations have confirmed that when individuals are asked to generate memories in response to cue words, the memories that they retrieve will tend to be rated as personally significant and highly emotional (e.g., Conway, 1990; Rubin & Kozin, 1984). These findings suggest that we may be more likely to remember emotional experiences as compared to non-emotional ones. When given open-ended cues, which could lead us to retrieve any type of memory, it seems that the events that spring to mind most easily are those that contain emotional relevance.

Beneficial effects of emotion on memory are frequently discovered in more controlled laboratory investigations as well. If presented with a series of pictures, some positive, some negative, and some neutral, people will tend to remember more of the positive and negative pictures than the neutral pictures. This beneficial effect of emotion on memory has been demonstrated with a variety of stimuli—not only pictures, but also words, sentences, and narrated slide shows (e.g., Bradley, Greenwald, Petry, & Lang, 1992; Cahill & McGaugh, 1995; Kensinger, Brierley, Medford, Growdon, & Corkin, 2002; see Figure 6.1). It often is this increased

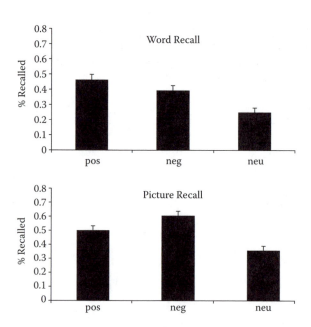

FIGURE 6.1 Young adults recall more positive and negative words or pictures than neutral words or pictures. This benefit in the quantity of information remembered often is referred to as the emotional memory enhancement effect. Data from Kensinger et al. (2002).

likelihood of remembering emotional information that is referred to as the *emotional memory enhancement effect*. As we have discussed in prior chapters, there are many other effects of emotion on memory aside from those on long-term declarative memory. However, when people refer to the emotional memory enhancement effect, they usually are speaking of the effect on long-term declarative memory.

A tremendous amount of research has examined the processes that give rise to the emotional memory enhancement effect. This research has been conducted primarily at two levels of analysis: concerning the cognitive processes and in reference to the neural processes that are recruited for emotional memory. This chapter discusses the findings from each of these levels of investigation. We also examine a closely related issue, which is to what extent the mnemonic benefit for emotional information results from the recruitment of processes that are specific to the processing of emotional information, and to what extent the memory advantage stems from additional engagement of the same processes that support memory for neutral information. Is there something "special" about how our memories of emotional events are recorded and retrieved or do emotional memories just represent one end of a mnemonic continuum?

□ Cognitive Processes Leading to the Emotional Memory Enhancement Effect

There is some evidence that, at the cognitive level, memory for emotional information may be enhanced because of features that tend to enhance memory for any type of information (emotional or non-emotional). In particular, emotional stimuli tend to be more highly *related* to one another, they tend to be more *distinct*, and individuals are more likely to carry out *elaborative* processes when the stimuli are encountered. In the following, we discuss the extent to which these features can account for the enhancing effects of emotion on memory (see also Talmi, Luk, McGarry, & Moscovitch 2007 for further discussion).

Emotion and Relatedness

Relatedness refers to how interconnected or thematically associated items are to one another. The issue of relatedness is particularly important in laboratory assessments of memory because a number of studies have demonstrated that individuals do better when asked to remember lists of items that are thematically associated with one another than when asked to remember lists of unrelated items. For example, if I ask you to remember the words *sink, counter, refrigerator, stove, fork, microwave, knife, dishwasher, cabinet* you will likely do better than if I ask you to remember the words *computer, avocado, purple, backpack, chess, telephone, wrench, cherry, toothpaste*. The connections between the items on the first list can help memory in a couple of ways. The connections can provide organization as the information is initially encountered on the study list, and they also can help with the generation of appropriate cues during retrieval attempts (e.g., Gardiner, Craik & Birtwistle, 1972; Hunt & McDaniel, 1993; Mandler, 1967). For example, as you were studying the list of kitchen items, you might have been able to use mental imagery (e.g., to imagine the sink next to the refrigerator) or inter-item associations (e.g., to group together the fork and the knife) to help you learn the information. At retrieval, you also might be better able to generate good cues to help you remember the information (e.g., trying to think of all the kitchen items that may have been on the list; trying to remember what item you had associated with fork). In contrast, these types of strategies would be harder to use with the second series of unrelated items.

If care is not taken to equate emotional and non-emotional items on their relatedness, it will tend to be the case that the emotional items will be more interconnected with one another than will the neutral words. "Emotion" can be thought of as a category, and the items that make up that category often have thematic relations with one another (e.g., negative items frequently refer to death, injury, illness).

There has been extensive discussion about the extent to which the semantic or thematic relatedness of emotional items can explain the emotional memory enhancement effect. One study showed that the emotional memory enhancement effect could be eliminated when memory for emotional words is compared to memory for closely interconnected neutral words (Talmi & Moscovitch, 2004). However, this effect has not been replicated for highly arousing emotional words (e.g., "taboo" words; Buchanan et al., 2006; Kensinger & Corkin, 2003c), and semantic relatedness also does not explain the entire emotional enhancement effect for emotional pictures (see also Talmi, Schimmack, Paterson, & Moscovitch, 2007), suggesting that although relatedness may contribute to an emotional memory advantage, it may not be a sufficient mechanism to explain the effect. Rather, as we discuss later, other emotion-specific effects, as well as effects not specific to emotional items, must be considered in order to understand the emotional enhancement effect.

Emotion and Distinctive Processing

Emotional items are not only more likely to be clustered around a theme than are neutral items, they also are more likely to be distinctive. Although distinctiveness is a somewhat nebulous term, in a general sense it refers to an item's "uniqueness" (Hunt & McDaniel, 1993). Distinctive items show less overlap with other items stored in memory, and they show little overlap with other items presented in a similar context. Thus, seeing a chainsaw in a kitchen would be more distinctive than seeing a chainsaw in a basement workroom because the chainsaw shares fewer features with items in the kitchen than with items in the workroom. Encoding manipulations that increase the distinctiveness of items (e.g., asking people to create unusual mental images to remember words on a list, or including pictures along with words on a study list) will increase the likelihood that people will remember presented information (e.g., Einstein & McDaniel, 1987; Schacter & Wiseman, 2006; Schmidt, 1994).

Emotional information is likely to be distinctive for a number of reasons (see Talmi et al., 2007; Schmidt, 1994 for further discussion). First, individuals are likely to have a physiological reaction to emotional items, thereby providing an additional dimension of experience for emotional items than for non-emotional ones. Second, emotional items are likely to be relevant to an individual's goals (Lazarus, 1991) and to be more personally relevant than non-emotional information. Third, emotional items are more likely to elicit regulation strategies and appraisal mechanisms than non-emotional items, thereby enhancing the cognitive processes associated with emotional experience. Therefore, emotional salience results in a number of additional dimensions (e.g., personal relevance, physiological response, cognitive appraisal) that are less likely to be present with neutral stimuli (e.g., Christianson & Engelberg, 1999; LeDoux, 2000). The presence of these additional dimensions is thought to increase what has been referred to as "absolute" distinctiveness. Regardless of what we are comparing them to, these items will have dimensions not present for other types of information (see Schmidt, 1991; Talmi, Luk et al., 2007 for further discussion).

However, emotional items may benefit not only from "absolute" distinctiveness but also from "relative" distinctiveness. That is, emotional items often will be less congruent within the context of a psychology experiment than non-emotional items. Seeing an emotional item among a list of items that one is trying to remember as part of a memory experiment may be akin to seeing a chainsaw on a kitchen counter. The emotional information is unexpected and so it stands out.

It is difficult to alter the effects of emotion on absolute distinctiveness. It is easier, however, to manipulate the relative distinctiveness of emotional items compared to other items presented on a study list. In fact, it has been demonstrated that if individuals are presented with a series of emotional items and a single neutral item is interspersed, participants will be more likely to remember the neutral item than to remember the emotional items (Schmidt, 2002). These data suggest that at least some of the effects of emotion on memory may arise because emotional items are relatively distinct (see also Pesta, Murphy, & Sanders, 2001; Kensinger & Corkin, 2004b for further discussion).

If relative distinctiveness were the sole contributor to the emotional memory enhancement effect, then the effect should be eliminated if participants were shown one list of emotional items and another list of neutral items and then memory was compared for the two lists. In this instance, the relative distinctiveness of the emotional and neutral items should be kept constant—participants should be expecting emotional items on the first list and non-emotional items on the second list. Results have been mixed with regard to whether this manipulation eliminates the emotional memory enhancement effect. Although some studies have reported stronger emotional memory enhancement effects on mixed lists (i.e., those that include emotional and non-emotional items on a single list) compared to pure lists (i.e., one list with emotional items and another list with non-emotional items; Dewhurst & Parry, 2000; Gruhn, Smith, & Baltes, 2005; Hadley & MacKay, 2006), other studies have found robust emotional memory enhancement effects even in a pure list condition (Kensinger & Corkin, 2003c). It is plausible that when the stimuli are selected to have particular personal relevance, or to elicit strong physiological responses, the absolute distinctiveness of those items will be sufficient to drive a mnemonic advantage (see Schmidt & Saari, 2007 for evidence that distinctiveness is a critical contributor to the emotional memory enhancement). Further research is needed to address this possibility.

Emotion, Elaboration, and Self-Referential Processing

We have known for decades that the encoding operations that are performed during the initial processing of information can influence the likelihood that the information can later be retrieved (Craik & Lockhart, 1972). In particular, "deep" encoding operations that focus on the meaning of information tend to produce a higher likelihood of later retrieval than encoding operations that focus on more superficial or "shallow" aspects of the incoming information, such as the information's perceptual features. It is likely that, in addition to benefits stemming from relatedness and distinctiveness, emotional items also benefit from deep encoding. We are more likely to focus on an item's meaning if that information is emotional whereas we may be more likely to attend only to the superficial characteristics of non-emotional information.

Elaborative encoding of emotional information may occur for a number of reasons. We are likely to process emotional information in regard to ourselves, a type of processing that is thought to elicit particularly deep, elaborative processing operations (e.g., Rogers, Kuiper, & Kirker, 1977; Symons & Johnson, 1997). We are likely to try to find meaning in emotional experiences. We are likely to think about the experience's broader significance to our personal lives or to our broader environment. We may try to reappraise the meaning of an event's experience to make it more or less emotionally evocative. Each of these factors can increase the likelihood that we elaborate on the occurrence of emotional events, thereby encoding them in a deep fashion.

Although many researchers have theorized about emotion's effects on elaborative encoding (e.g., Christianson, 1992; Ochsner, 2000), there are still many unanswered questions regarding the elaborative processes that are engaged. To what extent do these processes overlap with those involved during processing of self-referential information? Do the elaborative processes represent distinct processes that are not typically engaged when we contemplate the meaning of non-emotional information? How automatically do we engage elaborative processing of emotional information as compared to non-emotional information? That is, do we consciously try to think deeply about emotional information, or is it something that occurs relatively automatically because of the information's relevance to our goals? Further research is needed to clarify the nature of the elaborative processes that are engaged for emotional information and how those processes can enhance the likelihood that we will later remember emotional experiences.

☐ Neural Processes Leading to the Emotional Memory Enhancement Effect

The findings just described might lead one to believe that there is nothing "special" about emotional memories. Perhaps emotional items are remembered better than non-emotional ones because people benefit from some combination of relatedness, distinctiveness, and elaborative processing, all of which benefit memory for non-emotional information as well. As noted in Chapter 3, neuroimaging and neuropsychology are methods that have provided critical insights into whether behavioral enhancements in emotional memory arise from engagement of similar or distinct processes. Therefore, to examine this issue in detail, we turn our attention to studies of patients with amygdala damage and then to neuroimaging investigations of emotional memory.

Amygdala Damage Disrupts Emotional Memory Enhancement

Neuropsychological research has provided strong evidence for differences in the processes that contribute to long-term declarative memory for emotional information and for non-emotional information. In particular, studies of patients with damage to the amygdala have revealed that these individuals do not show a memory advantage for emotional information. They are just as likely to remember neutral events as they are to remember positive or negative ones. It is important to note, however, that these patients are not amnesic for emotional material. They can remember emotional information at above-chance levels. Thus, it does not appear that the amygdala is required in order for people to remember emotional experiences; however, the amygdala does appear to be necessary in order for people to receive a mnemonic boost for emotional as compared to non-emotional information.

One of the best-documented cases of emotional memory loss following amygdala damage is the patient SM046, originally reported by Tranel and Hyman (1990). This patient had bilateral mineralization of the amygdala, caused by Urbach-Wiethe disease, but relatively little damage to the remaining medial temporal lobe (although there was some damage to the entorhinal cortex). Across a range of paradigms, this patient showed a blunted emotional memory enhancement effect. Other patients with bilateral mineralization of the amygdala have shown a similar pattern of results, either showing equivalent recognition memory for emotional and neutral pictures, or poorer performance for the emotional pictures. These patterns of performance are in stark contrast to those of the control participants who were more likely to recognize the emotional pictures than the non-emotional ones (Markowitsch et al., 1994). Studies using the narrated slide show developed by Heuer and Reisberg (1990) and modified by Cahill and McGaugh (1995) have also demonstrated that while control participants remember more information about the arousing portions of the narrated slide show (e.g., those describing the boy's accident as described in Ch. 3) than the nonarousing portions, patients with bilateral amygdala damage showed no memory advantage for the arousing portions of the story (Adolphs, Cahill, Schul, & Babinsky, 1997; Cahill and McGaugh, 1995; Phelps et al., 1998; Hamann, Ely, Grafton, & Kilts, 1999).

It is important to note that the performance of patients with amygdala damage contrasts with the performance of patients with damage to other regions of the medial temporal lobe. Patients with medial temporal lobe damage that spares the amygdala often show a dense amnesia; they are impaired in their overall memory performance (see Corkin, 2002; Kensinger & Corkin, 2008). However, these patients show a normal memory enhancement for emotionally arousing material as compared to non-arousing material (Hamann, Cahill, & Squire, 1997; Hamann, Cahill, McGaugh, & Squire, 1997). These data emphasize the dissociable roles of the amygdala and other medial temporal lobe structures. It appears that while the hippocampal memory system is critical for the formation of new long-term memories, the amygdala plays a specific role in modulating the function of those medial temporal lobe regions in order to increase the likelihood that emotional memories are retained over time.

Clearly, studies of patients with amygdala damage have contributed a great deal to our understanding of emotional memory, and in the remainder of this section, I will focus on two questions that are actively being addressed within this patient population. First, to what extent are the effects of amygdala damage on emotional memory separable from effects on emotional processing? Second, are there distinct roles for the right and left amygdala in modulating emotional memory?

With regard to the first question, a number of studies have demonstrated that bilateral amygdala damage often affects both emotional memory and emotional perception. For example, patients with amygdala damage are often impaired in recognizing facial expressions (Adolphs, Tranel, Damasio, & Damasio, 1995; Anderson & Phelps, 2000; Broks et al., 1998; Calder et al., 1996; Schmolck & Squire, 2001; Sprengelmeyer et al., 1999). They also are no better at detecting emotional information presented in a rapid stream of items than they are at detecting neutral information, whereas controls will show an advantage for detecting emotional information (Anderson & Phelps, 2001). This leads to the question of whether the deficits in emotional processing and in emotional memory result from a single deficit or whether the two abilities may be dissociable. Brierley, Medford, Shaw, and David (2004) tackled this question by assessing participants' emotional processing ability (e.g., their ability to perceive affect from facial and vocal expressions) and participants' emotional memory ability (using the narrated slide show as well as another test of recognition memory). They reasoned that if emotional processing and emotional memory were intricately linked to one another, then the magnitude of the deficits should be similar in the two domains. In contrast to this hypothesis, they found that there was no correlation between performance on the tests of emotional perception and on the tests of emotional memory. This result is consistent with findings from another study in which a patient with amygdala damage demonstrated a normal emotional memory enhancement effect while at the same time showing impaired recognition of fear from both facial and vocal expressions (Papps, Calder, Young, & O'Carroll, 2003). These findings suggest that perception of emotional expressions and affective modulation of memory may be supported by separable processes. However, relatively few studies have examined this issue, and it is still not clear what neural dissociations may explain the independence between emotional processing and emotional memory.

With regard to the second question, many studies have examined the effects of unilateral as compared to bilateral amygdala damage on emotional memory. Patients with bilateral damage tend to have greater impairments in emotional memory than patients with unilateral damage (e.g., Brierley et al., 2004), but there has not been agreement regarding the effects of unilateral damage on emotional memory. For example, in one study in which memory was assessed for the narrated slide show, patients with left amygdala damage all showed a blunted emotional memory enhancement effect, whereas patients with right amygdala damage showed normal affective modulation of memory (Adolphs, Tranel, & Denburg, 2000). There have been a couple of other studies that have suggested that left amygdala damage may specifically disrupt emotional enhancement of verbal (and not nonverbal) material, whereas right amygdala damage may affect emotional memory for nonverbal material (e.g., LaBar & Phelps, 1998; Buchanan, Tranel, & Adolphs, 2006). These studies have only provided weak evidence for this type of lateralization, however, because many of these patients have shown overall deficits in verbal or visual memory (for neutral as well as emotional information) following left or right temporal lobe damage, respectively. Therefore, it is hard to know whether the laterality effects that have emerged result from lateralized damage to the amygdala or whether they might instead result from damage to surrounding medial temporal lobe regions. We know that other regions within the medial temporal lobe function in a modality-specific manner, with the left medial temporal lobe supporting memory for verbal information and the right medial temporal lobe critical for memory for nonverbal information (e.g., Kelley et al., 1998). Therefore, future studies are needed to resolve whether the amygdala operates in a modality-specific fashion as well or whether laterality effects in the amygdala are influenced by other factors. Neuroimaging studies are beginning to address the important question of what types of stimulus or participant characteristics are related to laterality effects in the amygdala (see the next section as well as Chapter 10 for more discussion of laterality effects in the amygdala).

These studies of patients with amygdala damage have been essential in demonstrating that the amygdala is not critical for the formation of all long-term memories, but that it plays an essential modulatory role in emotional memory, increasing the likelihood that emotional memories are retained over time. These studies suggest that there is something "special" about emotional memories, with the mnemonic benefits conferred because of amygdala engagement. Thus, although emotional memories can benefit from domain-general processes that contribute to the formation of all sorts of memories, they also appear to benefit from emotion-specific processes.

☐ Neuroimaging Investigations of the Amygdala's Role in Emotional Memory

Although patient studies have revealed a critical role for the amygdala in mediating the emotional memory enhancement effect, they have not been able to clarify the memory stage during which the amygdala exerts its influence. Neuroimaging methods provide a way to address this issue. These neuroimaging studies have demonstrated that the amygdala plays an important role in the encoding of emotional information. The role of the amygdala during the encoding of emotional information was first revealed in a PET study in which neural responses were measured as individuals listened to the narrated slide shows that we have discussed previously. Later, participants were asked to report what they remembered from the slide show. The individuals who showed the greatest amygdala activity during the initial viewing of arousing slides were those individuals who showed the greatest emotional memory enhancement (Cahill et al., 1996). Note that this first study was therefore a demonstration of a between-subjects effect of amygdala activity on emotional memory (i.e., people who showed greater amygdala activity also showed greater emotional memory enhancement). Although this finding provides a strong suggestion for the role of the amygdala in the encoding of emotional information, one could always argue that individual differences in amygdala reactivity are being measured, rather than effects specific to the encoding of emotional information.

More direct evidence for a role of the amygdala in the encoding of emotional information has come from fMRI studies in which researchers can look at variations in amygdala activity within a particular person. As described in Chapter 3, event-related neuroimaging methods allow researchers to examine the neural processes associated with the successful encoding of emotional information by comparing brain activity during the processing of items that will later be remembered to brain activity during the processing of items that will later be forgotten. Similarly, researchers can pinpoint the activity associated with the successful retrieval of emotional information by comparing brain activity associated with correct endorsements of studied items to brain activity associated with incorrect rejections of studied items. These studies have confirmed that, even within a single subject, the emotional items that elicit the greatest amygdala activity during encoding are those that will be most likely to be remembered (reviewed by Hamann, 2001; Phelps, 2004; Kensinger, in press). In contrast, the amygdala shows no comparable relation to memory for non-emotional information. These data provide strong evidence for a role of the amygdala during the encoding process.

The amygdala, of course, is not acting on its own to record emotional experiences. In fact, as evidenced by the patient data, the amygdala is not necessary for the retention of emotional information. Patients with damage to the amygdala are not amnesic for emotional information. They can remember at least some emotional experiences; they just do not remember them with a greater probability than they remember non-emotional experiences. Thus, rather than the amygdala being essential for the retention of emotional information, it appears that the amygdala serves a modulatory role, increasing the likelihood that emotional information is successfully encoded and retained over time. It has been proposed that, once activated during the processing of emotional information, the amygdala exerts its effects on emotional memory by modulating the functioning of sensory cortices to assure that the emotional information is attended (reviewed by Davis & Whalen, 2001; Dolan & Vuilleumier, 2003; LeDoux, 1995; see also Talmi, Anderson, Riggs, Caplan, & Moscovitch, 2008) and by enhancing mnemonic consolidation processes in the hippocampal formation to increase the likelihood that the emotional information is retained over time in a stable memory trace (reviewed by McGaugh, 2004; Phelps, 2004). The amygdala is well suited for these modulatory functions because of its extensive connections to cortical and subcortical regions; in fact, the amygdala is one of the more extensively connected subcortical regions of the brain (Amaral, Price, Pitkanen, & Carmichael, 1992; Amaral, 2003).

Recent neuroimaging studies have provided strong evidence for these modulatory effects of the amygdala on the functioning of both sensory processes and mnemonic ones. Within the sensory realm, a number of neuroimaging studies have shown strong correlations between the amount of activity in the amygdala and the amount of activity in sensory regions—such as the fusiform gyrus or the occipital cortex—during the processing of emotional information (e.g., Tabert et al., 2001; Talmi et al., 2008; Noesselt, Driver, Heinze, & Dolan, 2005). By scanning individuals with varying amounts of amygdala damage as they viewed fearful faces, Vuilleumier, Richardson, Armony, Driver, and Dolan (2004) discovered that the amount of amygdala preservation corresponded with the amount of fusiform modulation based on the emotional content of the attended faces. These results suggest that the amygdala can modulate visual processing in humans, increasing the likelihood that an emotional item in the environment is detected and attended (see Duncan & Barrett, 2007 for further discussion).

A number of neuroimaging studies also have provided evidence for amygdalar modulation of mnemonic processes and, in particular, for the amygdala's ability to modulate the activity in other regions of the medial temporal lobe (see review by Phelps, 2004; Labar & Cabeza, 2006). There are strong correlations between the amount of activity in the amygdala and the amount of activity in the hippocampus as participants encode emotional information (i.e., initially process that information to allow later memory for that information). The strength of those correlations corresponds with the mnemonic enhancement for emotional information (e.g., Dolcos, LaBar, & Cabeza, 2004; Hamann, Ely, Grafton, & Kilts, 1999; Kensinger & Corkin, 2004c; Kensinger & Schacter, 2005a). Although these correlational studies cannot identify the direction of modulation, nor can they distinguish a direct modulatory effect from an indirect one, they do provide evidence that the amygdala and hippocampal formation seem to work in concert to create robust memories of emotional experiences.

Evidence for bi-directional influences between the amygdala and the hippocampus came from a neuroimaging study investigating the encoding of emotional information in patients with varying amounts of amygdala and hippocampal damage (Richardson, Strange, & Dolan, 2004). While in the scanner, patients were asked to encode a series of aversive and neutral words. Those encoding trials were sorted on a post-hoc basis into those words that participants were later able to identify on a recognition memory task and those words that participants later failed to recognize as having been studied. The study revealed that the greater the extent of amygdala atrophy, the less activity there was in the hippocampus during the encoding of the emotional information; conversely, the amount of hippocampal atrophy also was inversely related to amygdala activity (Richardson et al., 2004). These correlations suggest that reciprocal connections between the amygdala and the hippocampus may be important for modulating the encoding of emotional information (see also Kilpatrick & Cahill, 2003).

It is important to point out that these neuroimaging studies cannot easily tease apart effects of encoding (i.e., of registering information into memory) from effects of consolidation (i.e., of creating a stable form of memory that can persist over long periods of time). From the animal literature, we know that a large role of amygdala modulation of hippocampal function seems to be in the modulation of consolidation processes (see McGaugh, 2004; Phelps & LeDoux, 2005 for reviews), so it is likely that some of the interactions between the amygdala and the hippocampus reflect influences on consolidation rather than initial encoding. One possible way to examine this issue is to ask whether the relation of amygdala-hippocampal interactions correlates more strongly with the ability to remember information over the very long term than with the ability to remember information over a relatively short delay. If the critical role of amygdala modulation of hippocampal function in humans relates to the types of details that are retained in a memory trace over time, then one might expect the effects of those interactions to be particularly influential on memory over longer delays. If, in contrast, amygdala modulation of hippocampal function also plays a critical role in influencing the types of details that are recorded during the stimuli's initial presentations, then the interactions between the amygdala and the hippocampus may be as effective in influencing emotional memory over short delays as over longer ones. Research in my laboratory, as well as in other laboratories, is just beginning to address this important question (see Talmi et al., 2008 for an important study examining the effect of emotion on memories assessed after a short time interval).

The amygdala also appears to play an important role in episodic retrieval (see Buchanan, 2007 for a thorough review of the research examining retrieval of emotional memories). Initial evidence of amygdala engagement during retrieval came from PET studies revealing increased amygdala activity during the retrieval of emotional as compared to neutral items (e.g., Dolan, Lane, Chua, & Fletcher, 2000; Taylor et al., 1998). Because PET requires use of a blocked design, with some blocks including emotional items, it was not clear from these studies whether amygdala activation during the retrieval phase was related to mnemonic processes per se or to more general emotional processing. To circumvent this difficulty, a few studies examined the amygdala's role in retrieval of neutral information that had been studied in an emotional context. Because the information presented during retrieval was itself non-emotional, amygdala engagement could not result simply from the emotional processing of the retrieval cue. These studies demonstrated that the amygdala was more active during the retrieval of information learned in an emotional context than during the retrieval of information learned in a non-emotional context, thus providing stronger evidence for a role of the amygdala in retrieval (e.g., Maratos, Dolan, Morris, Henson, & Rugg, 2001; Smith, Henson, Dolan, & Rugg, 2004). Note that in these studies, however, only correct retrieval trials were included. Even stronger evidence for a role of the amygdala in retrieval has come from demonstrations of an interaction between emotional content and successful retrieval (Dolcos, LaBar, & Cabeza, 2005; Kensinger & Schacter, 2005b; Kensinger & Schacter, 2007). This interaction highlights that the amygdala shows a stronger relation to successful retrieval (as compared to retrieval failures) for emotional items than for neutral items, underscoring the potential importance of amygdala engagement during the retrieval process. It is still difficult to rule out possible effects of emotion processing (e.g., if the items that elicit the greatest emotional reaction also are those that are most likely to be retrieved, then it is possible that the amygdala's correlation with accurate retrieval is not causal but rather is a secondary result of the increased emotional processing of that item). However, these results nevertheless suggest that the amygdala may be involved in the retrieval, as well as in the encoding, of emotional memories.

☐ Concluding Remarks

As this chapter has emphasized, a tremendous amount of research has focused on understanding how emotion enhances the quantity of information that is remembered. Although it is likely that at least some of the mnemonic benefits for emotional information result from encoding processes that are not unique to emotion (e.g., emotional items benefit from relatedness, distinctiveness, and elaborative encoding), neuropsychological and neuroimaging studies have provided strong evidence that there are emotion-specific processes that boost memory for emotional information. In particular, the amygdala appears to be critical for this quantitative memory boost. Through its interactions with other cortical and subcortical regions, the amygdala is able to modulate sensory functions as well as mnemonic ones, increasing the likelihood that emotional information in the environment is perceived and retained in a stable memory trace that can be effectively retrieved.

Aspects of Memory Enhanced by Emotion

We all are aware that we can remember prior experiences with varying amounts of detail. We may remember that we took a family vacation to Arizona, but we may fail to retrieve many details about the sites we saw, the places we stayed, or the food we ate. In contrast, we may remember another family vacation to Maine with a tremendous amount of detail, recalling the excitement we felt as we boarded the plane, the color of the rental car, the feel of the cool ocean water, or the excellent seafood we ate (for a review of the processes supporting these different types of memories, see Yonelinas, 2002).

Often, the hallmark of an emotional memory is the vividness with which one remembers the occurrence. For example, it would not be surprising to find that everyone who was of elementary-school age or older at the time can remember that John F. Kennedy was shot or that terrorist attacks occurred on September 11, 2001. What is amazing, however, is that people can tell you where they were, and what they were doing, when they first learned that these events had taken place. Interest in the detail with which people remember highly emotional public events dates back at least to the assassination of President Lincoln (Colgrove, 1899), but the systematic study of these emotional memories was launched in 1977 by Brown and Kulik. In their investigation of people's memories for the assassination of John F. Kennedy, Brown and Kulik demonstrated that 14 years after the fact, people still remembered where they were when they heard the news, how they learned the news, what they were doing at the time, and how the news impacted them. Because of the tremendous vividness with which people remembered these events, Brown and Kulik coined the term "flashbulb memory." It seemed as though, at the time that an emotional event took place, a flash of activity went off in the brain, recording in picture-perfect detail all aspects of the ongoing event.

Many studies have replicated Brown and Kulik's (1977) original finding that participants remember a variety of personal details, such as where they were, what they were wearing, and what they were doing when they first learned about an assassination (Christianson, 1989; Winograd & Killinger, 1983), a terrorist attack (Budson et al., 2004; Paradis, Solomon, Florer, & Thompson, 2004; Pezdek, 2003; Smith, Bibi, & Sheard, 2003; Wolters & Goudsmit, 2005), or a space shuttle explosion (Bohannon, 1988; Kensinger, Krendl, & Corkin, 2006; Neisser & Harsch, 1992). Although these highly emotional public events occur infrequently, studies of auto-biographical memories have also demonstrated that individuals remember emotional experiences in a particularly vivid manner (e.g., Conway, 1990; Rubin & Kozin, 1984; Schaefer & Philippot, 2005).

In fact, it turns out that many of emotion's effects become apparent *only* when the quality of a memory is considered. For example, recognition memory performance often is comparable for emotional items and for non-emotional ones (e.g., Dougal & Rotello, 2007; Ochsner, 2000; Sharot, Delgado, & Phelps, 2004). In other words, sometimes it is the case that individuals are no more likely to select previously presented emotional items than they are to select previously presented neutral items from among a list that intermixes studied with nonstudied items. However, if rather than asking people simply to select the studied items, you also ask them to indicate whether they vividly "remember" something specific about the item's prior presentation (e.g., something they thought when they saw the item, something that happened in the room when the item was presented) or simply "know" that the item was presented, robust effects of emotion often emerge. In particular, individuals are much more likely to vividly remember emotional items as compared to non-emotional ones (Dewhurst & Parry, 2000; Kensinger & Corkin, 2003c; Ochsner, 2000; Sharot et al., 2004; Figure 7.1).

☐ Effects of Emotion on Memory for Detail

As the prior section described, we often believe that our memories of significant life experiences are retained with particular detail and with a vivid quality that distinguishes them from our memories of more mundane events. When Brown and Kulik (1977) coined the term "flashbulb memory," they believed that memories for surprising and consequential events were formed by a separate memory mechanism, essentially a neural "now print" command, causing a permanent retention of all information present at the time that the emotional response was elicited.

However, there is now abundant evidence that emotional memories are not infallible. Even when people believe that they vividly remember the

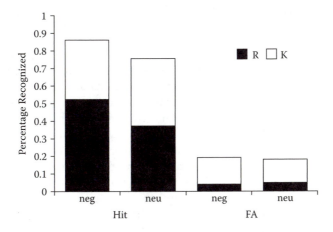

FIGURE 7.1   Participants were more likely to vividly "remember" studied negative items than studied neutral items (reflected by the larger R-based hit response to negative than to neutral words). The likelihood of falsely endorsing new words as studied ones was not affected by emotion (reflected by the similar false alarm rates for negative and neutral items). R = vividly remember. K = know, without remembering details. Hit = correct endorsement of a studied item. FA = false alarm, or incorrect endorsement of a novel item. neg = negative word, neu = neutral word. Data from Kensinger & Corkin (2003, Experiment 1).

context in which they experienced an emotional event, details of those memories can be quite inaccurate. Individuals' reports about where they were or what they were doing when they learned of a surprising event often change over time, and yet individuals retain high confidence in the accuracy of their memories. In fact, there often is little correlation between an individual's confidence in his or her memory and the consistency of that memory over time (Neisser & Harsch, 1992; Schmidt, 2004; Schmolck, Buffalo, & Squire, 2000; Talarico & Rubin, 2003). However, the fact that memory is not immune to distortion does not address the question of whether memories for emotional experiences are *more likely to be accurate* than memories for more mundane experiences. In other words, does emotion influence the accuracy with which information is remembered?

In order to examine this question, this chapter discusses two ongoing debates regarding the effects of emotion on memory. First, does emotion primarily inflate an individual's confidence in a memory, or does emotion also serve to increase the accuracy with which information is remembered? Second, does emotion affect memory for all types of details equally, or does emotion exert a greater influence on remembering some types of details more than other types of details?

☐ Inflated Confidence or Enhanced Detail?

Although we now recognize that memories for emotional experiences are not immune to distortion, the question remains as to whether our memories for emotional events contain more accurate detail than our memories of non-emotional events. There is some evidence to suggest that emotion primarily inflates a person's confidence in a memory, but does not actually enhance the accuracy or the level of detail with which a memory is retained. The strongest evidence to support this conclusion comes from looking at participants' false alarm rates on recognition memory tasks; that is, the likelihood that participants will falsely endorse a nonstudied item as a studied one. Across a number of recognition paradigms, participants have been more likely to falsely recognize emotional items (and particularly negative ones) compared to non-emotional ones (Budson et al., 2006; Dougal & Rotello, 2007; Ehlers, Margraf, Davies, & Roth, 1988; Windmann & Kruger, 1998; Windmann & Kutas, 2001). This enhancement in false alarm rates has occurred for words related to the studied items (e.g., those from similar semantic categories) but critically, such false endorsements also have been more likely to occur for negative items that are unrelated to the studied items (e.g., Budson et al., 2006). These findings suggest that individuals are biased to believe that they have seen an emotional item previously. When that bias is controlled for (i.e., when the false endorsements to items unrelated to studied items are considered), a number of studies have revealed that recognition memory is no better for emotional items than for non-emotional ones (e.g., Dougal & Rotello, 2007; Ochsner, 2000; Sharot & Phelps, 2004).

There are a couple of plausible contributors to this biasing effect of emotion. First, emotional items (and particularly negative ones) tend to be processed more fluently than neutral items (Bargh, Chaiken, Govender, & Pratto, 1992; Kityama, 1990; Ohman, 1988). In other words, individuals are faster at detecting and processing emotional items. It turns out that items that have been seen recently tend to be processed more fluently than items that have not been encountered recently (Whittlesea, 1993; Whittlesea & Williams, 2000). Therefore, participants often use fluency of processing as a heuristic (a "rule of thumb") to determine whether a particular item has been studied. If the item is processed in a highly fluent manner, it is more likely that the item has been encountered recently. Because of this use of fluency as an indicator of a recent encounter, participants may misinterpret the fluid processing of an emotional item on a recognition task as evidence that they have recently studied the item. Thus, enhanced fluency could lead individuals to endorse falsely more nonpresented negative items than nonpresented neutral items. Second, as we have discussed, emotional items are more likely to be related to one another than are neutral items (Talmi & Moscovitch, 2004). Novel items that are thematically associated with studied items tend to be endorsed falsely more often than unrelated items (Roediger, Watson, McDermott, & Gallo, 2001; Stradler, Roediger, & McDermott, 1999). Therefore, it is possible that the semantic cohesion and thematic relatedness of emotional items will lead to their increased false recognition rates.

The fact that individuals have higher false alarm rates for emotional items than for nonemotional ones has led to the suggestion that emotion may primarily inflate a person's confidence in a memory or bias the individual to believe that he or she vividly remembers information. In fact, a recent article (Dougal & Rotello, 2007) was titled "'Remembering' emotional words is based on response bias, not recollection," demonstrating that people claim they "remember" emotional words even when those words were not previously studied (but see Grider & Malmberg, 2008 for an alternative view).

Though these studies suggest that emotion's primary influence may be in inflating a person's confidence in a memory, there are findings that provide strong evidence for effects of emotion on memory accuracy. In two studies, Kensinger, Garoff-Eaton, and Schacter (2006, 2007a) showed participants a series of negative and neutral objects (e.g., a spider, a blender). Participants made a size decision about each object, and no mention was made about a later recognition task (Figure 7.2, Panel a). To the participants' surprise, a couple of days later they were asked to perform a memory task. They were shown a series of objects. Some were identical to studied objects (same); others shared the same verbal label as studied objects but differed in any number of visual features (similar); and still others were entirely novel objects unrelated to those that had been studied (new). Participants were asked to indicate whether each item was the "same," "similar," or "new" (Figure 7.2, Panel b). The analyses examined the likelihood that participants would recognize that a particular type of item had been studied (e.g., would remember that a snake had been studied—would call it "same" or "similar") and the likelihood that participants would recognize the exact visual details of a studied item (e.g., would correctly give a "same" response to a same blender). The critical finding was that participants were better able to remember the exact visual details of negative items compared with neutral items (Figure 7.2, Panel c).

Is there a way to reconcile these two seemingly disparate literatures, one suggesting that emotion biases individuals to believe they remember something vividly and the other suggesting that emotion boosts the likelihood that they remember something in a detailed fashion? Though these literatures seem contradictory at first glance, I believe they can be understood together. First, it is important to recognize that the enhancement in memory for detail can occur independently of any enhancement in overall recognition accuracy. For example, Kensinger, Garoff-Eaton, & Schacter

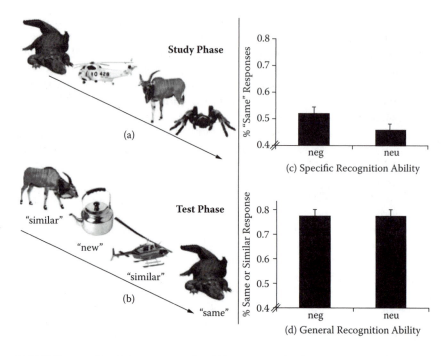

FIGURE 7.2 Participants studied a series of objects (a), and after a delay, participants were asked to indicate whether objects were the same (identical) as studied objects, similar to studied objects (sharing the verbal label but not the exact visual details), or new (nonstudied) objects (b). Participants were better at remembering the exact visual details of negative objects than of neutral ones (c) even though they were equally likely to remember whether a particular type of negative or neutral object had been studied (e.g., to know whether a spider or a kettle had been studied; d). Thus, even in an instance where the general ability to recognize a studied item was equal for negative and neutral items, the ability to remember the exact visual details of those objects was enhanced for the negative items. Data from Kensinger, Garoff-Eaton, and Schacter (2006).

(2006) found that the memory enhancement in memory for visual detail occurred even when the ability to recognize that a particular item type had been studied (e.g., to remember that a snake or a blender had been studied) was equivalent for the negative and neutral items (Figure 7.2, Panel c). In other words, emotion can have no effect on the likelihood that an item is remembered and yet—given that the item is retrieved—emotion can boost the likelihood that details of its presentation are remembered. Because of this finding, we cannot assume that increased "remember" responses without increased recognition performance occur because of a bias to believe that emotional information is "remembered." Rather, it may be true that people do not remember more emotional items than non-emotional ones, but that when they remember the emotional items, they remember them with increased vividness. In other words, their "remember" responses may be an accurate reflection of the increased details that they can retrieve about the emotional items. Second, false recollections need not always be spurious "noise" in the memory system. Rather, false recollections can sometimes be based on accurate (but misplaced) memory for detail. For example, let us imagine that I see the word "trash" on a study list. Perhaps because of associations that I form with that word, I later indicate that I saw the word "dirty." It is entirely possible that I could accurately remember associations that I had formed with the word trash and yet misattribute those to the word dirty (see Kahn et al., 2004 for neural evidence of such false recollections). Thus, falsely "remembering" emotional items need not result only from a bias to believe that an emotional item is remembered vividly; rather, such false endorsements also could occur if recollective components are recalled in response to the wrong retrieval cue (see also Dodson, Bawa, & Slotnick, 2007 for further discussion of misrecollection).

☐ Amygdala Activity and Emotional Memory: Enhancing Bias or Detail?

Although there is clear evidence that emotion can enhance memory for at least some types of details, these studies do not speak to the neural mechanisms through which such effects on accuracy arise. A particular point of debate has been whether engagement of emotion processing regions (and particularly the amygdala) during retrieval serves primarily to inflate a person's bias to believe that an item has been presented previously or whether engagement of emotion processing regions can correspond with the accuracy of retrieved memories.

Sharot et al. (2004) have suggested that amygdala activity at retrieval may primarily serve to inflate a person's estimate of a memory's vividness and level of detail. They found that amygdala activity at retrieval corresponded with an individual's self-reported vividness of memories for previously presented emotional items (see also Dolcos, LaBar, & Cabeza, 2005), while activity in the parahippocampal gyrus (associated with visual processing and visuospatial memory) corresponded with the self-reported vividness of memories for previously presented neutral items. Because the overall recognition rates were equivalent for emotional and neutral items, the authors interpreted their findings as indicating that when individuals say that they vividly remember neutral items, they are saying so because they remember particular details of that item's presentation (as deduced from the fact that activity in a visual-processing region corresponded with a vivid memory for a previously presented picture). In contrast, when individuals say that they vividly remember emotional items, they are saying so because amygdala engagement at retrieval leads them to feel as though they have a vivid memory because of the feeling of arousal and perceptual fluency that accompanies the remembrance of emotional items.

Other findings, however, have demonstrated that amygdala activity can correspond with retrieval of accurate detail (Kensinger & Schacter, 2005b; Smith, Stephan, Rugg, & Dolan, 2006) and not with false recognition of novel items (Kensinger & Schacter, 2007). For example, in one study (Kensinger and Schacter, 2005b), participants viewed a series of concrete nouns. Some referred to negative objects (e.g., snake, casket) and others to neutral objects (e.g., frog, canoe). Participants were shown photographs of half of the objects but only mentally imagined the other half of the objects. At retrieval, participants were shown a series of words and indicated whether they had seen the corresponding photo of the object (i.e., made a reality-monitoring decision; Johnson & Raye, 1981). We examined the regions in which activity was greater during the retrieval of items that were correctly attributed to imagination or perception compared to items that were misattributed. Critically, activity in the amygdala and the orbitofrontal cortex showed a correspondence to accurate retrieval of the negative items but showed no relation to accurate retrieval of the neutral items (Figure 7.3), suggesting a specific role for these regions in accurate retrieval of emotional information. Smith et al. (2006) revealed convergent findings in a study in which participants studied neutral objects in neutral or emotional scenes that either did or did not include people. Participants were scanned as they performed a recognition memory task in which they reported the context in which the neutral objects had been studied. In one condition, the options were "emotional context" or "neutral context"; in a second condition, the options were "context with people" or "context without people." The analyses revealed enhanced hippocampal-amygdala connectivity whenever individuals retrieved information studied in an emotional context, regardless of whether the task required reporting of the emotional context. When the retrieval of the emotional information was required for successful memory performance (i.e., when participants were deciding "emotional context" or "neutral context"), the connections between the hippocampus and the amygdala were strengthened, seemingly due to modulation from the orbitofrontal cortex.

Further research is needed to clarify whether there are instances in which amygdala activity at retrieval primarily inflates one's confidence in a memory. It is plausible that there are situations in which the amygdala—perhaps through its connections to ventromedial prefrontal cortex and other

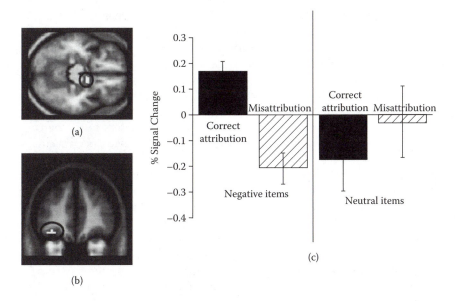

FIGURE 7.3 Retrieval-related activity in the amygdala (Panel a) and in the orbitofrontal cortex (Panel b) correspond with the likelihood that people correctly attribute negative items to imagination or perception. Activity in these regions showed no correspondence to accurate memory attributions for neutral items (Panel c; note that this panel depicts activity in the amygdala region; a similar pattern of activity was revealed in the orbitofrontal cortex). Data from Kensinger & Schacter (2005b).

regions tied to metamemory assessments (Schnyer, Nicholls, & Verfaellie, 2005)—leads a person to falsely believe that he or she has retrieved a vivid and detailed memory. However, the studies by Smith et al. (2006) and Kensinger and Schacter (2005b) emphasize that amygdala activity at retrieval is not always independent from memory accuracy. Rather, these studies provide strong evidence that amygdala engagement at retrieval can correspond with the accurate retrieval of detailed information.

□ What Details Are Enhanced by Emotion?

The first part of this chapter has emphasized that people believe that they vividly remember emotional experiences. Although our memories for emotional experiences are not perfect, it also seems that we are somewhat justified in our belief that we have retained more details about emotional experiences than about more mundane ones. Emotion has been found to enhance memory for many details, including the color of font in which a word was presented (Doerksen & Shimamura, 2001; Kensinger & Corkin, 2003c; D'Argembeau & van der Linden, 2004; MacKay et al., 2004), the spatial location of an item on a computer screen (D'Argembeau & Van der Linden, 2004; MacKay & Ahmetzanov, 2005; Mather & Nesmith, in press), or whether words or objects were visually presented or mentally imagined (Kensinger & Schacter, 2006d). These results suggest that emotion may have a broad effect on the ability to remember contextual (or "source") information. *Source memory* is a term that refers to the perceptual, spatiotemporal, or affective context in which an event occurs, and it often is contrasted with item memory, or memory for the item void of its context. For example, you may remember reading about a custody battle ("item memory") but have no memory for where you read the information (i.e., no "source memory"). In contrast, you may remember reading about a cake-decorating contest in your local newspaper last week, in which case you have retained both item memory and source memory.

While it is clear that at least some details are more likely to be remembered for items with negative emotional content than for items with neutral content, there are some questions that remain open to discussion. First, is this increased memory accuracy tied to the processing of the emotional information, or does it stem from engagement of the same processes that lead to accurate memory for neutral information? Second, does emotion enhance memory for all details, or are there instances in which emotion does not boost memory for detail?

The first question harkens back to the flashbulb memory literature. As noted earlier in this chapter, Brown and Kulik (1977) believed that there was a special memory mechanism that was triggered when an emotional event was experienced. This idea lost credibility over time because of the evidence that emotional memories were not immune to distortion. However, the issue re-emerged when, as described in Chapter 6, studies of patients with amygdala damage demonstrated a blunted emotional memory enhancement effect. If amygdala activity could enhance the quantity of remembered emotional information, perhaps it could also affect the amount of detail that people could remember about the emotional events. Conversely, the increased memory accuracy for negative arousing information could result from domain-general factors. Just as factors such as semantic relatedness or distinctiveness could contribute to the quantity of remembered information (as discussed in Chapter 6), such features could also influence the likelihood of memory distortion.

To examine the extent to which emotion-specific versus domain-general factors influenced the accuracy of emotional memories, Kensinger and Schacter (2006d) performed a series of neuroimaging investigations to examine the neural processes that underlie emotion's effects on reality-monitoring performance (i.e., participants' abilities to distinguish what they have imagined and what they have perceived; Johnson & Raye, 1981).

As noted above, individuals' reality-monitoring decisions are more accurate for negative items than for neutral ones (Kensinger & Schacter, 2006d). Accurate reality-monitoring is thought to occur when individuals encode, and later retrieve, details of an encoding episode that are diagnostic of whether the item was imagined or perceived (i.e., remember the cognitive operations used to imagine an item or the perceptual details of a perceived item; Johnson & Raye, 1981; Johnson, Hashtroudi, & Lindsay, 1993). Consistent with this proposal, two studies demonstrated that increased activity in visual processing regions corresponds with a person's assignment of a memory to perception (Figure 7.4), whereas increased activity in regions thought to be involved in self-generated information, or in self-referential processing, corresponds with an individual's assignment of a memory to imagination (Gonsalves & Paller, 2000; Kensinger & Schacter, 2006b; Figure 7.5).

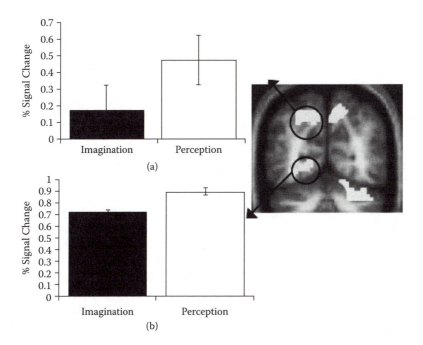

FIGURE 7.4 Activity in the precuneus (a) and in the fusiform gyrus (b), regions associated with visual perception (Fletcher et al., 1995; Kosslyn & Thompson, 2000) corresponded with attribution of a memory to perception rather than to imagination. This correspondence is consistent with the hypothesis that individuals use the amount of visual information retrieved to decide whether an item was visually presented (Johnson et al., 1993). Data from Kensinger & Schacter (2006b).

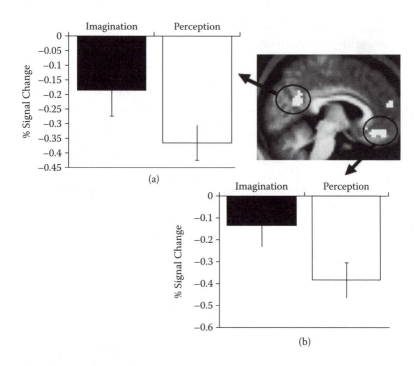

FIGURE 7.5 Activity in the posterior (a) and anterior (b) cingulate gyrus corresponds with a person's attribution of a memory to imagination rather than perception. This correspondence is consistent with the regions' roles in self-referential processing (e.g., Gusnard, Akbudak, Schulman, & Raichle, 2001). Data from Kensinger & Schacter (2006b).

Using fMRI, we investigated the encoding-related neural processes that led to later accurate memory attributions on the reality-monitoring task (Kensinger & Schacter, 2005a). As noted in Chapter 3, one of the most informative uses of fMRI for memory research has been the subsequent-memory paradigm, in which encoding-related activity can be sorted, on a post-hoc basis, based on participants' retrieval decisions. In this study, we were able to compare the encoding-related brain activity during the processing of items that participants later correctly attributed to perception or imagination to the brain activity for items that participants later mis-attributed. The results indicated that enhanced encoding-related activity in the posterior hippocampus was related to accurate memory attributions for negative arousing items as well as for non-emotional ones. This finding is quite consistent with prior research that had indicated that the hippocampus plays a critical role in encoding contextual information for non-emotional information (e.g., Davachi & Wagner, 2002), but critically, the results also indicated that the role of the hippocampus in encoding

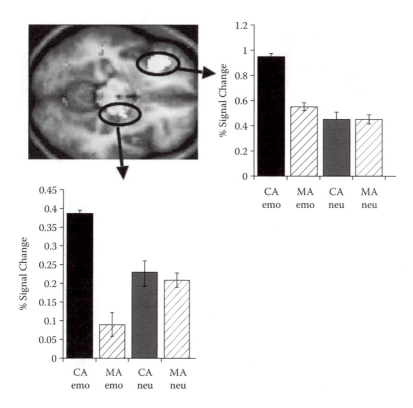

FIGURE 7.6 Increased activity in the amygdala and in the orbitofrontal cortex (two regions often engaged during emotional processing) corresponded with participants' abilities to later know whether a negative object had been presented as a picture or had only been imagined. CA = item later correctly attributed to perception or to imagination. MA = item later misattributed. Emo = negatively emotional item. Neu = neutral, nonemotional item. Data from Kensinger & Schacter (2005a).

contextual information was not limited to neutral information, but also extended to negative information.

In contrast to the hippocampal activity, enhanced encoding-related activity in the amygdala and the orbitofrontal cortex, regions often engaged during the processing of emotional information (e.g., Bechara, Damasio, & Damasio, 2000; Phan, Wager, Taylor, & Liberzon, 2002; Zald, 2003), corresponded with accurate memory attributions specifically for the negative arousing items and not for the neutral items (Figure 7.6). Thus, the enhanced accuracy for negative arousing items did not stem solely from the additional engagement of domain-general processes that enhance accuracy for all items. Rather, emotion-specific processing in the amygdala and

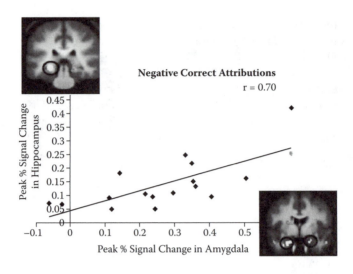

FIGURE 7.7   Activity in the amygdala and in the hippocampus was correlated during the encoding of negative items that were later correctly attributed to imagination or to perception: The participants who showed the greatest amygdala activity during the encoding of those negative items were also the participants who showed the greatest hippocampal activity. Data from Kensinger & Schacter (2005a).

orbitofrontal cortex increased the likelihood of accurate memory attributions for the emotional items. Part of the effect of these emotion-specific processes appeared to have been exerted via their interactions with regions that promote accurate encoding of non-emotional information. In particular, activity in the amygdala was highly correlated with activity in the hippocampus during the encoding of negative arousing items later accurately attributed to imagination or perception (Figure 7.7). The hippocampus is known to play a critical role in binding together a non-emotional item and its context. Patients with hippocampal lesions have difficulties remembering the context in which an item was studied (Giovanello, Verfaellie, & Keane, 2003; Shoqeirat & Mayes, 1991), and neuroimaging studies have revealed that hippocampal activity often corresponds specifically with the ability to remember contextual or associative information (e.g., Davachi & Wagner, 2002; Giovanello, Schnyer, & Verfaellie, 2004; Jackson & Schacter, 2004; but see also Stark & Squire, 2001). Thus, it appears that memory for the details of an emotional item's presentation can be enhanced not because individuals bring online an entirely distinct set of processes to help them remember the information, but rather because of modulation of the same processes (e.g., hippocampal-binding mechanisms) that typically are recruited for successful encoding of the details of non-emotional information. This finding is particularly important because there have been debates about whether the medial temporal lobe processes that underlie encoding of contextual detail may be different for emotional and non-emotional information (see Dougal, Delgado, & Phelps, 2006; Phelps, 2004; Sharot et al., 2004). This result suggests that similar medial temporal lobe regions may support the encoding of contextual details for emotional and non-emotional information (but see Dougal, Phelps, & Davachi, 2007 for evidence that distinct medial temporal lobe regions may support the encoding of contextual details for emotional versus non-emotional words).

It appears that the amygdala can exert its effects on memory for detail not only through modulation of medial temporal lobe processes, but also through modulation of perceptual-processing regions. Kensinger, Garoff-Eaton, and Schacter (2007c) conducted an fMRI scan as participants were shown negative and neutral objects. Outside of the scanner, participants were shown another series of objects and had to indicate whether each object was the "same" identical object, a "similar" object that shared the same verbal label as a studied object, or a "new" object. As described earlier in this chapter, participants are more accurate at distinguishing "same" from "similar" negative objects as compared to neutral ones (Kensinger, Garoff-Eaton, & Schacter, 2006; Kensinger et al., 2007c). We were interested in examining what neural processes might underlie that mnemonic enhancement.

We knew from prior research that the right fusiform gyrus (a region within the ventral visual-processing stream) plays a critical role in processing specific visual details and that activity in the right fusiform gyrus can correspond with memory for visual specifics (Garoff, Slotnick, & Schacter, 2005; Koutstaal et al., 2001). We were interested in examining whether, for the negative items, activity in the amygdala and in the right fusiform gyrus might relate to the improved memory for the details of negative items. Indeed, region of interest analyses revealed that activity in the amygdala and in the right fusiform gyrus showed robust relations to later memory for visual detail. Moreover, there was a strong correlation between activity in the two regions, suggesting that interactions between the amygdala and perceptual-processing regions were likely playing a critical role in enhancing memory for visual details.

These findings provide strong evidence that although memories for emotional experiences are not immune to distortion, they are more likely to be remembered with at least some types of details than are non-emotional memories. Moreover, engagement of emotion-processing regions (particularly the amygdala and the orbitofrontal cortex) predicts memory for many types of details regarding an emotional item's presentation (e.g., whether an item was imagined or perceived, and exactly what an object looked like). These regions seem to exert their effects, at least in part, by modulating the activity in mnemonic and visual regions typically recruited during the processing of non-emotional information.

☐ Types of Details Remembered About Emotional Events

Although it would be simple to conclude that emotional processing always enhances memory accuracy, the story does not appear to be so straightforward. Not all types of contextual details seem to be enhanced by emotional content. For example, in one study, we asked participants to encode positive, negative, and neutral pictures and words. For half of the items they were given a prompt indicating that they should decide whether the item depicted or described something animate. For the other half of the items, participants were prompted to decide whether the item depicted or described something common (that would be encountered in a typical month). We found that participants' abilities to remember whether they decided if an item was animate or if it was common was no better for emotional items than for non-emotional ones (Kensinger & Schacter, 2006a).

When participants underwent an fMRI scan as they encoded these items, the analyses revealed that amygdala activity showed no correspondence with memory for the decision made about the item (i.e., with "source memory"). Rather, amygdala activity was equally high during the encoding of the emotional items that people would later remember; encoding-related activity showed no relation to whether the person would later remember the decision that they had made about the item (Figure 7.8).

The results also revealed dissociations in medial temporal lobe function consistent with those demonstrated for non-emotional material. In particular, activity in the entorhinal cortex corresponded with memory for

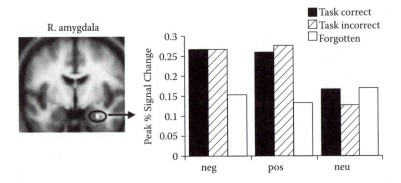

FIGURE 7.8 The amygdala was equally responsive during encoding of positive and negative stimuli, and amygdala activity was high regardless of whether or not the task performed with an item would be remembered. The amygdala showed no memory-related activity for the neutral items. Data from Kensinger & Schacter (2006).

emotional and non-emotional items, but not with memory for the context in which those items were studied. In contrast, activity in the hippocampus proper corresponded with memory for the decision made about the emotional and non-emotional items. These data are consistent with other findings from patient research and from neuroimaging, suggesting that the hippocampus proper plays a particularly important role in memory for source information while the entorhinal cortex plays a role in memory for intra-item features (Davachi et al., 2003; Davachi & Wagner, 2002; Giovanello et al., 2004; Kensinger & Schacter, 2006a; Ranganath, Johnson, & D'Esposito, 2003; Wan, Aggleton, & Brown, 1999). Importantly, these data suggest that the same dissociations within the medial temporal lobe that exist for non-emotional items also hold for emotional ones.

These results highlight the fact that the relation between amygdala activity during encoding and memory for event details may depend on the particular type of detail that is assessed. Emotion does not enhance memory for all aspects of an encoding episode, and amygdala engagement at encoding does not ensure that all details will be remembered accurately. A primary goal of the ongoing research in my laboratory is to understand the circumstances in which amygdala activity does, and does not, relate to the encoding of event details. Our working hypothesis is that amygdala activity guides encoding of details that are intrinsic to an item (e.g., its physical appearance or its gist), but does not enhance encoding of attributes that are extrinsic to an item (e.g., the task performed with the item; see Mather, 2007 for a related hypothesis).

If we look at the types of details for which memory has been assessed thus far, the findings seem consistent with this hypothesis. The types of details that are better remembered for emotional items than for neutral ones tend to be those that can be processed as intrinsic item attributes. Details such as a word's font or spatial location are integral to our ability to process the words. Similarly, individuals may have been more likely to remember neutral words occurring in an emotional sentence (Kensinger, Brierley, Medford, Growdon, & Corkin, 2002; Kensinger, Anderson, Growdon, & Corkin, 2004) because individuals processed the entire sentence as a single stimulus rather than as a series of individual words. In contrast, details that are more extrinsic to the emotional items may not be better remembered because of the emotional content. In fact, as will be discussed in the next chapter, the effects of emotion on memory are likely to be best understood in terms of trade-offs. Some attributes of an experience are more likely to be remembered because of the event's emotional importance, whereas other attributes are more likely to be forgotten (see Kensinger, 2007; Mather, 2007 for further discussion).

Some of these effects of emotion on memory for detail may relate to the connectivity between the amygdala and other medial temporal lobe regions. At least for non-emotional information, the specific neural substrates that relate to subsequent memory may differ depending on the level of detail encoded about the event. Within the medial temporal lobe, memories that are associative or that include binding of extrinsic contextual information with item information may be more likely to recruit the hippocampus proper or the parahippocampal gyrus (Brown & Aggleton, 2001; Davachi , Mitchell, & Wagner, 2003; Dobbins, Foley, Schacter, & Wagner, 2002; Eichenbaum, 2000; Jackson & Schacter, 2004; Ranganath, Johnson, & D'Esposito, 2000, 2003; Rugg, Fletcher, Chua, & Dolan, 1999; Sperling et al., 2001, 2003; but see Squire, Stark, & Clark, 2004). In contrast, the encoding of only item information, with relatively few extrinsic contextual associations appears more likely to rely on the entorhinal and perirhinal cortices (Brown & Aggleton, 2001; Cansino, Maquet, Dolan, & Rugg, 2002; Davachi et al., 2003; Holdstock et al., 2002; Kirwan & Stark, 2004; Mayes, Holdstock, Issac, Hunkin, & Roberts, 2002; Mayes et al., 2004; Ranganath et al., 2004). Because the amygdala has more robust connections with the entorhinal and perirhinal cortices than with more posterior medial temporal lobe regions (Phelps, 2004; Stefanacci, Suzuki, & Amaral, 1996), amygdala modulation may disproportionately influence the encoding of "intrinsic" item attributes (thought to be mediated by entorhinal/perirhinal activity; e.g., Brown & Aggleton, 2001; Davachi et al., 2003) compared to "extrinsic" contextual details. Ongoing research in my laboratory and in others' laboratories is currently examining the validity of this hypothesis.

☐ Concluding Remarks

This chapter has highlighted that emotion can have robust effects on the quality of a memory. Individuals believe that they remember emotional events vividly, and there is extensive evidence that emotion can enhance memory for at least some types of details. However, not all aspects of emotional events are remembered well. As will be described in the next two chapters, in order to understand the effects of emotion on memory for detail, one must consider both the type of detail being assessed (discussed in Chapter 8) and the content of the emotional information (most importantly, whether the information is positive or negative; discussed in Chapter 9). It turns out that both of these factors have dramatic effects on the amount of detail that is remembered.

CHAPTER

Emotion-Induced Memory Trade-Offs

As outlined in Chapter 7, individuals vividly remember many emotional experiences, and there is evidence that they are more likely to remember at least some types of details regarding emotional experiences compared to non-emotional ones. However, we also understand that emotion does not allow the formation of a picture-perfect memory, retaining all of the myriad details present at the time the information was processed. In fact, not only does emotion leave memory unaffected for some types of details, it also can have an impairing effect on memory for some types of information. This pattern is often described in terms of *trade-offs*. As implied by the term, although emotion has an enhancing effect on memory for some types of details, those beneficial effects of emotion can be accompanied by decrements in memory for other types of details.

☐ Characterizing the Emotion-Related Memory Trade-Off

Although many researchers would agree that emotion is likely to induce memory trade-offs, the exact nature of those trade-offs has been unclear. Two primary types of trade-offs have been described. One focuses on the relevance of the detail to the emotional information. This proposal purports that emotion causes a narrowing of attention so that details that are closely related to the emotional item are remembered well, whereas details further removed from the emotional item (in space, time, or theme) are more likely to be forgotten (e.g., Easterbrook, 1959; Loftus, 1979; referred to here as the *central/peripheral* trade-off). There has been a great deal of evidence supporting the existence of a central/peripheral trade-off. It often is the case that when individuals are shown a scene that includes

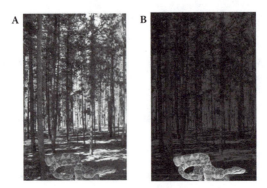

FIGURE 8.1 The central/peripheral trade-off in memory (e.g., Easterbrook, 1959; Loftus, 1979; Reisburg & Heuer, 2004) suggests that upon encountering information with an emotional element (A), attention will be focused on the emotional element and diverted away from the nonemotional elements (B). This attentional narrowing will lead to enhanced memory for the emotional element but impaired memory for the information more tangential to the emotional element.

an emotional element, participants will remember the emotional element well but will forget the surrounding, non-emotional elements (reviewed by Reisburg & Heuer, 2004). Individuals also often remember scenes as being "zoomed in" on the emotional element (i.e., they believe that a larger proportion of the scene was devoted to the emotional element; Mathews & Mackintosh, 2004; Safer, Christianson, Autry, & Oesterlund, 1998). These findings support the conclusion that participants' attention narrows on the emotional element in a scene, creating a very good memory for that element, but resulting in a poor memory for the information presented in the periphery (Figure 8.1). This type of attentional narrowing is also consistent with the "weapon-focus" effect. Individuals who witness a crime often remember the weapon used by the perpetrator but not other details such as the perpetrator's getaway vehicle or physical appearance (e.g., Loftus, 1979). This effect is likely to occur because attention is focused on the source of the emotional arousal (in this case, the gun) and diverted away from more tangential information.

Although a tremendous amount of research has focused on the central/peripheral trade-off, a second type of trade-off also has been described. Instead of focusing on the relevance of the information to the source of the emotional arousal, this framework instead focuses on the amount of detail remembered about the experience (referred to here as the *gist/detail trade-off*). Within this framework (proposed by Adolphs and colleagues; reviewed by Buchanan & Adolphs, 2002), emotion increases the likelihood that the "gist" or general theme of an experience is remembered, but it

a

b
Snake in forest

Brown and grey
spotted snake
c. on the mossy
ground,
Surrounded by
birch trees...

FIGURE 8.2 The gist/detail trade-off in memory (e.g., Buchanan & Adolphs, 2002) suggests that upon encountering information with an emotional element (a), the "gist" or general theme of the information will be easily extracted (b) whereas the details of the information will not be remembered (c).

reduces the probability that specific visual details of that event are remembered (Figure 8.2). Thus, if participants read stories, or are asked to view a series of photos, they will be better at remembering the general theme of the emotional stories compared to the non-emotional ones, and they will be more likely to remember the general types of information presented in the emotional photos compared to the non-emotional ones. However, the emotional content will hurt participants' ability to remember the exact details of the story or of the photos. Thus, although people will remember that they saw a picture of a dead person in the forest, they may not remember details such as the direction in which the dead body was facing or the type of trees in the forest (e.g., Adolphs, Tranel, & Buchanan, 2005).

It turns out, however, that the gist/detail trade-off tends to interact with the central/peripheral trade-off. That is, the effects of emotion on memory for detail are critically impacted by whether memory is assessed for the emotional element itself or for other, non-emotional, contextual elements. In a series of studies, Kensinger, Garoff-Eaton, and Schacter demonstrated that the gist/detail trade-off does not tend to occur for negative arousing objects. In fact, individuals often are *more likely* to remember the specific visual details, as well as the gist, of negative arousing objects compared to neutral objects (Kensinger, Garoff-Eaton, Schacter, 2006, 2007b; see also Burke, Heuer, & Reisberg, 1992). Thus, if young adults are presented with a snake and a chipmunk, they will be much better at remembering the visual details of the snake than they will be at remembering the visual details of the chipmunk. In contrast, a robust gist/detail trade-off occurs for more peripheral elements

	Specific Memory (For visual details of information)	**General Memory** (For general theme or "gist" of information)
Central Details (Tied to the emotional item)	Negative emotion enhances considerably	Negative emotion enhances considerably
Peripheral Details (Tangential to the emotional item)	Negative emotion impairs considerably	Negative emotion impairs slightly or has no effect

FIGURE 8.3 Summary of findings from Kensinger, Garoff-Eaton, and Schacter (2007a), demonstrating that the central/peripheral and gist/detail trade-offs interact with one another.

that are not directly linked to the negative arousing object. If participants are shown a snake in a forest or a chipmunk in a forest, the presence of the emotional element (i.e., the snake) will dramatically reduce participants' abilities to remember the details of the background (i.e., exactly what the forest looked like) but will have a lesser effect on their ability to remember the gist of the background (i.e., that it was a forest; Figure 8.3). In other words, the gist/detail trade-off occurs for non-emotional background (peripheral) elements of a scene, whereas both gist and visual detail are remembered well for the emotional (central) elements in a scene.

☐ Neural Processes Mediating the Trade-Off Effects

Research in my laboratory has been focused on understanding the neural processes that give rise to the focal effects of emotion, based on the extent to which a particular detail is tied to the emotional information. As discussed in Chapter 7, we found that amygdala activity during encoding corresponds with memory for visual detail but not with memory for the task performed with an item. Following up on this finding, we performed an fMRI task in which participants encoded objects by deciding either if they would fit in a shoebox or if the object was living. Outside of the scanner, participants' memories were tested for retention of the visual detail of the objects (assessed by their ability to distinguish identical from similar photos of the objects) and for retention of the task performed with the objects (Kensinger, Garoff-Eaton, & Schacter, 2007c).

Note that most explanations for the central/peripheral trade-off effect focus on attentional effects at encoding. We reasoned that, to the extent that the focal effects of emotion on memory arise from encoding processes (e.g., attention toward features directly tied to the emotional item), then there should be encoding-related activity that would both facilitate the successful encoding of the intrinsic details of an emotional item and also impede encoding of more extrinsic details regarding the item's presentation. An open question was whether this activity would be within the standard frontoparietal network that guides attention toward any task-relevant stimuli, or whether this network would instead include regions specifically tuned to the processing of emotional information (e.g., orbitofrontal cortex).

The results revealed that amygdala activity during encoding did not correspond with successful memory for all types of details of a negative item's presentation. Amygdala activity corresponded with later memory for a negative item's visual details but was not related to memory for the task performed with the negative items (Kensinger, O'Brien, Swanberg, Garoff-Eaton, & Schacter, 2007). These data emphasize that amygdalar engagement at encoding does not facilitate the encoding of all details present during an encoding episode.

The results also revealed that activity in the orbitofrontal cortex, ventral striatum, and anterior cingulate gyrus facilitated the encoding of the visual detail of a negative item but impeded the encoding of the task performed with the item. Interestingly, this network of regions has been implicated in the prioritized processing of emotional stimuli (Vuilleumier, Armory, Driver, & Dolan, 2001) and in tasks requiring attention to affective stimuli (e.g., Everitt, Cardinal, Hall, Parkinson, & Robbins, 2000; Robbins & Everitt, 1996; Schultz, 2000). Thus, the correspondence of these regions to a selective enhancement in encoding of an intrinsic item attribute is quite consistent with the proposal that at least some of the focal effects of emotion on memory arise from attentional focusing during encoding (see Kensinger, 2007; Mather, 2007 for further discussion). It appears that when individuals are most affectively focused on the item itself, they also are most likely to fail to encode the task that they performed with the item. Although the exact mechanism through which this affective attention network exerts its effects remains to be specified, it is plausible that activity within this network modulates the functioning of other sensory or mnemonic regions.

☐ Overcoming Emotion-Induced Memory Trade-Offs

In most of the experiments that have examined emotion-induced memory trade-offs, participants have passively viewed scenes and have been given no reason to attend to all aspects of the scenes. I have been very interested in understanding the extent to which the trade-offs that occur when individuals passively view scenes can be manipulated by directing participants' attention toward other aspects of the scenes. Can individuals overcome the attentional focus on emotional information in the environment and strategically direct their attention toward other, non-emotional, aspects of the environment?

In an initial study that I conducted with Suzanne Corkin, Anne Krendl, and Olivier Piguet, we asked some young adults to passively view scenes and made no mention of a later memory task. For other young adults, we warned them that their memories would be tested for various components of the scenes and that they should do their best to encode all elements of the scenes. Although the young adults in the passive viewing condition showed a robust central/peripheral memory trade-off, the young adults in the intentional encoding condition were able to overcome this trade-off. They no longer showed poor memory for peripheral elements that were presented with emotional objects as compared to peripheral elements that were presented with non-emotional objects (Kensinger, Piguet, Krendl, & Corkin, 2005; Figure 8.4).

This study provided evidence that young adults can overcome the central/peripheral trade-off. However, the open-ended intentional encoding instructions gave little insight into the processes that participants were using to overcome the emotion-induced memory trade-offs. Moreover, the fact that intentional encoding instructions were used made it hard to distinguish effects of attention at encoding from other factors (e.g., differential rehearsal) that also could have affected memory.

In order to more thoroughly examine the types of processes that young adults use to reduce the emotion-induced memory trade-offs, Daniel Schacter, Rachel Garoff-Eaton, and I performed a couple of experiments in which we asked young adults to tell a story about the scenes, incorporating as many scene elements as possible, or asked them to describe the scene so that another individual could use that description to paint a picture that would look similar to the one that they were viewing (Kensinger et al., 2007a). We asked participants to perform these tasks with a series of scenes, some containing a negative arousing object on a neutral background (e.g., a snake by a river) and others containing a neutral object on a neutral background (e.g., a monkey in a jungle). At test, participants were shown objects and backgrounds separately, presented one at a time, and they were asked to indicate whether each item was identical to what they had studied, was similar to what they had studied, or was new. In other words, if they saw a snake that they believed was identical to the snake that had been in a studied scene, they would indicate "same." If they saw a jungle and they believed that they had seen a jungle at encoding, but that this was not the same jungle, they would indicate "similar." If they saw a river but they believed that they had never studied a river, they would

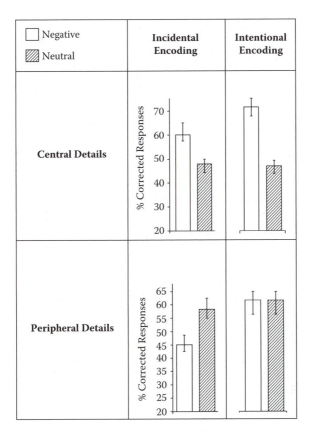

FIGURE 8.4   With incidental encoding instructions (left column), young adults showed a central/peripheral trade-off. They were more likely to remember central elements of a negative scene than of a neutral scene, whereas they were less likely to remember peripheral elements included in a negative scene. With intentional encoding instructions (right column), the central/peripheral trade-off no longer occurred; although young adults continued to show better memory for central elements of negative scenes, they showed equivalent memory for the periphal elements presented in negative and in neutral scenes. Data from Kensinger, Piguet, Krendl, & Corkin (2005).

indicate "new." Participants were shown same, similar, and new items; however, our primary interest was in examining their responses to the items that actually were the same as the items that they had studied. The critical question was whether emotion would affect the likelihood that participants could correctly identify that the objects and backgrounds had been studied (i.e., would know that they were not new) or would affect the likelihood that participants could correctly remember the visual details of the items (i.e., would know that they were same and not similar).

The results indicated that, with the storytelling instructions, participants were equally good at remembering the gist of the backgrounds presented with negative arousing objects and with neutral objects. With those instructions, however, participants still showed a memory decrement in remembering exactly what the backgrounds presented with the negative arousing items looked like. Thus, although having a negative object in the scene did not affect the ability to know whether the scene was new, it had a detrimental effect on knowing whether the background was the same or similar to a studied background. This pattern of results is perhaps not surprising given that the storytelling instructions would have focused participants' attention more on the gist of the scene than on the exact visual details. Indeed, when participants were asked to describe the visual details of the scene for an artist, their memory for the backgrounds was equated, both in terms of memory for gist and in terms of memory for detail.

These results provide strong evidence that attentional focusing during encoding plays an important role in elicitation of the trade-offs; by changing participants' focus at encoding, the strength of the trade-offs can be manipulated. Moreover, young adults are able to overcome some of this attentional focus. Although there does appear to be a strong attentional focusing on emotional elements in scenes, young adults can strategically deploy attention to other aspects of the scenes, thereby eliminating the trade-offs.

☐ Concluding Remarks

This chapter has highlighted that not all aspects of an emotional event are equally likely to be remembered. Although emotion may enhance memory for some details of an event, emotion is also likely to impair memory for other details. The robustness and pervasiveness of the trade-offs emphasize the need to assess memory for a variety of details of an emotional event, rather than relying on memory for a single type of detail as a way to estimate the accuracy of an emotional memory. The existing data also emphasize that although emotion-induced memory trade-offs often occur, the exact nature of those trade-offs appears to be somewhat malleable. The trade-off is influenced by changes in encoding methodologies and by individual differences in cognitive function and in affective state (see Chapter 10 for further discussion). This sensitivity to somewhat subtle task manipulations and participant characteristics emphasizes the need to carefully evaluate the particular encoding (and possibly retrieval) processes that lead to emotion-induced memory trade-offs. By doing so, we may begin to gain a fuller understanding of the way in which emotion elicits focal effects on memory for some, but not all, details of a previously experienced event.

Influences of Valence and Arousal on Emotional Memory

As you may have noticed, most of the studies discussed thus far have examined the quality or accuracy of *negative arousing* emotion on memory. This focus on the negative is likely due to a number of factors. First, many theories of emotion's modulation of memory have stemmed from the animal literature, in which paradigms such as fear conditioning have been the norm. Perhaps because of this, many theories about emotion's influence on memory have focused specifically on negative arousing emotions, with little discussion of what happens when something is positive or when something is negative but not particularly arousing. Second, negative arousing emotions tend to be easier to elicit than other types of emotions. This is probably not true in everyday life, but it certainly is true with regard to the types of stimuli that we show participants in the laboratory. It is relatively easy to find images of spiders, snakes, or injured people, that will cause people to have a strong negative response. In contrast, it can be quite difficult to find positive stimuli that will lead to high-arousal feelings of pleasure. Many of the positive stimuli instead elicit feelings of serenity. Similarly, it is harder to find stimuli that are negative but that do not elicit feelings of arousal than it is to find high-arousal negative stimuli.

Despite these difficulties, some research has examined the extent to which the valence of an event (whether it elicits positive or negative affect) and the arousal of an event (whether it elicits a feeling of excitation/agitation or whether it is calming/soothing) influences the likelihood that the event is remembered. This chapter describes the studies that have examined the effects of these two dimensions on memory for emotional information.

☐ Effects of Arousal on Memory

The vast majority of studies examining the effects of emotion on memory have focused on stimuli that are associated with high levels of arousal. For these stimuli, mnemonic influences appear to occur via interactions between the amygdala and the hippocampus. This proposal originated from the animal literature (see review by McGaugh, 2004) and has been confirmed more recently by studies using neuroimaging (reviewed by Phelps, 2004). For example, Kensinger and Corkin (2004c) asked participants to undergo an fMRI scan as they encoded some words that were negative and arousing (e.g., *slaughter*) and other words that were nonarousing (either negative words like *sorrow* or neutral words like *yellow*). While in the scanner, participants were asked to indicate whether each word was abstract or concrete, and no mention was made of a memory test. Later, outside of the scanner, participants performed a recognition memory task. They were shown a series of words, some of which had been studied, and they were asked to indicate whether they vividly "remembered" that the item was presented while they were in the scanner, "knew" the item had been presented but lacked any specific memory about its presentation, or believed that the item was "new." We compared the encoding-related activity for words that participants later vividly remembered and for words that participants later forgot. For the arousing words, activity in both the amygdala and the hippocampus corresponded with an increased likelihood that a participant later remembered the words, and the amount of activity in the two regions was correlated strongly (Figure 9.1). For the nonarousing words, hippocampal activity predicted subsequent memory, but amygdala activity did not. These findings suggest that amygdala activity during encoding relates to successful encoding of arousing items, but not of nonarousing ones (see also Dolcos, LaBar, & Cabeza, 2004 for evidence that amygdala activity during encoding leads to vivid memories of emotionally arousing information).

In order to examine the automaticity of the effect, Kensinger and Corkin (2004c) asked participants to study words either with full attention devoted toward the encoding task or with attention divided between the encoding task and a secondary sound discrimination task. We reasoned that if relatively automatic processes led to the mnemonic enhancement for the arousing words, then the benefit should remain even when participants' attention was divided. In contrast, if participants were using attention-demanding, elaborative encoding processes to help them remember the arousing words, then diverting their attention away from the encoding task should disrupt those processes and should therefore minimize the mnemonic benefit for the arousing words. The results revealed that adding the secondary task impaired the vividness with which the

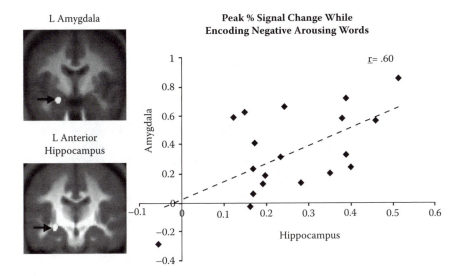

FIGURE 9.1 Acitivity in the amygdala and in the hippocampus corresponded with successful encoding of negative arousing words, and activity in the two regions was highly correlated. Data from Kensinger & Corkin (2004c).

nonarousing words were remembered, whereas it did not have a large effect on the vividness of memories for the arousing words (see also Bush & Geer, 2001; Kern, Libkuman, Otani, & Holmes, 2005; Figure 9.2). The finding that arousal-based influences on memory seem to occur relatively automatically is consistent with proposals that emotional information is privy to prioritized or relatively automatic processing (reviewed by Dolan & Vuilleumier, 2003; Pessoa, Kastner, & Underleider, 2003).

These studies emphasize that emotional arousal can be a critical factor contributing to the emotional memory enhancement effect (see also Cahill & McGaugh, 1995; McGaugh, 2004). However, while the vast majority of research has examined memory for high-arousal stimuli, an arousal response is not required for emotional modulation of memory. Items that lead to a feeling of pleasure or displeasure (i.e., that lead to changes in valence), but that do not elicit arousal, also can be remembered better than information that evokes neither valence nor arousal (Kensinger & Corkin, 2003c; Ochsner, 2000).

The processes that lead to the mnemonic enhancements for nonarousing items seem to be distinct from those mechanisms engaged for arousing information (Figure 9.3). In particular, the mnemonic boost for nonarousing stimuli appears to stem from increased engagement of the same sorts of processes that also support memory for non-emotional information (e.g., controlled and elaborative processing of the stimuli; see

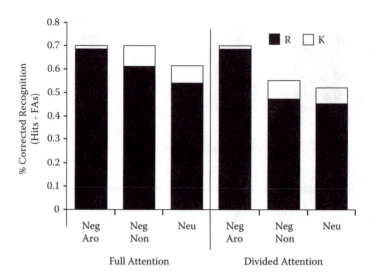

FIGURE 9.2 When young adults could devote their full attention toward encoding information, they showed an increased ability to vividly remember ("R" responses) negative arousing and negative nonarousing information as compared to neutral information. When their attention was divided during encoding, the enhanced ability to vividly remember the negative nonarousing items disappeared, whereas the ability to vividly remember the negative arousing items remained. R = vividly remember. K = know, without remembering details. Neg Aro = negative arousing word. Neg Non = negative nonarousing word. Neu = neutral word. FAs = False Alarms. Unpublished data from Kensinger & Corkin.

Kensinger, 2004 for further discussion). Thus, in contrast to the minimal effect of divided attention on participants' memories for arousing items (Bush & Geer, 2001; Kensinger & Corkin, 2004c), divided attention has a large detrimental effect on the likelihood that participants will vividly remember negative nonarousing items. In fact, when participants' attention is divided during encoding, the mnemonic enhancement for negative nonarousing words disappears (Kensinger & Corkin, 2004c). As discussed in Chapter 6, for nonarousing information, controlling for other factors such as the items' semantic relatedness also can sometimes reduce the effects on memory (Talmi & Moscovitch, 2004). These findings suggest that there is not a special memory mechanism supporting the encoding of negative nonarousing information. Rather, these items are remembered better because they are a class of stimuli that are particularly likely to benefit from organized and elaborative encoding strategies.

Evidence to support this conclusion has come from both patient and neuroimaging studies. Patients with amygdala damage, despite

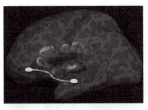

Negative Nonarousing Words:

-Benefit form additional elaboration

-Memory enhanced via
 prefrontal-hippocampal interactions

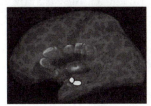

Arousing Words:

-Benefit from automatic focus

-Memory enhanced via
 amygdala-hippocampal interactions

FIGURE 9.3   Summary of results from Kensinger & Corkin (2004c): Memory for negative nonarousing words is enhanced due to distinct processes from those that enhance memory for negative arousing words.

showing no emotional memory enhancement for arousing informa-tion, tend to show a normal memory boost for negative nonarousing information (LaBar & Phelps, 1998). This pattern of results is consistent with the proposal that these individuals can benefit from elaborative encoding or from the additional organization imposed by the enhanced relatedness associated with emotional items. There is no reason to sup-pose that these types of processes would rely on the amygdala; rather, it would be logical to propose that these processes would instead rely on the same types of mnemonic functions that support memory for nonemotional information. Indeed, when Kensinger and Corkin (2004c) examined the neural processes that led to the successful encoding of negative nonarousing items, they found that it was increased activity in the prefrontal cortex and in the hippocampus that corresponded with subsequent memory. Critically, these were the same regions that were associated with successful encoding of neutral items in that same study (Kensinger & Corkin, 2004c) and that have often been implicated in elaborative encoding of non-emotional information (see Paller & Wagner, 2002 for review). This overlap in the neural processes engaged to remember neutral and negative nonarousing words is consistent with the conclusion that participants are remembering the negative nonar-ousing words not because of some "special" memory mechanism, but rather because of increased engagement of the same types of cognitive and neural processes that lead to a vivid memory for non-emotional information. This finding emphasizes that simply showing a memory benefit for emotional stimuli does not necessitate that a distinct mnemonic mechanism be postulated.

These findings also emphasize that there are stimuli for which the amygdala can show activity, but for which it does not appear to modulate mnemonic performance. Thus, we found that amygdala activity was greater for the negative nonarousing words than for the neutral words, but that amygdala activity did not correspond with subsequent memory for those items (Kensinger & Corkin, 2004c). Research by Anderson, Yamaguchi, Grabski, and Lacka (2006) has provided intriguing evidence that stimuli, such as fearful faces, that elicit amygdala responses but no arousal effect, may not be associated with the same mnemonic benefit as stimuli that elicit both amygdala activity and physiological arousal. Thus, it is plausible that amygdala engagement during encoding is not sufficient to elicit modulatory effects on memory. Rather, some type of physiological arousal effect may also be necessary.

☐ Effects of Valence on Memory

The studies described previously have focused on examining how differences in arousal level influence the types of memory mechanisms that are recruited. But what about differences in valence? To assess the effects of valence on memory, researchers have contrasted memory for positive arousing and negative arousing events. Because the positive and negative events are matched on arousal, if the two types of experiences have different memory characteristics, then it cannot be only the arousal of the events that influences memory. Rather, such differences would suggest that valence could affect memory as well.

When examining the effect of valence on the *quantity* of information remembered, almost every conceivable outcome has been observed. Sometimes, valence seems to have little effect on the quantity of retrieved information, with the emotional memory enhancement being comparable for positive and negative stimuli (e.g., Bradley, Greenwald, Petry, & Lang, 1992; Kensinger, Brierley, Medford, Growdon, & Corkin, 2002). However, particularly when testing memory for verbal or pictorial stimuli that are presented within a laboratory setting, the emotional enhancement has been found to be greater for negative items than positive ones (e.g., Charles, Mather, & Carstensen, 2003; Ortony, Turner, & Antos, 1983). In contrast, other studies (generally those assessing memory for autobiographical experiences or information encoded in reference to the self), have found that individuals remember more positive than negative information (e.g., D'Argembeau, Comblain, & van der Linden, 2005; Linton, 1975; Matt, Vazquez, & Campbell, 1992; White, 2002).

However, when examining the *quality* of a memory, more consistent effects of valence have been revealed. Negative events often are remembered with a greater sense of vividness than positive events (e.g., Ochsner, 2000; Dewhurst & Parry, 2000). Positive stimuli, in contrast, often are remembered with only a feeling of familiarity, or with general (nonspecific) information (e.g., Ochsner, 2000; Bless & Schwarz, 1999). This effect of valence on memory for detail can exist even when overall recognition rates are equated for negative and positive information (Kensinger, O'Brien, Swanberg, Garoff-Eaton, & Schacter, 2007; Kensinger, Garoff-Eaton, & Schacter, 2007b). Positive mood also has been associated with more memory reconstruction errors than negative mood, likely because individuals in a happy mood rely on gist-based information or on heuristics, while individuals in a negative mood are more likely to focus on the specific details of information (e.g., Bless et al., 1996; Storbeck & Clore, 2005).

These laboratory findings also appear to extend to real-world events infused with emotional importance. Three prior studies have examined whether a person's response to an event outcome (finding it positive or negative) affects what he or she remembers about the event (Bohn & Berntsen, 2007; Levine & Bluck, 2004; Kensinger & Schacter, 2006e). Levine and Bluck asked participants who were either pleased or displeased with the verdict decision in the O.J. Simpson trial to take a recognition memory task about particular events that had occurred during the trial. Kensinger and Schacter asked Red Sox fans and Yankees fans to report what they remembered about the final game of the 2004 playoff series, in which the Red Sox emerged victorious after overcoming a 0–3 deficit in the series. Bohn and Berntsen asked East and West Germans to remember details about the fall of the Berlin Wall. This event had been a highly positive one for some people, but a highly negative one for other people. The valence of the event did not affect the *quantity* of remembered information. The overall number of details remembered about the event was similar regardless of whether the person had found the event to be positive or negative. However, valence did affect the consistency and confidence of the memories. Levine and Bluck (2004) found that individuals who were happy about the O.J. Simpson verdict remembered the event more vividly and were more liberal in accepting that something had occurred. Similarly, Kensinger and Schacter found that Red Sox fans, who found the outcome positive, showed more memory inconsistencies and were more likely to be overconfident in their memories than were Yankees fans. Bohn and Berntsen also found that, although those who had found the fall of the Berlin Wall to be positive rated their memories as being more vivid than those who had found the event to be negative, the positive group actually remembered the facts of the event with less accuracy. Taken together, these studies provide strong evidence that positive and negative memories can be associated with different characteristics, with accurate details being more likely to be remembered about negative events than about positive ones.

☐ Concluding Remarks

Although a tremendous amount of research has examined the effect of emotion on memory, a lot of this research has not teased apart the effects due to stimulus arousal and those due to stimulus valence. However, as has been made clear by the studies discussed in this chapter, each of these dimensions can influence the mechanisms through which declarative memory is modulated. When comparing memory for arousing versus nonarousing information, it is clear that the amygdala plays a critical role in modulating memory for arousing information, whereas prefrontal elaboration processes seem to be more important for mediating enhancements for nonarousing information. It is less clear what types of neural differences give rise to the divergent effects of positive and negative valence on memory. The vast majority of neuroimaging studies have examined the amygdala's role in encoding *negative* information, and the one study to compare memory for negative and positive arousing stimuli found similar recruitment of medial temporal lobe processes during the encoding of both types of information (Kensinger & Schacter, 2006a). However, although the amygdala may be equally engaged during the processing of positive and negative information, its connections with other brain regions may be influenced by the information's valence. Indeed, there is evidence that outside of the medial temporal lobe, different neural processes may support the successful encoding of positive and negative information (Dolcos et al., 2004; Kensinger & Schacter, 2006c; Mickley & Kensinger, 2006). It also is plausible that many of the effects of valence on memory may arise from differences at retrieval rather than from differences during encoding or consolidation. As described earlier, positive affect often is associated with reliance on heuristics or schemas while negative affect is linked to analytical and detailed processes. These differences may lead to valence-related effects on retrieval orienting and on retrieval monitoring which could affect the types of information that people remember about positive and negative experiences.

Individual Differences in Young Adults' Emotional Memories

Cognitive psychologists and cognitive neuroscientists typically clump together all participants within a particular age range into a single participant group and analyze their data without regard to individual differences. In fact, all of the data that have been described thus far in this book has paid little attention to individual variability in cognitive or affective function. As we have seen, these group analyses have provided fundamental insights into emotion–memory interactions. However, they also have the potential to miss fundamental modulators of those interactions. In this chapter, we explore how differences in young adults' cognitive ability, their personalities, their affective traits, and their sex can influence the effects of emotion on memory.

☐ Effects of Cognitive Ability on Emotional Memory

Not everyone has the same types of cognitive resources available for information processing. Some individuals may have excellent verbal working memory but poor nonverbal working memory; others may have the opposite strengths. Some people may be very good at multi-tasking and at flexibly engaging and disengaging their attention as needed; others may find this type of dual tasking to be extraordinarily difficult. Though there has not been extensive research examining how individual differences in cognitive abilities may relate to emotional memory, recent research suggests that this will be a fruitful line for future research.

In one study, Waring, Payne, Schacter and Kensinger (in press) asked young adults to view a series of scenes with emotional or non-emotional objects placed against a non-emotional background. As described in Chapter 8, people tend to remember emotional objects well but they tend to forget the backgrounds against which the objects are presented. We wondered whether the magnitude of the trade-off that participants demonstrated would be related to their working memory and executive function ability (see Chapter 5 for further explanation of these constructs). We hypothesized that individuals with better working memory ability, and with good attention control, would be better able to disengage from the processing of the emotional object and to instead (or in addition) process the background elements of the scenes. To test this hypothesis, we correlated participants' emotion-related memory trade-off (i.e., the difference in memory between the emotional object in a scene and the non-emotional background on which the object was presented) with their performance on a series of working memory and executive function tasks. We found that the better a person's spatial working memory performance, and the better their executive functioning, the less likely they were to show an emotion-related memory trade-off (Waring et al., in press). These data suggest that individual differences in cognitive ability can influence the likelihood that participants will demonstrate an emotion-related memory trade-off.

☐ Effects of Personality and Affective Traits on Emotional Memory

Cognitive ability was not the only factor to influence performance on the scene memory task just described. We also assessed participants' trait anxiety (using the Beck Anxiety Inventory; Beck & Steer, 1990) and found that individuals who were most anxious were also those who showed the greatest emotion-induced memory trade-off (Waring et al., in press). These data are consistent with prior studies demonstrating that individuals who are anxious or stressed are more likely to focus on emotional information in the environment (reviewed by Mathews & MacLeod, 1994) and often are better able to remember emotional information but not non-emotional information compared to individuals who are less anxious (e.g., Matthews & Mackintosh, 2004).

These findings also are broadly consistent with data suggesting that personality variables can be related to the way in which information is processed and subsequently remembered. For example, Canli and colleagues (Canli et al., 2001; Canli, Silvers et al., 2002) found that individuals who are high in neuroticism have greater brain reactivity to negative stimuli, whereas individuals higher in extroversion have greater brain reactivity to positive stimuli (see Costa & McCrae, 1992 for discussion of the Big Five Personality traits, including extroversion and neuroticism). These findings suggest that personality variables may relate to the way in which information in the environment is perceived and processed. Results consistent with this hypothesis have been revealed in studies conducted by Barrett and colleagues (discussed in Duncan & Barrett, 2007), demonstrating that personality characteristics can influence the likelihood that rapidly presented fearful faces are detected.

Although these studies suggest an influence of personality on fairly automatic or rapid processing of emotional information, personality factors also may influence memory via individual differences in emotion regulation strategies. Richards and Gross (2006) demonstrated that memory for emotional information suffered when individuals were asked to suppress their affective responses to stimuli. In fact, this emotion regulation resulted in mnemonic decrements on par with those that resulted from distracting participants' attention away from the emotional information. It is plausible that successful regulation strategies in essence divert processing resources away from the incoming emotional information, thereby reducing both the types of information that initially are processed and the sorts of information that are later remembered.

☐ Effects of Gender on Emotional Memory

The extent to which functional sex-related differences exist in the brain has been a topic of extensive debate throughout the cognitive literature. There have been a number of domains in which sex differences in neural structure and activity have been reported. For example, there are sex differences in average brain weight and volume (greater in men than in women), in the asymmetry of the brain's hemispheres (greater in women), and in the amount of cortical blood flow (greater in women; see Casper, 1998 for review of sex differences). Most recently, sex differences in emotional processing and in emotional memory have captured the attention of cognitive psychologists and cognitive neuroscientists. Sex effects have appeared in nearly every domain of emotional long-term memory that we have discussed: on the quantity of remembered information, on the quality of remembered information, on the types of trade-offs induced by emotion, and on the neural processes that support memory for emotional information.

With regard to the quantity of remembered information, a number of studies have suggested that women often remember more emotional experiences than men do. This effect has been demonstrated in studies of autobiographical memory retrieval (Davis, 1999; Fujita, Diener, & Sandvik, 1991; Seidlitz & Diener, 1998) and confirmed by laboratory studies demonstrating that a greater proportion of the events that women remember are emotional, whereas men tend to remember a smaller proportion of emotional items (e.g., Canli, Desmond, Zhao, & Gabrieli, 2002).

There have been a few explanations for this effect of sex on emotional memory. The first relates to gender differences in willingness to report emotional experiences or in the ways in which the two genders rehearse the events. Perhaps women expect to remember emotional events better and are therefore more willing to recall these experiences (e.g., Fabes & Martin, 1991; Feldman Barrett, Robin, Pietromonaco, & Eyssell, 1998). Perhaps men also tend to "strip away" the emotional meaning of an event over multiple rehearsals, whereas women may be more likely to retain this emotional core of a memory (Bauer et al., 2003). These factors—particularly those that relate to gender differences in rehearsal—cannot be ruled out as important contributors. Nevertheless, it is important to note that gender differences in memory can arise even when methods that should encourage recall of as much information as possible—such as rewarding participants for correct responses—are used. The second explanation hinges on gender differences in the perceived arousal of the stimuli. Within this framework, the effects of sex arise because of differences in the perceived intensity of the stimuli. Because women experience many events as more arousing than men do, they will benefit more from the effects of arousal on memory (Fujita et al., 1991; Canli et al., 2002). Indeed, there is some evidence to support this hypothesis. Often, women rate emotional stimuli as more arousing than do men (e.g., Canli et al., 2002). Moreover, stimuli rated as more arousing by men than women (e.g., pornographic materials; Murnen & Stockton, 1997; Symons, 1979) also tend to be remembered better by men than by women (Geer & McGlone, 1990). A third framework purports that sex-related effects on memory arise not because of differences in perceived arousal, but rather because of differences in the way in which men and women encode, rehearse, or retrieve emotional information (Seidlitz & Diener, 1998).

In order to adjudicate between these alternatives, researchers have controlled for the arousal elicited by stimuli and then examined sex differences in emotional memory enhancements. If differences in arousal lead to the sex-related differences, then stimuli that are rated as equally arousing by men and women should also be remembered equally well by the two sexes. In contrast to this hypothesis, sex effects on memory sometimes do occur even when arousal is matched (Canli, Zhao, Brewer, Gabrieli, & Cahill, 2002; Hamann, Herman, Nolan, & Wallen, 2004; Karama et al., 2002). These findings have lent credence to the hypothesis that there are sex differences that arise during the encoding, rehearsal, or retrieval of prior emotional experiences.

Further support for the notion that sex-related effects on emotional memory do not arise solely from differences in perceived arousal have come from studies examining the effects of emotion on the quality and types of trade-offs induced by emotional information. Women tend to remember emotional events more vividly, and with greater detail, than do men (Seidlitz & Diener 1998; Canli et al., 2002). However, women also can show greater trade-offs related to the encoding of emotional information. For example, Strange, Hurlemann, & Dolan (2003) found that memory is impaired for neutral words presented in close temporal proximity to emotionally arousing words, but that this impairing effect was much larger in men than in women (see also Cahill, Uncapher, Kilpatrick, Alkire, & Turner, 2004 for evidence that sex-related characteristics can relate to the magnitude of emotion-induced trade-offs).

With regard to the neural processes that support memory for emotional information, the primary sex-related differences have seemed to be in the laterality of amygdala function. A few studies have demonstrated that women tend to show a correspondence between left amygdala activity and subsequent memory for emotional information, whereas men tend to show a stronger correspondence between right amygdala activity and subsequent memory for emotional stimuli (Cahill, McGaugh, & Weinberger, 2001; Cahill et al., 2004). It is not clear what sex differences underlie these differences in amygdala laterality, although some evidence points to differences in how the two sexes process emotional information. In particular, sex differences in emotional processing can emerge very early in the processing stream, as soon as 300 ms after presentation of a stimulus (Gasbarri et al., 2006). As we have discussed in preceding chapters, differences in the initial processing of incoming information can have robust effects on the likelihood that information is retained over the long term. Thus, differences in how men and women encode information may have profound effects on their later memory for emotional experiences.

In retrospect, it is perhaps not surprising that at least some studies have revealed sex effects. There are sex differences in the neuroanatomical structure and function of the amygdala and the hippocampus (e.g., Goldstein et al., 2001; Maren et al., 1994; Tanapat, Hastings, Reeves, & Gould, 1999), structures that we know to be essential for emotional memory. However, sex effects are by no means universally demonstrated. For every paper reporting an effect of sex, there seems to be another study that has conducted analyses to examine sex effects but has not found them. Moreover, studies examining the effects of amygdala damage on emotional memory tend not to find sex differences with regard to the effects of lateralized amygdala activity.

Although lack of statistical power could explain some of these null effects, it is not clear that this factor alone can explain the large number of studies that have revealed no effect of sex on emotional memory. An intriguing question for future research to address is under what conditions do sex effects in emotional memory become most apparent? One possible influence may relate to the encoding task used—tasks that are less constrained (e.g., passive viewing) may allow a greater influence of individual differences in how the information is processed and may lead to greater effects of sex than encoding tasks that are fairly constrained (e.g., deciding whether a picture shows something animate). Another important factor may prove to be the delay after which memory is assessed. To the extent that rehearsal or consolidation factors contribute to the effects of sex on memory, longer delays might be expected to reveal greater effects of sex than shorter ones. The particular demands of the retrieval task (e.g., whether the task assesses item recognition memory or memory for particular types of details) may also be an important factor.

It also is likely that the laterality effects may be circumscribed to particular nuclei within the amygdala. There is some recent evidence that it may be the ventral amygdala, in particular, that is sensitive to the sex of the participant (Mackiewicz, Sarinopoulos, Cleven, & Nitschke, 2006). In contrast, the dorsal amygdala may respond in a more sex-invariant fashion based on the arousal of the presented information (i.e., greatest response to highly arousing stimuli; Kensinger & Schacter, 2006c; Kim, Somerville, McLean, Johnstone, Shin, & Whalen, 2003). Particularly as fMRI increases in its spatial resolution, future research will do well to examine the influence of sex on activity in discrete subregions of the left and right amygdala.

☐ Concluding Remarks

There has been a lot of controversy about exactly how emotion and memory interact. The philosopher William James stated that emotions "leave a scar on the cerebral tissue" (James, 1890), yet others have argued that traumatic experiences interfere with the formation of a memory (e.g., Janet, 1889). As we have described in this chapter, it may be that both lines of argument are correct. The precise effects of emotion on young adults' memories can vary depending on the type of emotion (positive, negative, arousing, nonarousing), the type of information queried from memory (memory that an event happened, memory for a detail central to the emotion of an event, memory for a peripheral detail), and the cognitive and affective traits of the individual who is attempting to remember the information (anxious and stressed, happy and calm, good spatial working memory ability, male, female). As this chapter has described, great strides are being made in understanding the effects of emotion on young adults' memories as research moves away from examining the effects of "an emotion" on "a memory" to instead parse apart "emotion" and "memory" into their constituent subdivisions. In the next chapter, we examine how a similar breakdown of emotion and memory is beginning to shed light on how emotion–memory interactions change as adults age.

III

SECTION

*Emotional Memory
in Older Adults*

Cognitive and Neural Changes
With Advancing Age

Thus far, we have described the effects of emotion on memory performance in young (typically college-age) adults. In the following chapters, we shift our attention toward an examination of how the effects of emotion on memory change as adults age. In order to understand the effects of emotion on older adults' memories, first it is necessary to discuss how the aging process affects cognitive and emotional processing more broadly. This chapter reviews the effects of aging on cognitive ability, and in Chapter 12, we consider the effects of aging on emotional processing. After these discussions, we begin our query into the effects of aging on memory for emotional information, examining the effects of aging on working memory (Chapter 13) and on long-term memory (Chapters 14 and 15). We describe evidence for a "positivity effect" with aging (described by Mather & Carstensen, 2005) and discuss the situations in which this positivity effect does, and does not, occur (Chapter 15). We conclude with a comparison of the effects of healthy aging and Alzheimer's disease on emotional memory (Chapter 16).

The bulk of the research that we will discuss has used a cross-sectional approach. The performance of a group of young adults has been compared to the performance of a group of older adults. It is important to note that this methodology brings with it an inherent ambiguity in interpretation. One cannot distinguish differences attributable to aging processes from *cohort* effects that influence processing in one group of individuals more than the other does. Differences in memory performance between young and older adults could arise not only from processes specifically tied to the aging process but also from differences in, for example, the recentness with which participants have needed to memorize information (likely a much more common task for college-age students than for retirees). Nevertheless, these cross-sectional studies are beginning to provide a relatively clear picture of the types of cognitive changes that emerge with aging, backed by a few longitudinal studies that have followed the same cohort of individuals over a long period of time.

☐ Cognitive Declines With Healthy (Nonpathological) Aging

Although significant cognitive decline does not inevitably occur with aging, nearly all individuals report at least some cognitive changes as they age. Among the most common complaints of older adults are difficulty selecting relevant information and ignoring irrelevant information (e.g., listening to the person speaking to them from across the table while ignoring the conversation being held by the two people to their right), problems retrieving proper names from memory (e.g., generating the names of acquaintances, places visited, or movie or book titles), and troubles remembering the context in which information was learned (e.g., remembering which friend told them a particular story). In contrast to these changes, which older adults often report to be quite frustrating, many other areas of cognition remain relatively stable with aging. Thus, older adults remain just as good as younger adults at retrieving and using world knowledge that has been acquired throughout their lifetime (often referred to as "crystallized intelligence"; Cattell, 1971) and at performing tasks that rely on implicit memory. Thus, older adults are as good (and sometimes better) than young adults at defining and spelling words, at answering questions that rely on general world knowledge or on knowledge related to their areas of expertise, and at carrying out tasks that they have performed for many years (see Kensinger & Corkin, 2003a, 2004a for review).

It still is not clear which cognitive and neural changes explain these patterns of age-related impairment and preservation of cognitive impairment. Within the field of cognitive aging, there have been two main types of theories generated to explain the pattern of age-related cognitive changes. The first type of theory ("domain-general") posits that all age-related cognitive changes can be explained by changes in an ability that is shared by the various types of tasks on which older adults are impaired. In other words, there is some "core" process that is disrupted by aging, and this deficit leads to problems on a variety of cognitive tasks. The second type of theory ("domain-specific") proposes that there is a set of independent changes that occur with aging, each explaining one of the age-related deficits. This chapter briefly reviews the most often-cited domain-general and domain-specific theories of aging.

☐ Domain-General Theories of Cognitive Aging

There have been three primary domain-general theories of aging put forward. The first proposes that age-related changes in cognition relate to changes in sensory processing. The second suggests that a slowed speed of information processing can account for the age-related deficits that are seen across a range of tasks. The third purports that changes in inhibitory ability (the ability to ignore everything in the environment that is not task- or goal-relevant) lead to the age-related deficits.

The sensory deficit theory proposes that the cognitive changes that accompany aging can be attributed to age-related sensory deficits in hearing and vision (reviewed by Li & Lindenberger, 2002; i.e., Luchies et al., 2002). If information were not adequately perceived, then it would make sense that the information would be harder to attend to or process over the short term, and it also would follow that the information would be harder to retain in memory over the long term. Indeed, when young adults are asked to process information that has been perceptually degraded (e.g., to listen to words pronounced against a background of static), they often show cognitive deficits similar to those typically displayed by older adults (Murphy, Craik, Li, & Schneider, 2000). Older adults' cognitive deficits also often correlate with their sensory deficits. In other words, the older adults with the poorest sensory discrimination also tend to be those with the poorest cognitive performance (e.g., Tay et al., 2006). It is important to note that this relation does not necessitate a direct influence of sensory ability on cognitive function. It could be that there is a more global change (e.g., increased brain atrophy) that affects both sensation and cognition, thereby creating the correlation between older adults' performance in those two domains. However, the existence of such a relation does lend credence to the hypothesis that older adults' sensory deficits may explain, at least in part, their cognitive decline.

In contrast to the sensory hypothesis, the speed-of-processing hypothesis suggests that older adults' deficits may be explained by the sluggish way in which incoming information is processed and organized. It is well known that older adults have a slower speed of processing than young adults. Reaction time (the time that it takes a person to react to an event) tends to decrease steadily throughout the adult lifespan. This slowing is not due merely to changes in motor function; it also reflects a slowing at the cognitive level. Therefore, age-related differences in reaction time tend to be less pronounced when a simple task is performed (e.g., press a button whenever a tone is played) than when a more difficult task is performed (e.g., press one button when a high tone is played and a second button when a low tone is played; e.g., Luchies et al., 2002).

Salthouse and colleagues have suggested that this decline in processing speed may underlie many of the age-related changes in cognitive function (reviewed by Salthouse, 1996). In particular, they propose that slower speed of processing may make it difficult for older adults to process incoming information within the period that is often needed for successful cognitive performance. As an example, imagine that someone is reciting their phone number to a young adult and an older adult, who are both trying to remember the number. If it takes the older adult longer to process each digit of the phone number, then it is possible that while the older adult is trying to process the first few digits, he or she will have a harder time attending to the next string of numbers. In this way, slowed processing can affect performance on a range of tasks, even those that do not have an outright speed component. Cognitive performance can suffer because the slowed mental operations (in this case, memorizing the digits) cannot be carried out within the necessary time frame (in this case, within the time frame that the numbers were being recited). Slowed speed of processing can also reduce cognitive performance because the increased time between mental operations can make it more difficult to access previously processed information. The strongest evidence in favor of the slowing hypothesis has come from statistical analyses demonstrating that when speed of processing is controlled, many of the age differences on cognitive tasks disappear (discussed in Salthouse, 1996). These data suggest that the cognitive resources available to older adults may be determined by their speed of processing.

Both of the domain-general theories that we have discussed thus far have focused on the impact of aging on the processing of task- or goal-relevant information. The third domain-general hypothesis focuses instead on the impact that aging has on the ability to ignore information that is irrelevant to the task. Hasher, Zacks, and their colleagues have proposed that older adults' cognitive deficits may relate to their inability to ignore irrelevant information in the environment and instead to narrow their attention on the goal-relevant information (Hasher & Zacks, 1988). As an example, let us imagine that an older adult is seated at a long banquet table. She is trying to carry on a conversation with the couple sitting across the table from her. At the same time, the couple to her right is talking with one another, and the man to her left is talking to another person at the table. Because there are many conversations being carried out at the table, she must filter out the unwanted dialog and instead focus only on what the couple across from her is saying. In other words, she must *inhibit* (avoid) attending to the other conversations and instead focus only on the conversation in which she is taking part. Older adults often have difficulties in these types of situations, and laboratory studies have confirmed that inhibitory deficits are among the most pervasive sorts of deficits displayed by older adults. Importantly, these deficits are thought to affect not only older adults' performance on tasks that directly require inhibition of task-irrelevant information, but also their performance on a broader range of tasks. This is because if older adults are processing task-irrelevant information, they will likely have fewer resources available to process the task-relevant information.

☐ Domain-Specific Theories of Cognitive Aging

Although the three theories just described purport that age-related declines can be explained by core deficits that affect cognition broadly, other theories have proposed that some age-related deficits arise from changes in particular cognitive domains. These theories assert that, in order to understand the complex pattern of cognitive preservation and impairment that occurs with aging, one must consider domain-specific changes that have a larger impact on one area of cognition than on another. There are three primary domain-specific theories that have been proposed. The first focuses on older adults' difficulties in remembering specific words; the second focuses on older adults' difficulties remembering the context in which information was studied; and the third focuses on older adults' deficits in using self-initiated encoding strategies to help them learn information.

Older adults will tell you about their increased difficulties retrieving the appropriate name for a person or place. The deficits typically are most pronounced for proper names, but they can sometimes occur for common words as well. The word-finding problems of older adults have been demonstrated in the laboratory across a range of tasks. Older adults are more likely to make errors when asked to name items, they are slower at generating the appropriate names, and they are more likely to have "tip of the tongue" experiences, with access to the meaning of a word but not to its phonology (reviewed by Burke & Mackay, 1997).

Burke, Mackay, and colleagues have suggested that these increases in word-finding difficulties arise because aging weakens the connections that link one semantic concept to another (reviewed by Burke & Mackay, 1997). Thus, more links must be active in order for older adults to retrieve the name for which they are searching. To illustrate how this might work, let us imagine the links within the semantic memory network as a spider web, with connections between various units. The units may represent names (e.g., "banana") or properties of those items (e.g., "yellow," "fruit," "monkey"; Figure 11.1). If the links between those units are strong, it may be sufficient to have only a couple of links active in order for the appropriate name to become active (e.g., if I look at a yellow fruit, the convergence

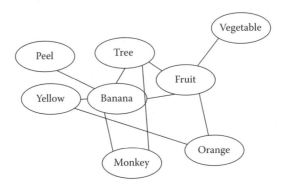

FIGURE 11.1 Schematic of a semantic memory network, showing semantic nodes linked to one another.

of these properties onto the word "banana" would likely be sufficient for me to retrieve the proper name). In contrast, for older adults, if the links become weaker, then they will need to have more linked units active in order to be able to retrieve the proper word. Consistent with this hypothesis, older adults tend to have more pronounced word-finding difficulties for words that have fewer associations (e.g., proper names; Evrard, 2002).

Although older adults' word-finding difficulties represent problems with semantic memory retrieval, many older adults' memory deficits exist within the domain of episodic memory. In broad terms, episodic memory can be thought of as consisting of memory for two different types of information: memory for the information that was previously encountered (e.g., remembering the content of a news article), and memory for the context in which that information was encountered (e.g., remembering in which newspaper the article appeared, or remembering the author of the article). Older adults tend to be nearly as good as young adults at remembering information that has been previously encountered. Where they show striking deficits, however, is in remembering the contextual details of an event. Naveh-Benjamin and his colleagues (see Old & Naveh-Benjamin, 2008, for a recent meta-analysis) have proposed that older adults have an associative binding deficit that leads to their episodic memory impairment; older adults seem to have difficulties binding together multiple event details into one cohesive memory (e.g., Chalfonte & Johnson, 1996; Craik & McDowd, 1987, Mantyla, 1993; Rugg & Morcom, 2005; Spencer & Raz, 1995).

Craik, Jennings, and colleagues have proposed that older adults' binding deficits, as well as their deficits on other episodic memory tasks, may stem from the fact that older adults do not spontaneously use encoding strategies to help them learn information (reviewed by Grady & Craik, 2000; Light, 1992). For example, if a young adult is in a situation where he must learn the names of a number of people in a short time, it is likely that he will adopt some strategy to help him learn the face–name associations. Perhaps he will try to associate each person's name with a memorable attribute (e.g., Phil studies physics) or with others who share a similar name (e.g., Tina looks like Aunt Katrina). Older adults will be much less likely to self-initiate the use of these types of strategies. If they are given a strategy to use, they usually will be effective at engaging the strategy; however, they will not spontaneously generate a strategy to help them learn information (reviewed by Johnson & Raye, 2000; Light, 2000).

☐ Neural Changes With Healthy (Nonpathological) Aging

Given the specificity of the age-related changes in cognition, perhaps it should not be surprising that not all regions of the brain are equally affected by aging. The largest structural and functional changes in the brain tend to occur in the prefrontal cortex and in the medial temporal lobe. Other cortical and subcortical regions, although they may undergo mild atrophy, tend to remain relatively preserved throughout adulthood.

Both structural and functional changes occur in the prefrontal cortex. At a structural level, there is gray matter atrophy, likely reflecting some combination of cell shrinkage and cell death (Figure 11.2; Coffey et al., 1992; Reuter-Lorenz, 2002). There are also white matter changes in the prefrontal cortex, reflecting axonal abnormalities. Because neuron-to-neuron communication occurs by sending pulses down the axon, these axonal abnormalities are likely to slow down neurotransmission, leading to sluggish cell-to-cell communication (Double et al., 1996).

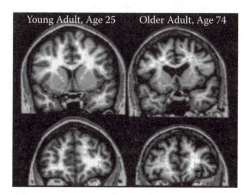

FIGURE 11.2 Coronal magnetic resonance images show the frontal atrophy that can occur with aging.

At a functional level, it is clear that older adults engage the prefrontal cortex in a different fashion than young adults. One of the most frequently demonstrated functional changes, as first noted by Cabeza and colleagues, is a hemispheric asymmetry reduction. Young adults often show increased activity in only one hemisphere of the prefrontal cortex during task performance. Older adults, in contrast, often show bilateral recruitment (Cabeza, 2002). It remains unclear exactly what this bilateral recruitment reflects. It may reflect compensatory activity (e.g., older adults may recruit additional brain regions to make up for less efficient responses in other regions), or it may arise because of pathological changes in the connections between the two hemispheres (e.g., perhaps in young adults, activity in one hemisphere inhibits activity in the other hemisphere, whereas perhaps aging disrupts this inhibition; Buckner & Logan, 2002). There is at least some evidence that this bilateral recruitment may reflect compensatory activity. In particular, some studies have found that bilateral recruitment is more often seen in older adults who perform well on a task than in older adults who perform the task poorly (Reuter-Lorenz et al., 2000). However, it remains to be determined whether compensatory recruitment can explain the broad range of tasks on which bilateral recruitment is seen in older adults.

The medial temporal lobe, and the hippocampus proper in particular, is another region that shows large age-related changes in structure and function. Although there is evidence of moderate atrophy in the hippocampus with advancing age, it remains unclear whether the atrophy results from cell loss, or whether cell shrinkage is the primary contributor (see reviews by Bastos-Leite, Scheltens, & Barkhof, 2004; Buckner, 2004). There also are frequently noted functional changes within the medial temporal lobe; most often, these appear as under-recruitment during both the encoding and the retrieval phases of memory tasks (e.g., Golomb et al., 1994; Sperling et al., 2001). These functional changes often correlate with older adults' reduced performance on tasks requiring memory for contextual details or memory for item-item associations. Given the essential role that the hippocampus proper plays in these types of memory tasks (reviewed by Corkin, 2002), it is perhaps not surprising that older adults who show less recruitment of this region during performance of memory tasks would also be those older adults who would show the most marked memory impairments.

☐ Concluding Remarks

As this chapter has emphasized, not all aspects of cognition decline uniformly with advancing age. Rather, age-related changes appear to be most pronounced on tasks that require rapid processing of incoming information, selective attention to task-relevant information, retrieval of proper nouns, and memory for the context in which information was studied. Although there still are debates about the cognitive and neural processes that underlie these cognitive changes, the alterations are intimately linked to age-related changes in the structure and function of the brain. Because the medial temporal lobes and prefrontal cortices are among the regions most affected by aging, tasks that rely on the integrity of those structures are the tasks on which older adults suffer the most age-related decline.

CHAPTER 12

Emotional Processing in Old Age

As discussed in Chapter 1, emotional processing can be measured through assessment of a person's subjective feelings, through examination of the time that it takes a person to detect or classify a particular stimulus, or through measurement of a person's physiological responses to a stimulus. Although the exact effects of aging on emotional processing can differ based on the type of assessment used, far fewer age-related differences are apparent in emotional processing as compared to cognitive processing.

☐ Evidence for Similar Emotional Processing in Young and Older Adults

When older adults are asked to rate the valence and arousal of stimuli, they typically give ratings that are comparable to those of young adults (e.g., Kensinger, Anderson, Growdon, & Corkin, 2004; Kensinger, 2008; Levenson, Friesen, Ekman, & Carstensen, 1991; Tsai Levenson, & Carstensen, 2000). Thus, the stimuli that older adults classify as positive or negative, or that they rate as eliciting excitation or agitation, tend to be largely overlapping with the stimuli that young adults classify within each of those categories. These findings suggest that a given stimulus will tend to elicit a similar type of emotion in both young and older adults (but see Gruhn & Scheibe, 2008, for evidence of some age-related changes).

Age-related preservation of emotional processing is apparent not only when subjective feelings are assessed but also when measuring a person's ability to detect or attend to information. Older adults, like young adults, are more likely to detect emotional information in the environment than they are to detect non-emotional information. For example, Leclerc and Kensinger (2008) asked young and older adults to view arrays of objects. Some arrays contained an emotional image embedded in an array of non-emotional images (e.g., a snake amid mushrooms); other arrays included a distinct neutral image among other non-emotional images (e.g., a teapot amid mushrooms); other arrays contained non-emotional images of one type, with no mismatched images (e.g., all mushrooms). Participants had to indicate, by button press, whether each array contained a mismatched image or not. The critical finding was that both young and older adults were faster at detecting the arrays with the mismatched emotional image than they were at detecting the arrays with the mismatched neutral image (Leclerc & Kensinger, 2008; see also Hahn, Carlson, Singer, & Gronlund, 2006; Mather & Knight, 2006). Interestingly, this benefit occurred only if the mismatched item was arousing (e.g., was a snake) and not if it was negative but nonarousing (e.g., was a trash can). A number of other tasks have revealed age-related preservation in the effects of emotion on attention focus. For example, young and older adults show a similar interfering effect of emotion when asked to ignore the printed word and to read the color of font in which the word is written (the emotional Stroop task). Both age groups find it harder to ignore the emotional words than to ignore the neutral words; thus, color naming is slowed for the emotional words as compared to the neutral words (MacLeod, 1991; Wurm, Labouvie-Vief, Aycock, Rebucal, & Koch, 2004). These findings support the conclusion that the attention of older adults, like that of young adults, is drawn toward emotional information in the environment.

☐ Evidence for Effects of Aging on Emotional Processing

Although young and older adults often perform similarly on tasks requiring detection or rapid processing of emotional information (see Mather, 2006 for further discussion), there are a couple of dimensions of emotional processing that appear to be altered with aging. There often are age-related changes in physiological responses to stimuli. There are also often age-related differences in a person's ability to control or regulate his or her emotional response to a stimulus. It currently is not clear whether these two age-related changes are associated or whether they stem from different effects of aging on emotional processing.

☐ Aging Affects Physiological Responses to Emotional Information

Even in situations in which older adults have cognitive responses to emotional stimuli similar to young adults, their physiological responses often are blunted. Thus, older adults show less pronounced physiological changes than do young adults as they reminisce about emotional experiences or view emotional film clips (Levenson et al., 1991; Tsai et al., 2000). Part of this blunting is likely because many physiological responses to emotional events rely on the response of the cardiovascular system, a system that is impacted by the aging process (Cacioppo et al., 1998). However, even physiological measurements that are less reliant on cardiovascular responses (e.g., skin conductance responses) are not always well aligned in young and older adults (e.g., Denburg et al., 2003; Gavazzeni et al., 2008).

☐ Aging Affects Emotional Regulation

Age-related differences also often occur when examining emotion regulation ability. In contrast to the cognitive realm, in which age-related changes often are in the direction of performance *decrements*, within the realm of emotion regulation, aging often is associated with *enhancements*. Older adults are often more effective than young adults at regulating their emotions. Thus, older adults show lower rates of depression than young adults do, they experience less negative emotion than do young adults, and when they do experience negative emotion, they are able to rebound from those negative mood states more rapidly than are young adults (Whittington & Huppert, 1998; Lachman & Bertrand, 2001; Mroczek & Spiro, 2003; Phillips & Allen, 2004). This reduction in negative affect does not reflect an overall blunting of emotional experiences. Older adults experience more positive affect than do young adults, and their good moods last longer than those of young adults (Malatesta, Fiore, & Messina, 1987; Moreno, Borod, Welkowitz, & Alpert, 1993; Gross et al., 1997; Calder et al., 2003).

It appears that this improvement in emotion regulation ability may be related to age-related changes in motivational goals (discussed by Carstensen, Mikels, & Mather, 2006). Although there are likely to be important individual differences, on the whole it appears that young adults tend to be motivated by knowledge-seeking goals (e.g., traveling the world, meeting new people, learning new skills). In contrast, older adults appear to be more motivated by emotion-relevant goals (e.g., spending time with close friends and family; Carstensen, 1992; Carstensen, Isaacowitz, & Charles, 1999). A number of hypotheses have been put forward to explain the basis for this shift, some focusing on the influence of reduced stress levels associated with retirement (Carstensen & Lockenhoff, 2003), and others focusing on differential rates of brain atrophy in regions related to cognitive processing versus emotional processing (e.g., Calder et al., 2003). Although it remains an open question to what extent environmental versus biological factors influence the motivational shifts with aging, it is intriguing to note that, in contrast to declines in many regions traditionally associated with cognitive function (e.g., the prefrontal cortex and hippocampal formation), regions associated with emotional processing (particularly, the amygdala and the orbitofrontal cortex) tend to undergo relatively little age-related decline. The atrophy in the amygdala and in the orbitofrontal cortex tends to be no greater than what can be accounted for by the age-related decline in whole-brain volume (e.g., Coffey et al., 1992; Good et al., 2001; Ohnishi, Matsuda, Tabira, Asada, & Uno, 2001; Raz et al., 1997; Sullivan, Marsh, Mathalon, Lim, & Pfefferbaum, 1995; Salat, Kaye, & Janowsky, 2001). Thus, it is plausible that age-related shifts toward emotion-based goals, and away from knowledge-seeking goals, may relate to the age-related preservation of emotion-processing regions compared to cognitive-processing regions.

At least in young adults, emotion regulation seems to occur via interactions between the network of regions that are active during relatively automatic processing of emotional information and regions that are involved in more controlled or strategic processing of emotional information (reviewed by Ochsner & Gross, 2005). The relatively automatic stage of processing can be thought of as a rigid, obligatory system, associated with an automatic coding of the affective salience of information in the environment. This system is slow-learning and fast-operating (see Kalisch, Wiech, Critchley, & Dolan, 2006; Satpute & Lieberman, 2006), and it is thought to arise via interactions between the orbitofrontal cortex, the basal ganglia, the amygdala, and the dorsal anterior cingulate gyrus (Satpute & Lieberman, 2006). In contrast to this relatively automatic emotional processing (see Pessoa, 2005 for discussion of whether emotional processing ever occurs in a truly automatic fashion), controlled emotional processing allows for a more flexible response to an environmental stimulus. This system is considered to be fast-learning and slow-operating, and it tends to require attentional resources. This controlled emotional processing tends to be mediated by activity in the lateral prefrontal cortex, the hippocampal formation, the parietal cortex, and the medial and prefrontal cortex (Kalisch et al., 2006; Satpute & Lieberman, 2006). A number of studies have now revealed that young adults, when asked to reappraise an emotional experience (e.g., to reinterpret a negative event in a more positive light), or to decrease their responses to a negative event, show increased activity in the regions associated with controlled emotion processing (e.g., in the lateral prefrontal cortex and parietal cortex), coupled with decreased activity in regions associated with more automatic emotional processing (e.g., in the amygdala; Ochsner, Bunge, Gross, & Gabrieli, 2002; Ochsner et al., 2004; Ray et al., 2005). Inverse correlations between the amount of activity in controlled emotional processing regions and in relatively automatic emotional-processing regions suggest that activity in the controlled processing regions can downregulate the activity in the automatic regions, thereby dampening an individual's reaction to an emotional event. Though these processes have yet to be directly compared in young and older adults, there is evidence that older adults show the same types of interactions between prefrontal and amygdalar regions during attempts at emotion regulation (Urry et al., 2006).

Given the cognitive and neural processes that underlie emotion regulation, it is intriguing that aging seems to enhance, rather than impair, emotion regulation ability. As discussed in Chapter 11, aging results in large decrements in cognitive resources and in functional and structural changes in lateral prefrontal cortices. Thus, it is surprising that older adults would be even better than young adults would be at regulating their emotional responses, given that emotion regulation requires executive control exerted by lateral frontal regions. At a cognitive level, Mather and colleagues (discussed in Mather, 2006) have proposed that despite older adults' reduced cognitive resources, they still show enhanced emotion regulation ability because they devote a greater proportion of their resources toward emotional regulation. This hypothesis seems plausible given the evidence that older adults may place more importance on emotional regulation goals than young adults. However, further research is needed in order to examine the validity of this hypothesis.

At a neurobiological level, it is possible that older adults' improved emotional regulation relates to their blunted physiological responses to emotional stimuli and to changes in the neural systems engaged during emotional processing (see Cacioppo, in press). As described earlier, older adults tend to show blunted physiological responses to emotional information. They also often show decreased amygdala engagement to negative information than do young adults (Mather et al., 2004). Although it is impossible to determine causality, it is plausible that older adults have an easier time regulating their emotional reactions to emotional information than do young adults because older adults do not experience the same physiological arousal or limbic activation from the information. However, very little research has examined the neural processes associated with emotional processing in older adults, and the studies that have been conducted have primarily focused on the amygdala (Fischer et al., 2005; Gunning-Dixon et al., 2003; Iidaka et al., 1999; Wright et al., 2003). Therefore, we currently understand little about the broader neural networks underlying older adults' processing of emotional information. The little evidence that does exist suggests that older adults may show less amygdala engagement during the processing of emotional as compared to neutral stimuli, at least when the stimuli are faces. Instead, the older adults' amygdala seems to be more sensitive to novelty detection than to emotion detection per se (Wright et al., 2003).

☐ Aging, Personality, and Emotional Processing

It is intriguing to think about how the amygdala response to novelty might relate to age-related changes in a personality characteristic referred to as "openness to experience." This dimension of the "five factor" theory of personality (Costa & McCrae, 1992) refers to a person's willingness to explore and tolerate new and unfamiliar experiences and ideas. Studies typically find that openness to experience declines with aging (e.g., Terracciano, McCrae, Brant, & Costa, 2005). It seems plausible that there could be a relation between the amygdala response to novelty and the age-related decline in openness to experience. In other words, the amygdala response to novel information may correlate with older adults' processing of new information as being somewhat aversive.

Although that idea is speculative, there is good evidence that age-related changes in personality can be tied to neurobiological impacts of aging. For example, Williams et al. (2006) found that older adults' responses in the medial prefrontal cortex differ from that of young adults. When young and older adults were asked to view blocks of happy faces or blocks of fearful faces, older adults showed more late-onset medial prefrontal activity for negative information than did young adults, consistent with the idea that older adults may be engaging more emotion regulation strategies. In contrast, they showed more early-onset medial prefrontal activity for happy faces than did young adults, perhaps suggesting that older adults' attention is automatically focused on positive information. Interestingly, Williams et al. found that these age-related changes correlated with age-related reductions on the personality measure of neuroticism. Thus, it seems that older adults' engagement of prefrontal processes in response to negative information relates to their decreased tendency to experience states of anxiety, anger, guilt, and depression in their daily lives (Matthews & Deary, 1998).

☐ Concluding Remarks

There is abundant evidence that older adults are better at emotion regulation than are young adults. However, the cognitive and neural basis for this improvement remains somewhat of a mystery. Regardless of the mechanisms underlying age-related changes in emotional regulation ability, the fact that this regulation of emotion is enhanced by aging suggests an interesting dichotomy between older adults' preserved rapid detection of emotional information and their altered controlled regulation of emotional experience. By teasing apart the contributions of relatively automatic versus more controlled emotional processing, it is likely that future research will make great strides in clarifying the ways in which emotional processing changes as adults age.

Effects of Aging on Emotional Working Memory

As discussed in the prior chapters, aging seems to have far fewer effects on emotional processing than on cognitive processing. This disjoint between a relatively intact emotion processing system and a more disrupted cognitive processing system leads to the intriguing question of how interactions between emotion and cognition change as adults age. This chapter addresses two lines of inquiry that have begun to tackle this question. The first line examines the effects of emotion on working memory—the ability to maintain and manipulate information over short periods of time (the construct of working memory was described in more detail in Chapter 5). The second line of inquiry examines how emotion can affect the ability of older adults to make decisions.

☐ How Aging Affects the Ability to Maintain Emotional Information Over Short Periods of Time

One of the primary ways in which researchers have examined the effects of aging on emotional working memory has been to vary the emotional content of the to-be-maintained information and to ask whether emotional information is more or less likely to be retained over short periods of time than non-emotional information. For example, if older adults are asked to repeat the words "death slander misery virus" in the opposite order as they were read, will they be any more or less likely to do so correctly than if they are asked to repeat in backwards order a string of neutral words such as "dash standard manicure vocal"? Preliminary data from my laboratory have suggested that older adults, like young adults, do not show a beneficial effect of emotion on working memory accuracy. Older adults are no more likely to maintain and manipulate emotional words in working memory than they are to maintain and manipulate non-emotional words.

If anything, maintaining emotional information in working memory seems to come at a cost for older adults, just as it can for young adults. Thus, when older adults are asked to perform an n-back matching task, indicating whether the face that they are currently viewing on a computer screen matches the face that they viewed n items previously, older adults are slower at making the matching decision when the face is fearful than when it is neutral. In fact, in the preliminary data that we have gathered thus far, the impairing (slowing) effects of emotion appear to be *greater* in older adults than in young adults (Kensinger, unpublished observations). Although the results are preliminary, and thus must be interpreted cautiously, a disproportionate impact of emotion on the working memory ability of older adults could arise because of older adults' increased deficits in inhibition (as discussed in Chapter 11). To the extent that the impairing effects of emotion on working memory performance arise because attention is drawn toward the emotional aspects of the face (e.g., toward the facial expression rather than to the facial identity), it would follow that if older adults are less able to inhibit the focusing on that irrelevant dimension (facial expression) and to focus their attention to a task-relevant dimension (facial identity), then they likely would show a greater working memory disruption with the faces displaying an emotional expression than would young adults (who should be able to more effectively inhibit the processing of the irrelevant dimension).

It also is interesting to consider these findings in light of the changes in emotional processing described in Chapter 12. The fact that young and older adults both show interference when needing to inhibit the processing of fearful facial expressions is consistent with the conclusion that, when examining relatively automatic stages of emotion processing, both young and older adults may be likely to focus on the negative information in their environment. Thus, these findings from the working memory realm may be interpreted as providing further evidence for age-related preservation of the relatively automatic processing of emotional information.

The research described thus far has focused on examining whether aging affects the ability to hold emotional information in mind over time. In contrast to this line of research, other research has examined whether aging influences the ability to hold an emotional feeling in mind over time. Mikels and colleagues (Mikels & Reuter-Lorenz, in press; Mikels, Larkin, Reuter-Lorenz, & Carstensen, 2005) asked young and older adults to view a series of picture pairs. One member of a pair was presented, and there was then a 3-second retention interval before the second member of the pair was presented. Participants were asked to judge how the second member of the pair compared to the first member on either an affective or a nonaffective dimension. In one condition, the members of the pair were always neutral, and participants were asked to indicate whether the second picture was visually brighter or less bright than the first image. Thus, in this condition, participants had to retain visual (nonaffective) information in their working memories. In a second condition, the members of the pair were either both positive or both negative, and participants were asked to indicate whether the emotion elicited by the second picture was more intense or less intense than the first picture. Therefore, in this condition, participants had to retain their emotional feeling over the delay in order to make the appropriate rating. The critical findings from this study were that older adults were impaired (compared to young adults) on the visual working memory task but performed as well as young adults on the emotional working memory task. Moreover, on the emotional working memory task, there was an age by valence interaction. Young adults were better at comparing the negative affect elicited by the two pictures, whereas older adults were better at comparing the positive affect.

Once again, these findings are worth considering within the context of the effects of aging on emotional processing. These data corroborate the view that older adults may be better at processing and maintaining positive affect and may be relatively impaired at processing or maintaining negative affect. However, it is important to consider the stage of processing that likely was assessed in this study. Because participants were required to maintain their emotional state over a 3-second period of time, it is likely that older adults invoked more controlled emotion processes, perhaps including emotion regulation attempts. Thus, it is interesting to consider that the results from the two lines of working memory research just described actually dovetail nicely with the hypothesis that aging may disproportionately impact the controlled stages of emotion processing and may leave the automatic stages of processing relatively intact (see Mather, 2006; Mather & Carstensen, 2005).

Although the two lines of research discussed thus far have examined the effect of transient emotional responses on working memory performance, other research has been geared toward understanding how mood states influence working memory in young and older adults. Some of the most consistent demonstrations have centered around the effects of anxiety on working memory performance. As described in Chapter 5, anxiety often has a detrimental effect on young adults' working memory performance, plausibly because of the cognitive resources that are devoted toward rumination and worry (see Eysenck, 1979). Interestingly, however, at least a few studies have revealed an even greater impact of anxiety on the working memory performance of older adults (e.g., Backman & Molander, 1991; Deputla, Singh, & Pomara, 1993). For example, Hogan

(2003) compared the performance of young and older adults on a word-comparison and rotary pursuit task under conditions of either full attention (i.e., only one task being performed) or divided attention (i.e., with two tasks being performed simultaneously). High anxiety did not exacerbate the effects of divided attention in the young adults on either task. In contrast, the effects of divided attention on the cognitive (word-completion) task were more detrimental to anxious older adults than to less anxious older adults, although anxiety did not affect older adults' performance on the motor (rotary pursuit) task. These results are consistent with the suggestion that anxiety may draw cognitive resources away from the task and toward rumination or worry. Because older adults have fewer cognitive resources to begin with, any additional cognitive load (as added by increasing anxiety) will be likely to critically affect their performance. In contrast, because young adults may have cognitive resources to spare (i.e., more resources than are required for successful task performance), additional anxiety may have a lesser impact on their performance (see Backman & Molander, 1991; Deputla et al., 1993 for further discussion).

☐ Link Between Older Adults' Affective Working Memory and Decision Making

Despite age-related declines in cognitive functioning (as discussed more fully in Chapter 11), older adults appear to make decisions in their everyday lives that are at least as good as those made by young adults (e.g., Denney & Pearce, 1989; Hartley, 1989; Marsiske & Willis, 1995; Cornelius & Caspi, 1987). One plausible explanation for older adults' preserved decision making is that they may rely on their intact affective processing to guide their decisions (discussed by Kensinger & Leclerc, in press; Peters, Hess, Auman, & Vastfjall, 2007). This hypothesis would be in keeping with the working memory literature just described. Older adults seem to do a good job of maintaining and remembering the emotions elicited by prior experiences, and they may be able to capitalize on that information to decide which of two (or more) options is best. Indeed, there is a reasonable amount of evidence to suggest that older adults' emotions influence their decisions more than is the case with young adults. For example, older adults are more likely to buy products that are marketed with emotion-relevant slogans than with other types of slogans (Fung & Carstensen, 2003), and they are more likely to have their decisions influenced by the amount of positive or negative information provided about a choice (Kim, Goldstein, Hasher, & Zacks, 2005). There are some types of emotion-related decisions for which older adults show impairments as compared to young adults

(Denburg, Tranel, & Bechara, 2005; Denburg, Rechnor, Bechara, & Tranel, 2006), so clearly older adults' emotional responses to stimuli do not always follow the most adaptable or task-advantageous patterns. Nevertheless, it seems likely that older adults' relatively good ability to maintain the emotional valence, or the reward value, of a stimulus coupled with their relatively poorer ability to maintain other types of mental representations in working memory has important consequences for the ways in which older adults make decisions in everyday life.

☐ **Concluding Remarks**

Only a handful of studies have examined the effects of aging on emotional working memory. Yet, each study has revealed that aging does affect the way in which emotion interacts with working memory ability. When examining participants' abilities to hold information in mind, it appears that the detrimental effects of emotion that are found in young adults are even more exaggerated in older adults. However, when examining participants' abilities to hold feelings in mind, it appears that older adults perform just as well as younger adults. Although it remains to be seen whether this dissociation between holding informational content in mind and holding a stimulus-linked feeling in mind will hold across a range of tasks, it appears that examining the effects of aging on emotional working memory will be a fruitful avenue for future research.

When Aging Influences Effects of Emotion on Long-Term Memory

As we have discussed, aging can sometimes have a less detrimental effect on emotion processing than on cognitive processing. Thus, older adults tend not to show declines in emotion processing, and they remain very good at maintaining and comparing emotional states that have occurred at varying time points. In the next two chapters, we explore the effects of emotion on older adults' declarative long-term memories. As discussed in Chapters 6 through 8, emotion can exert a variety of effects on young adults' long-term memories. Emotion can influence the likelihood that an event is remembered, it can influence the subjective vividness of a memory, and it can influence the types of details that are likely to be remembered about an event. In this chapter, we explore how aging influences each of these effects of emotion on memory.

☐ Effects of Emotion on the Quantity of Events That Older Adults Remember

The majority of studies have demonstrated that older adults, like young adults, remember more emotional than nonemotional information. The presence of an intact emotional memory enhancement effect in older adults has been revealed across a number of studies using stimuli ranging from advertisements to word lists (Carstensen & Turk-Charles, 1994; Fung & Carstensen, 2003; Kensinger, Brierley, Medford, Growdon, & Corkin, 2002). In fact, in some instances, emotional information seems to be remembered as well by older adults as by young adults. Whereas older adults often remember less neutral information than young adults, there have been a number of instances in which the proportion of remembered emotional information is similar in young and older adults (e.g., Carstensen, Fung, & Charles, 2003; Carstensen & Turk-Charles, 1994; Denburg, Buchanan, Tranel, & Adolphs, 2003). These findings may suggest that the emotional memory advantage seen in young adults is not only maintained, but also can be enhanced in older adults.

☐ Effects of Emotion on the Quality of Events That Older Adults Remember

Although most evidence points to an intact emotional memory enhance-ment effect in older adults, it has been less clear whether older adults remember emotional information with the same subjective vividness as young adults. This question is of particular interest because, as described in Chapter 11, older adults often show particularly large impairments in the ability to vividly remember prior events (e.g., Craik & McDowd, 1987; Mantyla, 1993; Rugg & Morcom, 2005; Spencer & Raz, 1995).

The vast majority of studies that have examined the effect of emotion on the vividness of older adults' memories have asked whether older adults form "flashbulb memories" with the same frequency as young adults. The results have been mixed. Some studies suggest that age does not have a detrimental effect on the likelihood of retaining vivid memories of an emo-tional event (e.g., for the assassination of John F. Kennedy as reported by Christianson, 1989; for the resignation of Margaret Thatcher as reported by Wright, Gaskell, & O'Muircheartaigh, 1998). In fact, Wright et al. (1998) found that up until age 75, there was an age-related *increase* in the vividness with which adults reported memories for the reception of the news of Margaret Thatcher's resignation. Other investigations, however, have demonstrated that aging can negatively impact the ability to remember the details of an emotional event after a delay (e.g., for the assassination of John F. Kennedy as reported by Yarmey & Bull, 1978; for the resignation of Margaret Thatcher as reported by Cohen, Conway, & Maylor, 1994; for the death of the eighth president of Turkey as reported by Tekcan & Peynircioglu, 2002).

Studies of this sort are quite difficult to carry out because surveys typi-cally must be administered very quickly after the occurrence of an event, and participants must be contacted again after a delay in order to assess their retention of details initially reported. Because of the complex design, it often is difficult to directly compare one study to another in order to determine what might account for contradictory findings. For example, although Wright et al. (1998) and Cohen et al. (1994) both examined older adults' memories for the resignation of Margaret Thatcher, Wright et al. did not include a baseline assessment of the memory's accuracy and therefore relied solely on the subjective reports of the adults. Cohen et al., in contrast, assessed the consistency of older adults' responses at two time points. Therefore, the fact that Cohen et al., but not Wright et al., found that aging had a detrimental effect on memory may suggest that while older adults have the same subjective increase in memory for emotional experiences as do young adults, in reality their memories for emotional events do not have the same accuracy. However, there also were other potentially important methodological differences between the two studies, which could explain their contrary results. The delay after which memory was assessed differed in the two studies (11 months in Cohen et al. and 3 years in Wright et al.). The methods used to query memory also differed. Wright et al. used a marketing phone interview, asking participants to respond "yes" or "no" to a series of questions, whereas Cohen et al. analyzed written survey responses. It is, therefore, impossible to determine whether the divergence resulted principally from the reliance on assessments of subjective memory vividness versus objective memory accuracy.

Another difficulty with most of these studies of older adults' flash-bulb memories is that they did not include a non-emotional control event. Thus, at least in the studies where a detrimental effect of aging was noted, it is difficult to determine whether this deficit reflected a general effect of age on memory vividness or a specific reduction in the effect of emotion on memory's vividness. That is, we would expect older adults to show a reduced ability to vividly remember any type of information (emotional or nonemotional). Therefore, without a nonemotional control event, it is hard to know whether older adults' difficulties vividly remembering an emotional experience reflect a general deficit in their ability to vividly remembering any type of information or a more specific lack of enhancement in their ability to vividly remember an emotional event.

Two studies have now circumvented this problem by including a nonemotional control event. Davidson & Glisky (2002) asked young and older adults to report what they remembered about the deaths of Princess Diana and Mother Theresa and to report what they remembered about their Labor Day weekend activities, which occurred in close proximity to the two deaths. Their study revealed that young and older adults remembered more information about the deaths than they did about the control event and that aging had no effect on the frequency with which flashbulb memories were formed.

Kensinger, Krendl, and Corkin (2006) reached a similar conclusion after comparing young and older adults' memories for the Columbia shuttle explosion (a highly emotional event) and for the Super Bowl (a less emotional event that occurred in close temporal proximity to the Columbia shuttle explosion). They asked participants to tell them what they remembered about these two events shortly after their occurrence (within a couple of weeks) and then again after a 7-month delay. They found that although older adults had poorer memory overall, they remembered more information about the shuttle explosion than they did about the Super Bowl game. In fact, the effect of age on the amount of information remembered was less pronounced for the shuttle explosion than it was for the Super Bowl game (Kensinger et al. 2006). These results, coupled with those of Davidson & Glisky (2002), suggest not only that older adults show a qualitative memory benefit for emotional events but also that age-related deficits in the ability to vividly remember prior experiences may be mitigated when events contain emotional relevance.

☐ Effects of Emotion on the Details That Older Adults Remember About Events

The results just described suggest that emotion may lead to age-related enhancements in the ability to vividly remember previously encountered information. However, these studies do not speak to whether the types of details that older adults remember about emotional experiences match those that are most likely to be remembered by young adults. Comblain, D'Argembeau, van der Linden, & Aldenhoff (2004) have suggested that because older adults are more likely than are young adults to focus on their internal state, older adults also are less likely to vividly remember the external details associated with the presentation of emotional information. Indeed, two studies have suggested that older adults will often remember the feelings elicited by an emotional event but not other details of the event. In fact, there are instances in which older adults' memories seem to consist primarily of details related to the feelings elicited by an event rather than details of the event itself. In contrast, young adults will be more likely to remember spatio-temporal details of an event than they will their thoughts or feelings about an event (Hashtroudi, Johnson, & Chrosniak, 1990). Older adults also appear to be better able to remember emotion-relevant source information (e.g., was a name associated with a "good person" or a "bad person"; was a food "safe" or "unsafe" to eat) than neutral source information (e.g., was a name read by a male or a female voice; in which location was the food presented; Rahhal, May, & Hasher, 2002; May, Rahhal, Berry, & Leighton, 2005). This effect occurs even when the two types of source information are directly correlated (i.e., participants are told that all names read by a female voice refer to "good people" and all names read by a male voice refer to "bad people"; Rahhal et al., 2002).

The research that I have conducted with my colleagues also has suggested that older adults may remain more focused on emotional information, preventing them from encoding other contextual information. In one experiment (Kensinger et al., 2002), we asked young and older adults to read aloud sentences, half of which were negatively emotional (e.g., "He would abuse the children at every party" or "There was a fire in the forest") and half of which were neutral (e.g., "He would amuse the children at every party" or "There was a road in the forest"). The sentences were identical with the exception of the critical word (e.g., fire versus road), and the version of the sentence that was studied was counterbalanced across participants (no participant studied both the emotional and the nonemotional version of a particular sentence). After reading aloud these sentences, we asked the participants to take a forced-choice recognition memory task. Participants were shown three words and were asked to pick the member of the triplet that had been included in a studied sentence. We found that young adults had better memory for the words that had been studied in an emotional context than for the words that had been studied in a neutral context. Thus, if a young adult had studied the sentences "He would abuse the children at every party" and "There was a road in the forest," that young adult would show better recognition of words like party (i.e., words included in emotional sentences) than words like forest (i.e., words included in nonemotional sentences). Older adults did not show any contextual memory effect. Although, like the young adults, the older adults were more likely to recognize emotional words than neutral ones (e.g., "abuse" and "fire" versus "amuse" and "road"), they showed no difference in recognition rates for nonemotional words included in emotional versus neutral sentences.

As often is the case in studies of older adults' memories, there was variability in performance. Some older adults showed at least some contextual memory advantage for the emotional words, whereas other older adults showed no glimmer of contextual enhancement. We found that the older adults who showed at least some contextual benefit were the same individuals who performed well on other measures of source memory (e.g., on tasks requiring them to remember who had told them particular facts; Figure 14.1). These results led us to hypothesize that, in general, older adults do not show contextual memory benefits for emotional information because of their relatively poor source memory ability. In other words, many older adults may not effectively bind the emotional information to its context, thereby preventing an emotion-mediated contextual memory enhancement. Another possibility, however, is that older adults may have been more focused on the emotional content of the sentences and less focused on the contextual details of the sentences. Perhaps those older adults who performed best on the source memory measures were also those individuals who were able to expand their attention focus beyond the emotional word in the sentence and to the broader context in which that word occurred. Because both source memory and flexible deployment of attention rely on prefrontal processes (see Roberts, Robbins, & Weiskrantz, 1998), it is quite likely that these two abilities would go hand-in-hand.

Emotional Memory Measure	Measures of Source Memory (check-mark indicates significant correlation, $r > .45$, $p < .05$)			
	Source experiment	Source color	Source person	Temporal order
Emo vs. Neu word-context recall	✓	✓	✓	✓
Pos vs. Neu word-context recall	✓	✓	✓	✓
Neg vs. Neu word-context recall	✓	✓		✓
Neg vs. Neu sentence context recognition	✓			

FIGURE 14.1 There were robust correlations between older adults' performance on measures of source memory and their ability to show emotion-related contextual-memory enhancements. Data from Kensinger et al. (2002).

The results described thus far suggest that aging can fundamentally affect the types of details that are remembered about an emotional event. There do appear, however, to be some circumstances in which young and older adults remember similar aspects of emotional experiences. In particular, older adults, like young adults, tend to show the same sorts of emotion-induced memory trade-offs. As discussed in Chapter 8, there are two primary types of trade-offs that have been described. The gist/detail trade-off refers to individuals' abilities to extract the general theme, or the "gist" of an emotional event, but to have poor memory for its specific sensory details. The central/peripheral trade-off refers to individuals' abilities to remember the information directly tied to the emotional arousal elicited by the event but to have poor memory for more tangential details. Denburg, Buchanan, Tranel, and Adolphs (2003) examined the ability of young, middle-aged, and older adults to remember the gist versus the visual detail of scenes and demonstrated that all age groups showed a gist/detail trade-off. Although all age groups were better at recalling the general types of emotional photos that they had studied as compared to the neutral photos, they were worse at distinguishing the studied emotional images from slightly altered images.

Kensinger, Piguet, Krendl, and Corkin (2005) demonstrated that the central/peripheral trade-off also occurs for older adults as well as for young adults. They asked individuals in the two age groups to study a series of pictures, each containing a negative or a neutral object placed against a neutral background. After a brief delay, they showed participants fragments from the photos and asked them to indicate whether those fragments had been included in any of the photos that they had studied. When

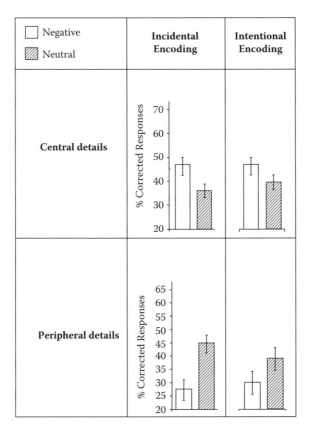

FIGURE 14.2   Older adults showed a central/peripheral trade-off when given either incidental encoding instructions (left column) or intentional encoding instructions (right column). In either instance, they showed better memory for the negative central elements than for the neutral ones, but poorer memory for the peripheral elements included in a scene with a negative element. These results contrast with those of the young adults (see Figure 8.4), who were able to overcome the trade-off effect with the intentional encoding instructions. Data from Kensinger et al. (2005).

the participants had been asked to passively view the photos initially, both young and older adults showed a pervasive memory trade-off. They were more likely to remember the fragments of the negative objects than they were to remember the fragments of the neutral objects, whereas they were less likely to remember the background fragments that had been presented with a negative object than with a neutral object (Kensinger et al., 2005; Figure 14.2). These results are in keeping with evidence that young and older adults' attention may be automatically directed toward things in the environment that are emotional, thereby enhancing memory for those elements but impairing memory for elements that are more tangential or peripheral.

This type of focus on central details also has been noted within the flashbulb memory literature, with individuals retaining the types of details (either event-related or personal) that were directly associated with their emotional reaction to an event (see Pezdek, 2003 for discussion). For example, for people near the September 11th terrorist targets, the details of the events themselves were likely to have high emotional salience. Thus, those individuals tended to retain those details over time, and to remember those event-related details better than details that are more personal. In contrast, for individuals more removed from those targets, the personal context was likely to elicit as great an emotional response as the event-related details. Those individuals tended to remember the personal details as well as, or better than, the event details (Pezdek, 2003; Smith, Bibi, & Sheard, 2003; Tekcan, Ece, Gülgöz, & Er, 2003). Thus, memory was best for the information that elicited the emotional response. In the case of individuals close to the terrorist targets, those were event-related details, but in the case of individuals further away from the terrorist targets, the emotional elicitation often stemmed from a more personal interaction. This type of memory narrowing—onto the information that spurred the emotional reaction—occurs not only in young adults, but also in older adults (see Budson et al., 2004).

More recently, Kensinger, Gutchess, and Schacter (2007) showed that the same interactions between the gist/detail and the central/peripheral trade-offs that exist for young adults (see Chapter 8 for more discussion) also exist for older adults. Like young adults, older adults are more likely to remember the gist *and* the visual detail of central emotional elements in a scene, whereas they often show a gist/detail trade-off for the more peripheral nonemotional elements in a scene. Thus, the central/peripheral trade-off is more apparent when assessing memory for specific visual detail than when examining memory for gist-based information.

Interestingly, in both Kensinger et al. (2005) and Kensinger et al. (2007), although young and older adults showed similar trade-off effects with passive viewing of scenes, age differences emerged when other encoding instructions were given. In Kensinger et al. (2005), young adults were able to overcome the central/peripheral trade-off when they were given instructions to intentionally encode the scenes so that they could remember the scenes in a later memory task. In contrast, even with these intentional encoding instructions, older adults were not able to overcome the central/peripheral trade-off. Similarly, in Kensinger et al. (2007), young adults were able to overcome the central/peripheral trade-off effect when they were given incidental encoding instructions that emphasized elaborative encoding of the entire scene. Older adults, in contrast, continued to show a robust trade-off. Consistent with the results described earlier from the study of memory for sentences (Kensinger et al., 2002), these results suggest that older adults have more difficulty flexibly disengaging attention from the negative arousing elements, thereby preventing them from successfully processing other elements. Further research is required to examine whether older adults show stronger attention capture by the negative arousing elements in scenes or sentences than do young adults (thus making it harder for them to divert attention away from those elements), whether older adults' difficulties arise because of age-related impairments in flexible attention (thus impeding their ability to shift attention away from the emotional information once it has captured their attention), or whether both factors contribute.

☐ Concluding Remarks

The fact that older adults often show normal enhancement for emotional information is consistent with the neural evidence indicating that the amygdala and other limbic regions (e.g., orbitofrontal cortex) are relatively spared in healthy aging. The amygdala shows minimal atrophy with healthy aging; the volumetric decline in the amygdala is on par with the decline in whole-brain volume (e.g., Coffey et al., 1992; Good et al., 2001; Raz et al., 1997; Tisserand, Visser, van Boxtel, & Jolles, 2000). Similarly, the orbitofrontal cortex may be relatively spared in aging, particularly in comparison to other regions of the prefrontal cortex (Salat, Kaye, & Janowsky, 2001). The amygdala and orbitofrontal cortex are regions often associated with the successful encoding and retrieval of emotional information (e.g., Kensinger & Schacter, 2005a, 2006b; Smith, Stephan, Rugg, & Dolan, 2006). Thus, it is likely that the circuitry underlying the emotional memory enhancement is relatively preserved across the adult lifespan (see also Kensinger & Schacter, 2008 and Figure 14.3 for evidence that the core of the emotional memory network is preserved across the adult lifespan). However, as has been described in this chapter, despite this age-related preservation in many aspects of emotional memory, the types of details that older adults remember about an emotional experience are not always in line with those remembered by young adults. Thus, emotion appears to affect some but not all aspects of emotional memory. As we will discuss in the next chapter, the effects of aging on emotional memory sometimes become even more divergent when one distinguishes not only emotional from nonemotional but also positive from negative.

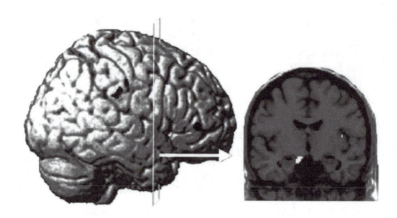

FIGURE 14.3   For both young and older adults, encoding-related activity in the orbitofrontal and ventrolateral prefrontal cortex, and in the amygdala, corresponds with subsequent memory for positive and negative items. Thus, the core of the emotional memory network appears to be relatively preserved across the adult lifespan (data from Kensinger & Schacter, 2008).

Age-Related Positivity Biases

As we discussed in Chapter 12, older adults may be more likely than young adults to attend to positive information in the environment. This effect often has been referred to as a "positivity effect," although there are debates about whether this effect is best characterized by a focus on the positive or by an avoidance of the negative (Blanchard-Fields, 2005; Mather, 2006). This positivity effect appears, at least in some instances, to alter the valence of information that older adults remember best. In particular, the effect results in interactions between age and valence, with older adults remembering proportionally more positive items than young adults, but proportionally fewer negative items than young adults (e.g., Charles, Mather, & Carstensen, 2003; Kennedy, Mather, & Carstensen, 2004).

☐ Positivity Bias in Older Adults' Memories

This type of positivity effect has now been demonstrated in a number of studies (but see Murphy & Isaacowitz, 2008 for evidence that it does not always occur). In one of the first demonstrations, Charles et al. (2003, Experiment 1) asked young, middle-aged, and older adults to view a series of positive, negative, and neutral photos each presented for 2 seconds. Participants were asked to view the photo stream as if they were watching television. The critical finding was that middle-aged and older adults were more likely to recall positive images than negative images, whereas young adults recalled a similar proportion of positive and negative images. In a second experiment within that study, participants again viewed photos, but this time in a self-paced condition. In this experiment, young adults showed mnemonic enhancement only for negative images, whereas older adults showed equivalent mnemonic enhancement for negative and positive images.

Since the original report of Charles et al. (2003), there have been a number of studies that have reported positivity effects with aging (Kennedy, Mather, & Carstensen, 2004; Leigland, Schulz, & Janowsky, 2004). Not all studies have reported these effects, however (e.g., Denburg, Buchanan, Tranel, & Adolphs, 2003; Gruhn, Smith, & Baltes, 2005). For example, Kensinger, Brierley, Medford, Growdon, and Corkin (2002) demonstrated no evidence of a positivity effect. Using both word lists and photo streams, young and older adults showed mnemonic enhancements for positive and negative items, and there was no interaction between age and valence. It is unclear what led to these contrary findings, although one likely contributor may relate to the type of encoding task used with participants. As discussed in more detail by Mather (2006), the studies that have tended to show the most pervasive and consistent positivity effects in older adults have asked participants to passively view the stimuli. In contrast, studies that have used more constrained encoding tasks (e.g., Kensinger et al. [2002] asked participants to rate each stimulus as positive, negative, or neutral) have tended to show less pronounced positivity effects. It is plausible that these more constrained encoding tasks, particularly those that focus participants on the emotional content, may be likely to eliminate age differences in how the information is processed, thereby diminishing the differential effects of valence on young and older adults' memories. However, there is some evidence that positivity effects in memory do not always stem from differential attention toward positive information during encoding. For example, Thomas and Hasher (2006) demonstrated that although older adults did not give preferential attention to positive information during encoding, they nevertheless showed better memory for positive items than for negative or neutral ones. Thus, further research is needed to understand the potential importance of encoding instructions and attention focus during encoding on the occurrence of the positivity effect.

☐ Links Between Older Adults' Self-Referential Processing and Their Positivity Effect

Recent research in my laboratory has led us to hypothesize that part of what may account for older adults' positivity effect is a shift in the types of information that are most likely to elicit self-referential processing. It is well known that thinking about how information relates to the self is an effective encoding strategy and one that benefits adults of all ages (Rogers, Kuiper, & Kirker, 1977; Gutchess, Kensinger, Yoon, & Schacter, 2007). Thus, it makes sense that if older adults were to process positive information in a more self-relevant fashion, this could lead to enhancements in their memory. Self-referential processing also is thought to be a type of controlled, elaborative encoding process, and therefore a link between self-referential processing and older adults' positivity effect would be consistent with proposals that the effect occurs because of age-related changes in the controlled processing of emotional information (Mather & Knight, 2005).

Neuroimaging studies in young adults have clarified the network of regions that are critical for this type of self-referential encoding, implicating regions of the ventromedial prefrontal cortex and midline structures lining the cingulate gyrus (reviewed by Northoff & Bermpohl, 2004). Recent neuroimaging studies in my laboratory have confirmed that while young adults engage these regions more during the processing of negative items than during the processing of positive items, the opposite is true for older adults. Older adults' recruitment of these regions is greater during the processing of positive information (Leclerc & Kensinger, 2008). Furthermore, older adults' recruitment of regions such as the ventromedial prefrontal cortex and regions of the cingulate gyrus correspond with their ability to later remember positive items (Kensinger & Schacter, 2008). These results suggest that at least part of what may differ between young and older adults is the likelihood that they think about how positive information relates to them and how their internal feeling state is altered by positive items. Older adults seem to do this more than young adults do, and this change may be a contributor to their positivity effect (see Kensinger & Leclerc, in press, for further discussion).

☐ Limits on the Positivity Effect— Positive Items Are Not Remembered With More Detail

Although older adults often remember more positive than negative information, an important boundary condition with regard to the existence of a positivity effect appears to relate to the level of detail assessed in memory. In two studies that Schacter, Garoff-Eaton and Kensinger conducted in collaboration with two then-undergraduate students, Jackie O'Brien and Kelley Swanberg, young and older adults were asked to distinguish whether they had seen or had imagined positive, negative, and neutral items (Kensinger, O'Brien, Swanberg, Garoff-Eaton, & Schacter, 2007). In one experiment, we asked participants to listen as a series of words were pronounced over a headset (a positive word might have been *love*, a negative word might have been *jail*, and a neutral word might have been *book*).

Participants were asked to indicate whether the first letter of the word was lower in height than the last letter of the word. The answer to *jail* would be "yes" (because the *j* is lower in height than the *l*), whereas the answer to *love* or *book* would be "no." After studying this series of words, participants performed a surprise recognition test. They listened to another series of words pronounced over the headset, and for each word, they indicated whether they had seen the word on the computer screen, had imagined the word, or had not studied the word. We were interested in distinguishing two types of memory: *general recognition* (the ability to remember that an item had been studied, regardless of whether it was properly attributed to the seen or imagined study condition) and *source recognition* (the ability to correctly attribute a studied item to the seen or imagined conditions). We found that young adults showed a general recognition and a source recognition advantage only for the negative items as compared to the positive or the neutral items. The older adults, in contrast, showed a general recognition advantage for the positive as well as the negative items, but they showed enhanced source recognition ability only for the negative items.

A similar pattern of results was demonstrated in a study that Kensinger conducted with Garoff-Eaton and Schacter (2007b). Using methods described in Chapter 7, we presented young and older adults with a series of positive, negative, and neutral objects and then at test asked them to distinguish *same* objects from objects that were *similar* (shared the same verbal label but differed in visual details) or *new*. As in Kensinger, O'Brien, et al. (2007), we focused on two types of memory: *general recognition* (the ability to know that an object was not *new*, regardless of whether it was correctly identified as being *same* or *similar*) and *specific recognition* (the ability to correctly distinguish *same* from *similar* exemplars). We found that young and older adults showed enhanced specific recognition for negative objects as compared to positive or neutral ones. Thus, as in Kensinger, O'Brien et al. (2007), only negative (and not positive) emotional content was associated with enhanced memory for detail. Also consistent with Kensinger, O'Brien et al. (2007), divergent effects of aging were demonstrated when assessing general recognition ability. While young adults showed a general recognition advantage only for negative objects, older adults showed equivalently elevated general recognition for the negative and positive objects.

The results of these two studies are important in indicating that in both young and older adults, negative (but not positive) information is likely to confer particular benefits on memory for detail. As discussed in Chapter 9, it has been suggested that negative emotion elicits a more detailed and analytic processing than positive emotion, thereby promoting memory accuracy (e.g., Clore, Gasper, & Garvin, 2001; Fiedler, 2001; Gasper & Clore, 2002). It appears that this detail-oriented processing of negative information occurs in older adults as well as in young adults. Thus, despite evidence for age-related changes in attention focus and in general memory for positive information, older adults nevertheless remember more detail about negative items than about positive ones. The fact that young and older adults show this consistent effect of negative emotion on memory for detail despite age-related changes in the self-relevance of the information (i.e., with negative information having more self-relevance to young adults and positive information having more self-relevance to older adults; Baumeister, Bratslavsky, Finkenauer, & Vohs, 2001; Mather & Carstensen, 2005) suggests that there is something fundamentally different about the way in which positive and negative information is processed and remembered and that this difference is preserved across the adult lifespan.

☐ Concluding Remarks

A number of studies have demonstrated that older adults are more likely to show a memory advantage for positive information than are young adults. Although there is some evidence that this positivity effect may be tied to differences in attention during encoding, it is not always the case that attentional effects at encoding predict the magnitude of the positivity effect at retrieval (e.g., Thomas & Hasher, 2006). Thus, more research is needed in order to understand the processes that lead to positivity effects in older adults' memories. Although it seems likely that older adults' positivity effect relates to the controlled way in which they process incoming information (Mather, 2006), it also appears that there are important limitations on the positivity effect. The positivity effect is not always present, and even when it is noted in general recognition ability, there is not always a corresponding benefit in memory for detail. Thus, although aging appears to enhance the likelihood that the "gist" or general theme of a positive item can be remembered, the way in which older adults process positive items may not allow them to remember the details of the presentations of those items. These results raise the intriguing question of whether there are particular types of details for which older adults will show a positivity effect in memory, or whether the effect typically will exist only in memory for more general, nonspecific information.

Emotional Memory
in Alzheimer's Disease

Although many older adults note at least some cognitive decline with advancing age, for most of them, the changes do not critically affect the way in which they function in daily life. For a subset of older adults, however, aging is associated with more pronounced cognitive decline. Some of these individuals will meet the criteria for dementia. The most common form of dementia is Alzheimer's disease, characterized by the accumulation of extracellular neuritic plaques and intracellular neurofibrillary tangles (see Goedert & Spillantini, 2006 for review). Because these pathological changes affect the medial temporal lobe first, long-term memory deficits tend to be the best indicator of mild Alzheimer's disease (Locascio, Growdon, & Corkin, 1995).

☐ Effects of Emotion on the Explicit Memory Performance of Alzheimer's Disease Patients

Most assessments of long-term memory retention in patients with Alzheimer's disease have used standardized memory tasks that assess memory for non-emotional information. However, over the last few years, there has been an increased interest in examining the extent to which Alzheimer's disease patients show emotional memory enhancement effects comparable to those of age-matched healthy individuals. At a neural level, there is reason to believe that Alzheimer's disease patients might show a disruption in their memory for emotional events. In contrast to healthy

Healthy Older Adult   **Patient With Mild AD**

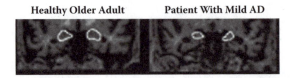

FIGURE 16.1 Depiction of the amygdala (outlined in white) in a healthy older adult and in an age- and gender-matched individual with Alzheimer's disease. These MR images visually depict what a number of quantitative assessments of amygdalar volume have revealed: Normal aging relatively spares the amygdala, whereas pronounced amygdala atrophy is present even in mild Alzheimer's disease.

aging, which results in minimal atrophy to the amygdala, Alzheimer's disease results in significant changes within the amygdala. Volumetric reductions in the amygdala tend to range from approximately 20% to 50%, and the volumetric decline usually is apparent even in relatively mild cases of the disease (Figure 16.1; Chow & Cummings, 2000; Krasuski et al., 1998; Mizuno, Wakai, Takeda, & Sobue, 2000; Chan et al., 2001; Galton et al., 2001; Jack et al., 1999; Scott, 1993; Scott, DeKosky, & Scheff, 1991; Scott, DeKosky, Sparks, Knox, & Scheff, 1992; Smith et al., 1999). Neuritic plaques and neurofibrillary tangles also are abundant in the amygdala (Arriagada, Growdon, Hedley-Whyte, & Hyman, 1992; Unger, Lapham, McNeill, Eskin, & Hamill, 1991; Vogt, Human, van Hoesen, & Damasio, 1990). Given the important role of the amygdala in emotional memory (see Chapters 2 and 3 for further discussion), it could logically follow that patients with Alzheimer's disease would show disruption in the emotional memory enhancements often noted in healthy older adults.

Indeed, a number of studies have demonstrated a disruption in the emotional memory enhancement effect in patients with Alzheimer's disease. The blunted emotional enhancement appears even in patients with relatively mild Alzheimer's disease. For example, Kensinger, Brierley, Medford, Growdon, and Corkin (2002) asked young adults, older adults, and patients with mild Alzheimer's disease to complete a series of tasks examining memory for positive, negative, and neutral information. In two tasks, one using pictures and the other using words, we found that young and older adults were able to recall more positive or negative pictures or words than neutral pictures or words. The patients with Alzheimer's disease, in contrast, were equally likely to recall positive, negative, or neutral pictures or words; these patients showed no memory benefit for the emotional information (Figure 16.2). This blunted emotional memory enhancement effect in Alzheimer's disease patients has now been demonstrated in a number of studies (Abrisqueta-Gomez, Bueno, Oliveira, & Bertolucci, 2002; Hamann et al., 2000; see also Boller et al., 2002; Kazui et

Stimulus	Memory Enhancements?		
Picture Recall	Young	✓	Pos and Neg
	Older	✓	Pos and Neg
	AD	✗	
Word Recall	Young	✓	Pos and Neg
	Older	✓	Pos and Neg
	AD	✗	
Word Recognition	Young	✓	Neg
	Older	✓	Neg
	AD	✗	

FIGURE 16.2   Summary of findings from Kensinger et al. (2002). Young and older adults showed a memory enhancement for positive and negative information compared to neutral information. Alzheimer's disease patients, in contrast, showed no memory benefit for the emotional information.

al., 2000; Kazui, Mori, Hashimoto, & Hirono, 2003; Moayeri, Cahill, Jin, & Potkin, 2000 for some evidence of emotional memory enhancement in Alzheimer's disease patients).

Although these results provided suggestive evidence that the amygdala atrophy that occurred in Alzheimer's disease might be sufficient to eliminate the emotional memory enhancement effect, Corkin, Growdon and Kensinger had some concerns about the generality of this claim. First, most studies had been conducted with small samples of patients (usually under 20 patients were tested), leading to the concern that perhaps the statistical power simply had not been great enough to detect potential impacts of emotion on memory. Second, the memory performance of the Alzheimer's disease patients typically was much poorer than the performance of the healthy older adults, leading us to worry that perhaps "floor" (i.e., near-chance recognition or near-absent recall) memory performance in the Alzheimer's disease patients had obscured any beneficial effects of emotion on their memory performance. In order to address these limitations, we created alternate versions of the stories from the NYU Stories standardized test often administered to Alzheimer's patients as part of their standard neuropsychological examination (Randt, Brown, & Osborne, 1981). We modified the stories by replacing key words with substitutions that differed in their emotional valence but not in their word frequency, familiarity, or imageability. For example, a neutral story would tell participants about a newspaper reporter that visited the theater district and interviewed performers. The emotional version of that story would tell participants about an earthquake that struck the theater district and trapped performers. In this way, we created six matched neutral and emotional versions of the stories. Each participant was read one emotional and one neutral story (never both versions of the same story), and the emotionality of each story was counterbalanced across participants. Participants were asked to freely recall elements from the story, and they were asked to take a recognition test regarding information that had been included in the story.

We tested a large sample of 80 Alzheimer's disease patients as well as two groups of older adults. One group was tested after the same short delay as the Alzheimer's disease patients. The other group was tested after a longer delay, in order to equate the overall memory performance levels of those older adults with the memory performance of the Alzheimer's disease patients. The results paralleled those that we had found earlier. Although both groups of older adults showed better memory for the emotional stories than for the neutral ones, the Alzheimer's disease patients showed no effect of emotion on the amount that they could recall or that they could recognize (Kensinger, Anderson, Growdon, & Corkin, 2004). These findings lend credence to the hypothesis that there is a disruption in the emotional memory enhancement effect with Alzheimer's disease. It does not appear that the lack of emotional memory benefit in these patients is an artifact of low statistical power or of "floor" memory performance.

Although many have postulated that these changes in emotional memory may be tied to the changes in the amygdala, the behavioral data cannot speak to the neural correlates underlying older adults' impaired emotional memory. In fact, one might reason that the blunted emotional enhancement effect emerges not because of changes in emotional memory per se, but rather because of the dramatic declarative memory deficits that accompany the disease. There are, however, some lines of evidence that argue against this type of interpretation. First, Hamann and colleagues (Hamann, Cahill, & Squire, 1997; Hamann, Cahill, McGaugh, & Squire, 1997) have demonstrated that amnesic patients with extensive medial temporal lobe damage (but without damage to the amygdala) show a normal emotional memory enhancement effect. Although their overall memory performance is low, they are more likely to remember emotional information than they are to remember neutral information. Second, Mori and colleagues (1999) found that amygdalar volume strongly correlated with the likelihood that Alzheimer's disease patients remembered personal information about the Kobe earthquake. The volume of other medial temporal lobe regions, in contrast, did not correspond with the ability of the patients to remember these details of their emotional experience. These results suggest that the blunted emotional memory enhancement effect in Alzheimer's disease patients is likely tied to the amygdala atrophy that accompanies the disease.

Assessments of overall memory performance are not the only explicit memory domains in which Alzheimer's disease patients show unusual effects of emotion. Budson et al. (2006) assessed the performance of young adults, older adults, and Alzheimer's disease patients on a task designed to elicit high levels of false recognition. Participants studied a series of words that were associated with a nonpresented lure word (e.g., participants might study *steal, robber, crook, thief,* which are all associated with the nonpresented word *burglar*; or they might study *bed, nap, dream, snore,* which are all associated with the nonpresented word *sleep*). Half of the studied words were associated with non-emotional lure words, while the other half were associated with emotional lure words. After studying these words, participants performed a recognition memory task. They were presented with a series of words, including the studied words, the nonstudied lure words, and additional nonstudied words that were unrelated to the studied items. Participants had to indicate whether each word had been included on the study list. We found that young and older adults were more liberal in accepting that an emotional word had been studied previously. Thus, they showed not only higher correct endorsements of the emotional items from the study lists but also higher false endorsements of emotional items that had never been studied. The Alzheimer's disease patients, in contrast, did not show this pattern of response. They were actually more conservative in endorsing an emotional item as compared to a non-emotional item.

These results open the possibility that Alzheimer's disease has a broad effect on multiple aspects of emotion's influence on explicit memory performance. Patients with Alzheimer's disease not only show a blunted emotional memory enhancement effect (as discussed previously), they also do not show the typical emotion-related changes in their bias to endorse previously studied information. Future studies will be required to examine the extent to which Alzheimer's disease disrupts a person's ability to discriminate studied from nonstudied emotional items, and the extent to which the disease influences a person's bias to endorse an emotional item as one that was previously studied.

☐ Effects of Emotion on the Implicit Memory Performance of Alzheimer's Disease Patients

The effects of Alzheimer's disease on emotional memory extend beyond the realm of explicit memory; Alzheimer's disease patients also have impairments in at least some domains of emotionally mediated implicit memory. For example, in a fear-conditioning paradigm, Alzheimer's disease patients have difficulties learning that a particular stimulus predicts an aversive event (Hamann, Monarch, & Goldstein, 2002). They also do not always show normal affective priming, at least for positive stimuli (Padovan, Versace, Thomas-Anterion, & Laurent, 2002), although there is some evidence for preserved priming for negative stimuli (Padovan et al., 2002; Labar et al., 2005). Interestingly, in at least one paradigm, Alzheimer's patients showed an advantage of emotion within implicit memory but not within explicit memory, suggesting dissociation between the processes supporting emotional memory enhancement in the two instances (Labar et al., 2005). These results open up intriguing questions regarding the extent to which the pattern of spared and impaired effects of emotion on the performance of Alzheimer's disease can be explained by global amygdala atrophy and the extent to which the deficits may be better explained by understanding disease-related changes in the connectivity between the amygdala and other brain regions. One possibility, worth further investigation, is that Alzheimer's disease may preferentially affect connections between the amygdala and other medial temporal lobe regions, whereas amygdala connections to sensory regions may remain relatively preserved.

☐ Emotional Processing in Alzheimer's Disease

In contrast to the widespread changes in emotional memory, Alzheimer's disease seems to have a lesser impact on emotional processing. In fact, a number of studies have suggested that emotional processing remains relatively intact in Alzheimer's disease, in contrast to the pervasive cognitive decline that accompanies the disease (e.g., Albert, Cohen & Koff, 1991; Cadieux & Greve, 1997; Roudier et al., 1998). Thus, Alzheimer's disease patients tend to focus their attention on emotional rather than on non-emotional information in the environment (LaBar et al., 2000). They show normal ratings of emotional information and normal skin conductance responses to a range of emotional stimuli (Kensinger et al., 2002; Kensinger et al., 2004; Hamann et al., 2000). They report similar intensities of emotion to real-life events as do healthy older adults (Budson et al., 2004).

Although Alzheimer's disease patients do sometimes show impairments on tasks that require processing emotional stimuli (Albert et al., 1991; Allender & Kaszniak, 1989; Brosgole, Kurucz, Plahovinsak, & Gumiela, 1981; Cadieux & Greve, 1997), many of these deficits seem secondary to perceptual or cognitive difficulties (Albert et al., 1991; Brosgole et al., 1981; Burnham & Hogervorst, 2004; Cadieux & Greve, 1997). When cognitive or perceptual performance is taken into account, usually the deficits within the patient groups no longer remain. Moreover, on tasks with relatively low perceptual and cognitive requirements, Alzheimer's disease patients tend to perform well (Bucks & Radford, 2004; Burnham & Hogervorst, 2004; Shimokawa et al., 2003).

These findings suggest that although there are changes in the limbic system with Alzheimer's disease, these changes are not sufficient to affect the ability to detect emotion or to experience emotion. The intact processing of emotional information also suggests an interesting dissociation between the neural substrates that may support emotional processing versus emotional memory. These results are consistent with recent findings from patients with temporal lobectomies (Brierley, Medford, Shaw, & David, 2004) that found little correlation between patients' emotional memory performance and their performance on tasks of emotional perception.

The fact that emotional processing seems at least mostly preserved in Alzheimer's disease patients also alleviates the concern that disease effects on emotional processing are mediating the effects on emotional memory. If a patient with Alzheimer's disease did not have an emotional reaction to an event, or did not recognize its emotional importance, it would not be surprising to find that the person would not have enhanced memory for that event. However, Alzheimer's disease patients often can show intact perception of emotional information even in instances in which their memory is not enhanced for that information. For example, a few studies (Abrisqueta-Gomez et al., 2002; Kensinger et al., 2002, 2004) have found that Alzheimer's disease patients and healthy older adults cognitively classify stimuli in the same manner in terms of their valence and arousal. Yet, despite this similarity in initial assessment, only the healthy older adults show a memory enhancement for the items classified as emotional. The fact that Alzheimer's disease patients seem to have normal attentional orienting toward emotional information, and also seem to have normal cognitive and physiological responses to emotional information, suggests that the disease-related changes in emotional memory do not arise from a more general deficit in responding to an emotional event.

☐ Concluding Remarks

This chapter has highlighted fundamental differences between the effects of healthy aging and mild Alzheimer's disease on emotional memory. Although healthy aging leaves many of the influences of emotion on memory relatively intact, Alzheimer's disease appears to disrupt many of those influences. However, discrepancies remain concerning the extent to which Alzheimer's disease affects emotional memory. Although some studies have suggested that the emotional memory enhancement effect is eliminated in Alzheimer's disease, many studies have found at least some mnemonic benefit in Alzheimer's disease patients. As has been emphasized throughout this book, emotion seems to have numerous effects on long-term memory, influencing not only the quantity of remembered information, but also the subjective vividness of memories and the types of details remembered about prior experiences. A clearer view of the effects of emotion on the memories of Alzheimer's disease patients may arise as research begins to tease apart these disparate influences of emotion. Nevertheless, the existing data seem to suggest that complete ablasion of the amygdala is not needed in order for significant disruptions in emotional memory to result. Rather, the amygdala atrophy that occurs early in Alzheimer's disease appears to be sufficient to disrupt many of the effects of emotion on memory.

Summary and Conclusions

Research examining emotion–memory interactions has, by necessity, moved beyond thinking about "emotion" and "memory" as monolithic constructs. It is readily apparent that there are myriad interactions between emotion and memory, differing based on the nature of the memory being retrieved, the emotion elicited by an experience, and the characteristics of the person remembering the event (e.g., gender, personality, or age). In this final chapter, I briefly summarize the influences that each of these dimensions can have in guiding emotion–memory interactions, highlighting the need to carefully parse emotion and memory into their constituent components in order to understand the ways in which the two can influence one another. I also discuss some general areas in which emotion's effects on memory seem to cut across different domains of memory and across different age groups. I conclude by noting some directions for future research that I believe will be particularly enlightening.

☐ The Inherent Complexity of Emotion–Memory Interactions

There are innumerable answers to the question "How does emotion affect memory?" The answer depends on the type of memory about which we are talking. For example, there are some types of information that are better remembered over the long term but that are not more likely to be held in mind over the short term (Chapter 5). Even within the realm of declarative long-term memory, the effects of emotion can vary depending on the type of information that we are asking a person to remember. If we are assessing the effects of emotion on the *quantity* or the *subjective quality* of declarative long-term memory, then the effects tend to be in the direction of memory enhancements (Chapters 6 and 7). Individuals remember a larger amount of emotional than non-emotional information, and they tend to remember the emotional information vividly. However, if we are interested in the effects of emotion on the types of details retained in long-term memory, then the effects of emotion often are better described as trade-offs rather than pure enhancements (Chapter 8). Thus, emotion often helps individuals to remember some event details well, but it prevents them from remembering other event details.

The effects of emotion on memory also depend on the nature of the experienced emotion. Items that elicit arousal can be remembered differently than items that elicit no arousal but that are perceived as negative. This effect is seen not only in declarative long-term memory but also in nondeclarative memory (Chapters 4 and 9). Moreover, the mechanisms leading to declarative emotional memory enhancements appear to differ based on whether the information is arousing or not. Arousing information is remembered due to amygdala–hippocampal interactions during encoding, whereas nonarousing information is remembered because of prefrontal–hippocampal interactions (Chapter 9). Even for information that is arousing, memory differs based on the information's valence (i.e., whether it is positive or negative). Across a range of paradigms, and in both young and older adults, positive information is remembered less accurately than negative information, and there is less correspondence between participants' confidence in a memory and the accuracy of that memory when the event in question is positive (Chapters 9 and 15).

Not only do stimulus and task characteristics influence the nature of emotion–memory interactions, but the characteristics of the person who is remembering the information can influence them as well. As we have discussed at length, with advancing age there may be a bias to remember the positive (Chapter 15), and there may be a tendency to show even greater emotion-induced trade-offs (Chapter 14). Even within an age group, individual differences can dramatically influence the effects of emotion on memory (Chapter 10). The sex of an individual can influence the magnitude of the emotional memory enhancement effect and the neural processes that lead to the enhancement. The personality of an individual also can influence the types of information that are attended to and the way in which information is encoded and stored over the long term.

☐ Effects of Emotion That Cross-Cut Memory Domains and Age Groups

The fact that there can be such divergent effects of emotion on memory highlights the need to move beyond a simplistic conception of how emotion influences memory. However, it is equally important to note that there are common themes that can help to explain emotion's innumerable effects on memory. By recognizing these commonalities, we may begin to appreciate not only the intricacies of emotion–memory interactions but also the core influences of emotion that cut across multiple domains of memory.

☐ Effects of Emotion on Memory for Detail

A theme throughout this book has been that it is important to consider not only whether an event is remembered or forgotten but also what types of details are remembered about an event. Across a number of memory domains, emotion exerts an effect on the types of details recorded and remembered about prior events. This effect of emotion on the ability to remember details of an event was most clearly delineated when discussing the effects of emotion on declarative memory trade-offs. Although emotion enhanced memory for some types of details, it left memory for other details unaffected, and impaired the ability to remember other types of details (Chapters 7 through 9). However, while trade-off effects in declarative memory have been discussed extensively, the effects of emotion on memory for detail are not restricted to this domain. Within working memory, there is evidence that emotion can have a focal beneficial influence on memory. Individuals are good at holding in mind information tied to the emotional meaning of an item (e.g., a fearful facial expression), but they do poorly at holding in mind information void of emotional relevance (e.g., the facial identity of the person; Chapter 5). Thus, across multiple domains of memory, there are instances in which emotion has a narrow beneficial influence on memory. Emotion enhances the ability to retain details intrinsically tied to the emotional meaning of an event but impairs the ability to remember details that are more extrinsic. (See also Mather, 2007 for an excellent review of evidence supporting a similar proposal that emotion enhances memory for intra-item features but not necessarily for inter-item features).

☐ Controlled Versus Automatic Processing

Not only is it important to consider the types of details remembered about an event, it also is important to consider *how* one is processing the event. It has been particularly fruitful to distinguish controlled from automatic processing of emotional information (see also Mather, 2006, 2007 for further discussion of the importance of distinguishing these processes). In both young and older adults, it appears that many of the mnemonic benefits and trade-offs for arousing information arise because of the relatively automatic way in which that arousing information is processed. Thus, declarative memory enhancements for arousing information can occur even when participants' attention is divided during encoding (Chapter 9), and memory trade-offs tend to occur not only when participants are intentionally directing their attention toward emotional information but also when they are passively viewing presented information (Chapter 8). It appears that attention is automatically directed toward arousing information in the environment, prioritizing the processing of that information and thus yielding memory benefits for the information intrinsically linked with that arousing information. This automatic focus on arousing information appears to have effects not only within declarative long-term memory (Chapter 8) but also within the domains of working memory (Chapter 5) and nondeclarative memory (Chapter 4).

Although the arousal-based mnemonic effects can occur relatively automatically, they also can be influenced by the use of controlled processes. For example, although young adults' attention is automatically focused on emotionally arousing information in the environment, it appears that they can divert their attention away from those arousing elements when they are given encoding tasks that emphasize processing of all scene elements or when they are given incentives to remember the entire scene presented to them (Chapter 8). The fact that the trade-off effects can be overcome underscores that the strength of the automatic focusing on emotional information in the environment can be altered by a person's goals to remember other information less tied to the source of the arousal. However, there appear to be important individual differences in the effectiveness of such controlled processes. Thus, individuals who are older (Chapter 14), who are more anxious (Chapter 10), or who have poorer cognitive control ability (Chapter 10), are less able to overcome the trade-offs. It remains to be seen whether these individuals are more focused on the arousing information, whether they engage controlled processes less effectively, or whether there is something different about their emotional processing circuitry that prevents controlled processing of incoming information from having the same regulatory effect on automatic focusing on arousing information.

☐ Emotion-Specific Versus Domain-General Processing

At a neural level, there have been many debates regarding the extent to which emotional memory represents a "special" memory mechanism, separable from the mechanisms used to remember non-emotional events. The existing literature provides little evidence that emotion fundamentally alters the circuits that are used to remember information. In fact, in some instances (e.g., when remembering nonarousing negative information), memory enhancements for emotional information seem to arise due to enhanced engagement of exactly the same processes that we use to remember non-emotional information (Chapter 9). Even in instances in which emotion-specific processes are brought online (e.g., when remembering arousing information), it is not the case that these processes supplant the mnemonic processes typically used to remember nonarousing information. For example, within the explicit domain, the medial temporal lobe regions that correspond with accurate encoding and retrieval of non-emotional information also are related to accurate encoding and retrieval of emotional information (Chapters 6 and 9). Within nondeclarative or working memory, similar processes also seem to support memory for non-emotional and emotional information (Chapters 4 and 5). Thus, engagement of emotion-processing regions appears to lead to enhancements in the functioning of the neural networks typically required for memory formation.

☐ Promising Avenues for Future Research

The field of emotional memory is still relatively young, and the study of emotional memory in older adults is in its infancy. Yet, the field is quickly expanding, with more and more researchers entering the emotional memory fold. In the following, I briefly outline two of the avenues for future research that I believe will be particularly likely to yield new insights into how emotional memory changes across the adult lifespan.

Understanding the Neural Connections of Emotional Memory

To date, the vast majority of neuropsychological and neuroimaging studies of emotional memory have been geared toward understanding the regions that are brought online during the successful encoding or retrieval of emotional information. Now that a clear picture has begun to emerge with regard to the regions that are "key players" in emotional memory, it is time to begin to investigate how these regions interact with one another in order to influence memory for emotional experiences. It is likely that we will understand far more about emotional memory by examining how emotion affects the connections between regions than by examining only how emotion affects the particular regions recruited during successful memory performance.

Individual Differences in Emotional Memory

We also must start to consider carefully the effects of individual differences on emotion–memory interactions. Currently there are only a handful of studies examining these effects, leaving this area of research ripe for expansion. In addition to focusing on the effects of individual differences on young adults' emotional memories, we also need to understand how individual differences map on to age-related changes in emotional memory. As we saw in our discussion of young adults' emotional memories, the interactions between emotion and memory seem to be dramatically affected by the particular characteristics of the person (mood, stress level, personality, and gender). Presumably, these factors will continue to have an impact throughout the lifespan, but it is not clear whether the influences of these individual differences are mitigated or enhanced in older age. On one hand, individual differences have had a longer time to operate in older adults than in young adults. Thus, to the extent that individual differences serve to change how information in the environment is processed throughout a lifetime, one might expect to see greater effects of individual differences in older adults than in young adults. On the other hand, if most of the age-related changes in emotional memory occur because of age-related brain atrophy, then we may see less of an influence of individual differences in older adults than in young adults. That is, if the pattern of atrophy is relatively consistent across all individuals, regardless of their personality, gender, or other individual attributes, then we might expect the atrophy to account for most of the age-related changes and other individual differences to account for only a few of them. Of course, this assumption presupposes that the rates of brain atrophy would not be tied to personality characteristics, which may be too simplistic of an assumption. For example, there is evidence that chronic stress levels, which may be tied to personality, can influence the pattern of age-related brain atrophy (Lupien et al., 1998; Porter & Landfield, 1998). A challenge for future research will be to move beyond investigating the effects that emotion has on memory for nearly all individuals and to examine the effects of emotion on memory that differ substantially across individuals.

REFERENCES

Abrisqueta-Gomez, J., Bueno, O.F., Oliveira, M.G., & Bertolucci, P.H. (2002). Recognition memory for emotional pictures in Alzheimer's disease. *Acta Neurologica Scandanavica, 105,* 51–54.

Adolphs, R., Cahill, L., Schul, R., & Babinsky, R. (1997). Impaired declarative memory for emotional material following bilateral amygdala damage in humans. *Learning and Memory, 4,* 291–300.

Adolphs, R., Tranel, D., Bechara, A., Damasio, H., & Damasio, A.R. (1996). Neuropsychological approaches to reasoning and decision making. In A.R. Damasio (Ed.), *Neurobiology of decision making* (pp. 157–179). Berlin, Germany: Springer Verlag.

Adolphs, R., Tranel, D., Damasio, H., & Damasio, A.R. (1995). Fear and the human amygdala. *Journal of Neuroscience, 15,* 5879–5891.

Adolphs, R., Tranel, D., & Denburg, N. (2000). Impaired emotional declarative memory following unilateral amygdala damage. *Learning and Memory, 7,* 180–186.

Aggleton, J.P. & Brown, M.W. (1999). Episodic memory, amnesia, and the hippocampal-anterior thalamic axis. *Behavioral and Brain Sciences, 22*(3), 425–444.

Albert, M.S., Cohen, C., & Koff, E. (1991). Perception of affect in patients with dementia of the Alzheimer type. *Archives of Neurology, 48,* 791–795.

Allender, J., & Kaszniak, A.W. (1989). Processing of emotional cues in patients with dementia of the Alzheimer's type. *International Journal of Neuroscience, 46,* 147–155.

Amaral, D., Price, J., Pitkanen, A., & Carmichael, S. (1992). The amygdala: Neurobiological aspects of emotion, memory, and mental dysfunction. In J.P. Aggleton (Ed.), *The amygdala: Neurobiological aspects of emotion, memory, and mental dysfunction* (pp. 1–66). New York: Wiley-Liss.

Amaral, D.G. (2003). The amygdala, social behavior, and danger detection. *Annals of the New York Academy of Sciences, 1000,* 337–347.

Amaral, D.G., & Insausti, R. (1990). Hippocampal formation. In G. Paxinos (Ed.), *The human nervous system* (p. 711). London: Academic.

Amaral, D.G., Insausti, R., & Cowan, W.M. (1984). The commissural connections of the monkey hippocampal formation. *Journal of Comparative Neurology, 224,* 307–336.

Anderson, A.K. (2005). Affective influences on the attentional dynamics supporting awareness. *Journal of Experimental Psychology: General, 134,* 258–281.

Anderson, A.K., & Phelps, E.A. (2000). Expression without recognition: Contributions of the human amygdala to emotional communication. *Pychol Sci.* Mar. *11*(2), 106–11.

Anderson, A.K., & Phelps, E.A. (2001). Lesions of the human amygdala impair enhanced perception of emotionally salient events. *Nature, 411,* 305–309.

Anderson, A.K., Yamaguchi, Y., Grabski, W., & Lacka, D. (2006). Emotional memories are not all created equal: Evidence for selective memory enhancement. *Learning and Memory, 13,* 711–718.

Anderson, J.R. (1983). *The architecture of cognition.* Cambridge, MA: Harvard University Press.

Aristotle. (1991). *The art of rhetoric* (H.C. Lawson-Tancred, Trans.). London: Penguin.

Arnsten, A.F., & Goldman-Rakic, P.S. (1998). Noise stress impairs prefrontal cortical cognitive function in monkeys: Evidence for a hyperdopaminergic mechanism. *Archives of General Psychiatry, 55,* 362–368.

Arriagada, P.V., Growdon, J.H., Hedley-Whyte, E.T., & Hyman, B.T. (1992). Neurofibrillary tangles but not senile plaques parallel duration and severity of Alzheimer's disease. *Neurology, 42,* 631–639.

Ashby, F.G., Valentin, V.V. & Turken, A.U. (2002). The effects of positive affect and arousal on working memory system and executive attention: Neurobiology and computational models. In S. Moore & M. Oakford (Eds.). *Emotional cognition: From brain to behavior* (pp. 245–287). Amsterdam: John Benjamins.

Baas, D., Aleman, A., & Kahn, R.S. (2004). Lateralization of amygdala activation: A systematic review of functional neuroimaging studies. *Brain Research Reviews, 45,* 96–103.

Backman, L., & Molander, B. (1991). On the generalizability of the age-related decline in coping with high-arousal conditions in a precision sport: Replication and extension. *Journal of Gerontology, 46,* P79–P81.

Baddeley, A. (1998). Recent developments in working memory. *Current Opinion in Neurobiology, 8,* 234–238.

Baddeley, A.D., & Hitch, G.J. (1974). Working memory. In G.A. Bower (Ed.), *Recent advances in learning and motivation* (Vol. 8, pp. 47–90). New York: Academic Press.

Bahar, A., Samuel, A., Hazvi, S., & Dudai, Y. (2003). The amygdalar circuit that acquires taste aversion memory differs from the circuit that extinguishes it. *European Journal of Neuroscience, 17,* 1527–1530.

Barbas, H. (2000). Connections underlying the synthesis of cognition, memory, and emotion in primate prefrontal cortices. *Brain Research Bulletin, 52,* 319–330.

Bargh, J.A., Chaiken, S., Govender, R., & Pratto, F. (1992). The generality of the attitude activation effect. *Journal of Personality and Social Psychology, 62,* 893–912.

Barrett, L.F. (2006). Are emotions natural kinds? *Perspectives on Psychological Science, 1,* 28–58.

Barrett, L.F., Lindquist, K., Bliss-Moreau, E., Duncan, S., Gendron, M., Mize, J., & Brennan, L. (2007). Of mice and men: Natural kinds of emotion in the mammalian brain? *Perspectives on Psychological Science, 2,* 297–312.

Barrett, L.F., & Wager, T. (2006). The structure of emotion: Evidence from the neuroimaging of emotion. *Current Directions in Psychological Science, 15,* 79–85.

Baston-Leite, A.J., Scheltens, P., & Barkhof, F. (2004). Pathological aging of the brain: An overview. *Topographical Magnetic Resonance Imaging, 15,* 369–389.

Bauer, P.J., Stennes, L., & Haight, J.C. (2003). Representation of the inner self in autobiography: Women's and men's use of internal states of language in personal narratives. *Memory, 11,* 27–42.

Baumeister, R.F., Bratslavsky, E., Finkenauer, C., & Vohs, K.D. (2001). Bad is stronger than good. *Review of General Psychology, 5,* 323–370.

Baxter, M.G., & Murray, E.A. (2000). Reinterpreting the behavioral effects of amygdala lesions in nonhuman primates. In J.P. Aggleton (Ed.), *The amygdala: A functional analysis* (pp. 545–568). Oxford, England: Oxford University Press.

Bechara, A., Damasio, H., & Damasio, A.R. (2000). Emotion, decision making and the orbitofrontal cortex. *Cerebral Cortex, 10,* 295–307.

Beck, A.T., & Steer, R.A. (1990). *Manual for the Beck anxiety inventory.* San Antonio, TX: Psychological Corporation.

Blanchard-Fields, F. (2005). Introduction to the special section on emotion-cognition interactions and the aging mind. *Psychology and Aging, 20,* 539–541.

Blaney, P.H. (1986). Affect and memory: A review. *Psychological Bulletin, 99,* 229–246.

Bless, H., Clore, G.L., Schwarz, N., Golisano, V., Rabe, C., & Wolk, M. (1996). Mood and the use of scripts: Does a happy mood really lead to mindlessness? *Journal of Personality and Social Psychology, 71,* 665–679.

Bless, H., & Schwarz, N. (1999). Sufficient and necessary conditions in dual process models: The case of mood and information processing. In S. Chaiken & Y. Trope (Eds.), *Dual process theories in social psychology* (pp. 423–440). New York: Guilford Press.

Bohannon, J.N. (1988). Flashbulb memories for the space shuttle disaster: A tale of two theories. *Cognition, 29,* 179–196.

Bohannon, J.N., & Symons, L.V. (1992). Flashbulb memories: Confidence, consistency, and quantity. In E. Winograd & U. Neisser (Eds.), *Affect and accuracy in recall: Studies of flashbulb memories* (pp. 65–91). Cambridge, England: Cambridge University Press.

Bohn, A., & Bernstein, D. (2007). Pleasantness bias in flashbulb memories: Positive and negative flashbulb memories of the fall of the Berlin Wall among East and West Germans, *Mem Cognit, 35,* 565–77.

Boller, F., El Massioui, F., Devouche, E., Traykov, L., Pomati, S., & Starkstein, S.E. (2002). Processing emotional information in Alzheimer's disease: Effects on memory performance and neurophysiological correlates. *Dementia, Geriatrics and Cognitive Disorders, 14,* 104–112.

Bolmont, B., Thullier, F., & Abraini, J.H. (2000). Relationships between mood states and performances in reaction time, psychomotor ability, and mental efficiency during a 31-day gradual decompression in a hypobaric chamber from sea level to 8848 m equivalent altitude. *Physiological Behavior, 71,* 469–476.

Bornstein, R.F. (1989). Exposure and affect: Overview and meta-analysis of research, 1968–1987. *Psychological Bulletin, 106,* 265–280.

Bradley, M.M., Greenwald, M.K., Petry, M.C., & Lang, P.J. (1992). Remembering pictures: Pleasure and arousal in memory. *Journal of Experimental Psychology: Learning, Memory, & Cognition, 18,* 379–390.

Bradley, M.M., & Lang, P.J. (1999). *Affective norms for English words (ANEW).* Gainsville, FL: The NIMH Center for the Study of Emotion and Attention, University of Florida.

Bradley, M.M., & Lang, P.J. (2000). Measuring emotion: Behavior, feeling, and physiology. In R.D. Lane & L. Nadel (Eds.), *Cognitive neuroscience of emotion* (pp. 242–276). New York: Oxford University Press.

Braga, M.F.M., Aroniadou-Anderjaska, V., Manion, S.T., Hough, C.J., & Li, H. (2004). Stress impairs 1A adrenoceptor-mediated noradrenergic facilitation of GABAergic transmission in the basolateral amygdala. *Neuropsychopharmacology, 29,* 45–58.

Brierley, B., Medford, N., Shaw, P., & David, A.S. (2004). Emotional memory and perception in temporal lobectomy patients with amygdala damage. *Journal of Neurology, Neurosurgery, and Psychiatry, 75,* 593–599.

Broks, P., Young, A.W., Maratos, E.J., Coffey, P.J., Calder, A.J., Isaac, C.L., et al. (1998). Face processing impairments after encephalitis: Amygdala damage and recognition of fear. *Neuropsychologia, 36,* 59–70.

Brosgole, L., Kurucz, J., Plahovinsak, T.J., & Gumiela, E. (1981). On the mechanism underlying facial-affective agnosia in senile demented patients. *International Journal of Neuroscience, 15,* 207–215.

Brown, M.W., & Aggleton, J.P. (2001). Recognition memory: What are the roles of the perirhinal cortex and hippocampus? *Nature Reviews Neuroscience, 2,* 51–61.

Brown, M.W., Wilson, F.A., & Riches, I.P. (1987). Neuronal evidence that inferomedial temporal cortex is more important than hippocampus in certain processes underlying recognition memory. *Brain Research, 409,* 158–162.

Brown, R., & Kulik, J. (1977). Flashbulb memories. *Cognition, 5,* 73–99.

Buchanan, T.W. (2007). Retrieval of emotional memories. *Psychological Bulletin, 133,* 761–779.

Buchanan, T.W., & Adolphs, R. (2002). The role of the human amygdala in emotional modulation of long-term declarative memory. In S. Moore & M. Oaksford (Eds.), *Emotional cognition: From brain to behavior* (pp. 9–34). Amsterdam: John Benjamins Publishing.

Buchanan, T.W., Denburg, N., Tranel, D., & Adolphs, R. (2001). Verbal and nonverbal emotional memory following unilateral amygdala damage. *Learning and Memory, 8,* 326–335.

Buchanan, T.W., Etzel, J.A., Adolphs, R., & Tranel, D. (2006). The influence of autonomic arousal and semantic relatedness on memory for emotional words. *Int J Psychophysiol, 61,* 26–33.

Buchanan, T.W., Tranel, D., & Adolphs, R. (2006). Memories for emotional autobiographical events following unilateral damage to medial temporal lobe. *Brain, 129,* 115–127.

Buckner, R.L. (2004). Memory and executive function in aging and AD: Multiple factors that cause decline and reserve factors that compensate. *Neuron, 44,* 195–208.

Buckner, R.L., & Logan, J.M. (2002). Frontal contributions to episodic memory encoding in the young and elderly. In A.E. Parker, E.L. Wilding, & T. Bussey (Eds.), *The cognitive neuroscience of memory encoding and retrieval* (pp. 59–82). Philadelphia: Psychology Press.

Bucks, R.S., & Radford, S.A. (2004). Emotion processing in Alzheimer's disease. *Aging and Mental Health, 8,* 222–232.

Budson, A.E., Simons, J.S., Sullivan, A.L., Beier, J.S., Soloman, P.R., Scinto, L.F., et al. (2004). Memory and emotions for the September 11, 2001, terrorist attacks in patients with Alzheimer's disease, patients with mild cognitive impairment, and healthy older adults. *Neuropsychology, 18,* 315–327.

Budson, A.E., Todman, R.W., Chong, H., Adams, E.H., Kensinger, E.A., Krandel, T.S., et al. (2006). False recognition of emotional word lists in aging and Alzheimer's disease. *Cognitive and Behavioral Neurology, 19,* 71–78.

Burke, A., Heuer, F., & Reisberg, D. (1992). Remembering emotional events. *Memory and Cognition, 20,* 277–290.

Burke, D.M., & Mackay, D.G. (1997). Memory, language, and ageing. *Philosophical Transactions of the Royal Society of London, B Series (Biological Sciences), 352,* 1845–1856.

Burke, J., Knight, R.G., & Partridge, F.M. (1994). Priming deficits in patients with dementia of the Alzheimer type. *Psychological Medicine, 24,* 987–993.

Burnham, H., & Hogervorst, E. (2004). Recognition of facial expressions of emotion by patients with dementia of the Alzheimer type. *Dementia and Geriatric Cognitive Disorders, 18,* 75–79.

Burton, L.A., Rabin, L., Vardy, S.B., Frohlich, J., Wyatt, G., Dimitri, D., et al. (2004). Gender differences in implicit and explicit memory for affective passages. *Brain and Cognition, 54,* 218–224.

Bush, S.I., & Geer, J.H. (2001). Implicit and explicit memory of neutral, negative emotional and sexual information. *Archives of Sexual Behavior, 30,* 615–631.

Cabeza, R. (2002). Hemispheric asymmetry reduction in older adults: The HAROLD model. *Psychology and Aging, 17,* 85–100.

Cacioppo, J.T. (1998). Somatic responses to psychological stress: The reactivity hypothesis. In M. Sabourin, F. Craik, & M. Robert (Eds.), *Advances in psychological science, Vol. 2: Biological and cognitive aspects* (pp. 87–112). Hove, England: Psychology Press.

Cacioppo, J.T., Berntson, G.G., Bechara, A., Tranel, D., & Hawkley, L.C. (in press). Could an aging brain contribute to subjective well being?: The value added by a social neuroscience perspective. In A. Tadorov, S.T. Fiske, & D. Prentice (Eds.), *Social neuroscience: Toward understanding the underpinnings of the social mind.* New York: Oxford University Press.

Cadieux, N.L., & Greve, K.W. (1997). Emotion processing in Alzheimer's disease. *Journal of the International Neuropsychological Society, 3,* 411–419.

Cahill, L., Haier, R.J., Fallon, J., Alkire, M.T., Tang, C., Keator, D., et al. (1996). Amygdala activity at encoding correlated with long-term, free recall of emotional information. *Proceedings of the National Academy of Sciences, USA, 93,* 8016–8021.

Cahill, L., & McGaugh, J.L. (1995). A novel demonstration of enhanced memory associated with emotional arousal. *Conscious Cognition, 4,* 410–421.

Cahill, L., McGaugh, J.L., & Weinberger, N.M. (2001). The neurobiology of learning and memory: Some reminders to remember. *Trends in Neuroscience, 24,* 578–581.

Cahill, L., Uncapher, M., Kilpatrick, L., Alkire, M.T., & Turner, J. (2004). Sex-related hemispheric lateralization of amygdala function in emotionally influenced memory: An fMRI investigation. *Learning and Memory, 11,* 261–266.

Calder, A.J., Keane, J., Manly, T., Sprengelmeyer, R., Scott, S., Nimmo-Smith, I., et al. (2003). Facial expression recognition across the adult life span. *Neuropsychologia, 41,* 195–202.

Calder, A.J., Young, A.W., Rowland, D., Perrett, D.I., Hodges, J.R., & Etcoff, N.L. (1996). Face perception after bilateral amygdala damage: Differentially severe impairment of fear. *Cognitive Neuropsychology, 13,* 699–745.

Canli, T., Desmond, J.E., Zhao, Z., & Gabrieli, J.D. (2002). Sex differences in the neural basis of emotional memories. *Proceedings of the National Academy of Sciences, USA, 99,* 10789–10794.

Canli, T., Sivers, H., Whitfield, S.L., Gotlib, I.H., & Gabrieli, J.D. (2002). Amygdala response to happy faces as a function of extraversion. *Science, 296,* 2191.

Canli, T., Zhao, Z., Brewer, J., Gabrieli, J.D., & Cahill, L. (2000). Event-related activation in the human amygdala associates with later memory for individual emotional experience. *Journal of Neuroscience, 20,* RC99.

Canli, T., Zhao, Z., Desmond, J.E., Kang, E., Gross, J., & Gabrieli, J.D. (2001). An fMRI study of personality influences on brain reactivity to emotional stimuli. *Behavioral Neuroscience, 115,* 33–42.

Cansino, S., Maquet, P., Dolan, R.J., & Rugg, M.D. (2002). Brain activity underlying encoding and retrieval of source memory. *Cerebral Cortex, 12,* 1048–1056.

Carstensen, L.L. (1992). Social and emotional patterns in adulthood: Support for socioemotional selectivity theory. *Psychology and Aging, 7,* 331–338.

Carstensen, L.L., Fung, H., & Charles, S. (2003). Socioemotional selectivity theory and the regulation of emotion in the second half of life. *Motivation and Emotion, 27,* 103–123.

Carstensen, L.L., Isaacowitz, D.M., & Charles, S.T. (1999). Taking time seriously: A theory of socioemotional selectivity. *American Psychologist, 54,* 165–181.

Carstensen, L.L., & Lockenhoff, C.E. (2003). Aging, emotion, and evolution: The bigger picture. *Annals of the New York Academy of Sciences, 1000,* 152–179.

Carstensen, L.L., Mikels, J.A. & Mather, M. (2006). Aging and the intersection of cognition, motivation, and emotion. In J. Birren, & K.W. Schaie (Eds.), *Handbook of the psychology of aging,* Sixth Edition, (pp. 343–362). San Diego, CA: Academic Press.

Carstensen, L.L., & Turk-Charles, S. (1994). The salience of emotion across the adult life course. *Psychology and Aging, 9,* 259–264.

Carver, C.S., Peterson, L.M., Follansbee, D.J., & Scheier, M.F. (1983). Effects of self-directed attention on performance and persistence among persons high and low in test anxiety. *Cognitive Therapy and Research, 7,* 333–354.

Casper, R.C. (1998). *Women's health: Hormones, emotions, and behavior.* Cambridge: Cambridge University Press.

Cassell, M.D., Freedman, L.J., & Shi, C. (1999). The intrinsic organization of the central extended amygdala. *Annals of the New York Academy of Sciences, 877,* 217–241.

Cattell, R.B. (1971). Abilites: Their structure, growth, and action. New York: Houghton Mifflin.

Chalfonte, B.L., & Johnson, M.K. (1996). Feature memory and binding in young and older adults. *Memory and Cognition, 24,* 403–416.

Chan, D., Fox, N.C., Scahill, R.I., Crum, W.R., Whitwell, J.L., Leschziner, G., et al. (2001). Patterns of temporal lobe atrophy in semantic dementia and Alzheimer's disease. *Annals of Neurology, 49,* 433–442.

Charles, S.T., Mather, M., & Carstensen, L.L. (2003). Aging and emotional memory: The forgettable nature of negative images for older adults. *Journal of Experimental Psychology: General, 132,* 310–324.

Cheng, P.W., & Holyoak, K.J. (1985). Pragmatic reasoning schemas. *Cognitive Psychology, 17,* 391–416.

Chow, T.W., & Cummings, J.L. (2000). The amygdala and Alzheimer's disease. In J.P. Aggleton (Ed.), *The amygdala: A functional analysis* (pp. 656–680). Oxford, England: Oxford University Press.

Christianson, S.A. (1986). Effects of positive emotional events on memory. *Scandinavian Journal of Psychology, 27,* 287–299.

Christianson, S.A. (1989). Flashbulb memories: Special, but not so special. *Memory and Cognition, 17,* 435–443.

Christianson, S.A. (1992). Emotional stress and eyewitness testimony: A critical review. *Psychological Bulletin, 112,* 284–309.

Christianson, S.A., & Engelberg, E. (1999). Organization of emotional memories. In T. Dalgleish & M. Power (Eds.), *The handbook of cognition and emotion* (pp. 211–227). Chichester, England: John Wiley & Sons, Ltd.

Clore, G.L., Gasper, K., & Garvin, E. (2001). Affect as information. In J.P. Forgas (Ed.), *Handbook of affect and social cognition* (pp. 121–144). Mahwah, NJ: Lawrence Erlbaum Associates.

Coffey, C.E., Wilkenson, W.E., Parashos, I.A., Soady, S.A., Sullivan, R.J., Patterson, L.J., et al. (1992). Quantitative cerebral anatomy of the aging human brain: A cross-sectional study using magnetic resonance imaging. *Neurology, 42,* 527–536.

Cohen, G., Conway, M.A., & Maylor, E.A. (1994). Flashbulb memories in older adults. *Psychology and Aging, 9,* 454–463.

Colgrove, F.W. (1899). Individual memories. *American Journal of Psychology, 10,* 228–255.

Collins, M.A., & Cooke, A. (2005). A transfer appropriate processing approach to investigating implicit memory for emotional words in the cerebral hemispheres. *Neuropsychologia, 43,* 1529–1545.

Comblain, C., D'Argembeau, A., van der Linden, M., & Aldenhoff, L. (2004). The effect of ageing on the recollection of emotional and neutral pictures. *Memory, 12,* 673–684.

Conway, M.A. (1990). Conceptual representation of emotions: The role of autobiographical memories. In K.J. Gilhooly, M.T.G. Keane, R.H. Logie, & G. Erdos (Eds.), *Lines of thinking: Reflections on the psychology of thought: Vol. 2, Skills, emotion, creative processes, individual differences and teaching thinking* (pp. 133–143). Oxford, England: Wiley.

Corkin, S. (1984). Lasting consequences of bilateral medial temporal lobectomy: Clinical course and experimental findings in H.M. *Seminars in Neurology 4,* 252–262.

Corkin, S. (2002). What's new with the amnesic patient H.M.? *Nature Reviews Neuroscience 3,* 153–160.

Cornelius, S.W., & Caspi, A. (1987). Everyday problem solving in adulthood and old age. *Psychology and Aging, 2,* 144–153.

Costa, P.T., Jr., & McCrae, R.R. (1992). *Revised NEO Personality Inventory (NEO-PI-R) and NEO Five-Factor Inventory (NEO-FFI): Professional Manual.* Odessa, FL: Psychological Assessment Resources.

Cowan, N. (1988). Evolving conceptions of memory storage, selective attention, and their mutual constraints within the human information-processing system. *Psychology Bulletin, 104,* 163–191.

Cowan, N. (1995). Sensory memory and its role in information processing. *Electroencephalography and Clinical Neurophysiology Supplement, 44,* 21–31.

Craig, A.D. (2002). How do you feel? Interoception: The sense of the physiological condition of the body. *Nature Reviews Neuroscience, 3,* 655–666.

Craik, F.I.M., & Lockhart, R.S. (1972). Levels of processing: A framework for memory research. *Journal of Verbal Learning and Verbal Behavior, 11,* 671–684.

Craik, F.I.M., & McDowd, J.M. (1987). Age differences in recall and recognition. *Journal of Experimental Psychology, 13,* 474–479.

Cutting, J.E. (2006). The mere exposure effect and aesthetic preference. In P. Locher, C. Martindale, L. Dorfman, V. Petrov, and D. Leontiv (Eds.), *New directions in aesthetics, creativity, and the psychology of art* (pp. 33–46). Amityville, NY: Baywood Publishing Company.

D'Argembeau, A., Comblain, C., & van der Linden, M. (2005). Affective valence and the self-reference effect: Influence of retrieval conditions. *British Journal of Psychology, 96,* 457–466.

D'Argembeau, A., & van der Linden, M. (2004). Influence of affective meaning on memory for contextual information. *Emotion, 4,* 173–188.

Davachi, L., Mitchell, J.P., & Wagner, A.D. (2003). Multiple routes to memory: Distinct medial temporal lobe processes build item and source memories. *Proceedings of the National Academy of Sciences, USA, 100,* 2157–2162.

Davachi, L., & Wagner, A.D. (2002). Hippocampal contributions to episodic encoding: Insights from relational and item-based learning. *Journal of Neurophysiology, 88,* 982–990.

Davidson, P.S., & Glisky, E.L. (2002). Is flashbulb memory a special instance of source memory? Evidence from older adults. *Memory 10,* 99–111.

Davidson, R.J., & Irwin, W. (1999). The functional neuroanatomy of emotion and affective style. *Trends in Cognitive Sciences, 3,* 11–20.

Davis, M. (1997). Neurobiology of fear responses: The role of the amygdala. *Journal of Neuropsychiatry and Clinical Neuroscience, 9,* 382–402.

Davis, M., & Whalen, P.J. (2001). The amygdala: Vigilance and emotion. *Molecular Psychiatry, 6,* 13–34.

Davis, P.J. (1999). Gender differences in autobiographical memory for childhood emotional experiences. *Journal of Personality and Social Psychology, 76,* 498–510.

Denburg, N.L., Buchanan, D., Tranel, D., & Adolphs, R. (2003). Evidence for preserved emotional memory in normal elderly persons. *Emotion, 3,* 239–254.

Denburg, N.L., Rechnor, E.C., Bechara, A., & Tranel, D. (2006). Psychophysiological anticipation of positive outcomes promotes advantageous decision-making in normal older persons. *International Journal of Psychophysiology, 61,* 19–25.

Denburg, N.L., Tranel, D., & Bechara, A. (2005). The ability to decide advantageously declines prematurely in some normal older persons. *Neuropsychologia, 43,* 1099–1106.

Denney, N.W., & Pearce, K.A. (1989). A developmental study of practical problem solving in adults. *Psychology and Aging, 4,* 438–442.

Deputla, D., Singh, R., & Pomara, N. (1993). Aging, emotional states, and memory. *American Journal of Psychiatry, 150,* 429–434.

Dewhurst, S.A., & Parry, L.A. (2000). Emotionality, distinctiveness, and recollective experience. *European Journal of Cognitive Psychology, 12,* 541–551.

Dobbins, I.G., Foley, H., Schacter, D.L., & Wagner, A.D. (2002). Executive control during episodic retrieval: Multiple prefrontal processes subserve source memory. *Neuron, 35,* 989–996.

Dodson, C.S., Bawa, S., & Slotnick, S.D. (2007). Aging, source memory, and misrecollections. *J Exp Psychol Learn Mem Cogn, 33,* 169–81.

Doerksen, S., & Shimamura, A. (2001). Source memory enhancement for emotional words. *Emotion, 1,* 5–11.

Dolan, R.J., Lane, R., Chua, P., & Fletcher, P. (2000). Dissociable temporal lobe activations during emotional episodic memory retrieval. *NeuroImage, 11,* 203–209.

Dolan, R.J., & Morris, J.S. (2000). The functional anatomy of innate and acquired fear: Perspectives from neuroimaging. In R.D. Lane & L. Nadel (Eds.), *Cognitive neuroscience of emotion* (pp. 225–241). New York: Oxford University Press.

Dolan, R.J., & Vuilleumier, P. (2003). Amygdala automaticity in emotional processing. *Annals of the New York Academy of Sciences, 985,* 348–355.

Dolcos, F., LaBar, K.S., & Cabeza, R. (2004). Interaction between the amygdala and the medial temporal lobe memory system predicts better memory for emotional events. *Neuron, 42,* 855–863.

Dolcos, F., LaBar, K.S., & Cabeza, R. (2005). Remembering one year later: Role of the amygdala and the medial temporal lobe memory system in retrieving emotional memories. *Proceedings of the National Academy of Sciences, USA, 102,* 2626–2631.

Double, K.L., Halliday, G.M., Kril, J.J., Harasty, J.A., Cullen, K., Brooks, W.S., Creasey, H., & Broe, G.A. (1996). Topography of brain atrophy during normal aging and Alzheimer's disease. *Neurobiology of Aging, 17,* 513–521.

Dougal, S., Delgado, M.R., & Phelps, E.A. (2006, April). *Medial temporal lobe correlates of recognizing personally relevant emotional stimuli.* Poster presented at the annual meeting of the Cognitive Neuroscience Society, San Francisco, CA.

Dougal, S., Phelps, E.A., & Davachi, L. (2007). The role of medial temporal lobe in item recognition and source recollection of emotional stimuli. *Cogn Affect Behav Neurosci, 7,* 233–42.

Dougal, S., & Rotello, C.M. (2007). "Remembering" emotional words is based on response bias, not recollection. *Psychonomi Bulletin and Review, 14,* 423–429.

Doya, K. (2000). Complementary roles of basal ganglia and cerebellum in learning and motor control. *Current Opinion in Neurobiology, 10,* 732–739.

Drevets, W.C., & Raichle, M.E. (1998). Reciprocal suppression of regional cerebral blood flow during emotional versus higher cognitive processes: Implications for interactions between emotion and cognition. *Cognition and Emotion, 12,* 353–385.

Duncan, S., & Barrett, L.F. (2007). Affect as a form of cognition: A neurological analysis. *Cognition and Emotion, 21,* 1184–1211.

Duncan, S., & Barrett, L.F. (2007). The role of the amygdala in visual awareness. *Trends in Cognitive Science, 11,* 190–192.

Easterbrook, J.A. (1959). The effects of emotion on cue utilization and the organization of behavior. *Psychological Review, 66,* 183–201.

Ebbinghaus, H. (1964). *Memory: A contribution to experimental psychology* (H.A. Ruger & C.E. Bussenius, Trans.). New York: Dover. (Original work published in 1885).

Ehlers, A., Margraf, J., Davies, S., & Roth, W.T. (1988). Selective processing of threat cues in subjects with panic attacks. *Cognition and Emotion, 2,* 201–219.

Eichenbaum, H. (2000). A cortical-hippocampal system for declarative memory. *Nature Reviews Neuroscience, 1,* 41–50.

Einstein, G.O., & McDaniel, M.A. (1987). Distinctiveness and the mnemonic benefits of bizarre imagery. In M.A. McDaniel & M. Pressley (Eds.), *Imagery and related mnemonic processes: Theories, individual differences, and applications* (pp. 78–102). New York: Springer-Verlag.

Elliott, R., Friston, K.J., & Dolan, R.J. (2000). Dissociable neural responses in human reward systems. *Journal of Neuroscience, 20,* 6159–6165.

Ellis, H.C., & Asbrook, P.W. (1991). In D. Kuiken (Ed.), *Mood and memory: Theory, research, and applications* (pp. 1–22). London: Sage Publications.

Engle, R.W., Kane, M.J. & Tuholski, S.W. (1999). Individual differences in working memory capacity and what they tell us about controlled attention, general fluid intelligence and functions of the prefrontal cortex. In A. Miyake & P. Shah (Eds.), *Models of working memory: Mechanisms of active maintenance and executive control* (pp. 102–134). New York: Cambridge University Press.

Engle, R.W., & Oransky, N. (1999). The evolution from short-term to working memory: Multi-store to dynamic models of temporary storage. In R. Sternberg (Ed.), *The nature of human cognition.* Cambridge, MA: MIT Press.

Evrard, M. (2002). Ageing and lexical access to common and proper names in picture naming. *Brain and Language, 81,* 174–179.

Everitt, B.J., Cardinal, R.N., Hall, J., Parkinson, J.A., & Robbins, T.W. (2000). Differential involvement of amygdala subsystems in appetitive conditioning and drug addiction. In J.P. Aggleton (Ed.), *The amygdala: A functional analysis* (2nd ed., pp. 353–359). Oxford, England: Oxford University Press.

Eysenck, H.J. (1979). The origins of violence. *Journal of Medical Ethics, 5,* 105–107.

Eysenck, M.W., & Calvo, M.G. (1992). Anxiety and performance: The processing efficiency theory. *Cognition and emotion, 6,* 409–434.

Fabes, R.A., & Martin, C.J. (1991). Gender and age stereotypes in emotionality. *Personality and Social Psychology Bulletin, 17,* 532–540.

Feldman, L.A. (1995). Variations in the circumplex structure of emotion. *Personality and Social Psychology Bulletin, 21,* 806–817.

Feldman-Barrett, L., Robin, L., Pietromonaco, P.R., & Eyssell, K.M. (1998). Are women the "more emotional sex?" Evidence from emotional experiences in social context. *Cognition and Emotion, 12,* 555–578.

Fiedler, K. (2001). Affective states trigger processes of assimilation and accommodation. In L.L. Martin & G.L. Clore (Eds.), *Theories of mood and cognition: A user's guidebook* (pp. 86–98). Mahwah, NJ: Erlbaum.

Fischer, H., Sandblom, J., Gavazzeni, J., Fransson, P., Wright, C.I., & Backman, L. (2005). Age-differential patterns of brain activation during perception of angry faces. *Neuroscience Letters, 386,* 99–104.

Fitts, P.M. (1964). The information capacity of dicrete motor responses. *J Exp Psychol, 67,* 103–112.

Fletcher, P.C., Frith, C.D., Baker, S.C., Shallice, T., Frackowiak, R.S., & Dolan, R.J. (1995). The mind's eye—precuneus activation in memory-related imagery. *NeuroImage, 2,* 195–200.

Frijda, N.H., & Sundararajan, L. (2007). Emotion refinement: A theory inspired by Chinese poetics. *Perspectives on Psychological Science, 2,* 227–241.

Fujita, F., Diener, E., & Sandvik, E. (1991). Gender difference in negative affect and well-being: The case for emotional intensity. *Journal of Personality and Social Psychology, 61,* 427–434.

Fung, H.H., & Carstensen, L.L. (2003). Sending memorable messages to the old: Age differences in preferences and memory for advertisements. *Journal of Personality & Social Psychology, 85,* 163–178.

Gabrieli, J.D., Keane, M.M., Stranger, B.Z., Kjelgaard, M.M., Corkin, S., & Growdon, J.H. (1994). Dissociations among structural–perceptual, lexical–semantic, and event–fact memory systems in Alzheimer, amnesic, and normal subjects. *Cortex, 30,* 75–103.

Gabrieli, J.D., Milberg, W., Keane, M.M., & Corkin, S. (1990). Intact priming of patterns despite impaired memory. *Neuropsychologia, 28,* 417–427.

Gabrieli, J.D.E., & Bergerbest, D. (2003). Memory: Priming and procedural. In L. Nadel (Ed.), *Encyclopedia of cognitive science.* London: Macmillan Ltd.

Galton, C.J., Patterson, K., Graham, K., Lambon-Ralph, M.A., Williams, G., Antoun, N., et al. (2001). Differing patterns of temporal atrophy in Alzheimer's disease and semantic dementia. *Neurology, 57,* 216–225.

Garavan, H., Pendergrass, J.C., Ross, T.J., Stein, E.A., & Risinger, R.C. (2001). Amygdala response to both positively and negatively valenced stimuli. *Neuroreport, 12,* 2779–2783.

Gardiner, J.M., Craik, F.I.M., & Birtwistle, J. (1972). Retrieval cues and release from proactive inhibition. *Journal of Verbal Learning and Verbal Behavior, 11,* 778–783.

Garoff, R.J., Slotnick, S.D., & Schacter, D.L. (2005). The neural origins of specific and general memory: The role of the fusiform cortex. *Neuropsychologia, 43,* 847–859.

Gasbarri, A., Arnone, B., Pompili, A., Marchetti, A., Pacitti, F., Calil, S.S., et al. (2006). Sex-related lateralized effect of emotional content on declarative memory: An event related potential study. *Behavioral Brain Research, 168,* 177–184.

Gasper, K., & Clore, G.L. (2002). Attending to the big picture: Mood and global versus local processing of visual information. *Psychological Science, 13,* 34–40.

Gavazzeni, J., Wiens, S., & Fischer, H. (2008). Age effects to negative arousal differ for self-report and electrodermal activity. *Pyschophysiology, 45,* 148–51.

Geer, J.H., & McGlone, M.S. (1990). Sex differences in memory for erotica. *Cognition and Emotion, 4,* 71–78.

Geschwind, N. (1965). Disconnection syndromes in animals and man. I. *Brain, 2,* 237–294.

Giovanello, K.S., Schnyer, D.M., & Verfaellie, M. (2004). A critical role for the anterior hippocampus in relational memory: Evidence from an fMRI study comparing associative and item recognition. *Hippocampus, 14,* 5–8.

Giovanello, K.S., Verfaellie, M., & Keane, M.M. (2003). Disproportionate deficit in associative recognition relative to item recognition in global amnesia. *Cognitive, Affective, and Behavioral Neuroscience, 3,* 186–194.

Goedert, M., & Spillantini, M.G. (2006). A century of Alzheimer's disease. *Science, 314,* 777–781.

Goldstein, J.M., Seidman, J.L., Horton, N.J., Makris, N., Kennedy, D.N., Caviness, V.S., et al. (2001). Normal sexual dimorphism of the adult human brain assessed by *in vivo* magnetic resonance imaging. *Cerebral Cortex, 11,* 490–497.

Golomb, J., Kluger, A., de Leon, M.J., Ferris, S.H., Convit, A., Mittelman, M.S., et al. (1994). Hippocampal formation size in normal human aging: A correlate of delayed secondary memory performance. *Learning and Memory, 1,* 45–54.

Gonsalves, B., & Paller, K.A. (2000). Neural events that underlie remembering something that never happened. *Nature Neuroscience, 3,* 1316–1321.

Good, C.D., Johnsrude, I.S., Ashburner, J., Henson, R.N.A., Friston, K.J., & Frackowiak, R.S.J. (2001). A voxel-based morphometric study of ageing in 465 normal adult human brains. *NeuroImage, 14,* 21–36.

Gordon, P.C., & Holyoak, K.J. (1983). Implicit learning and generalization of the "mere exposure" effect. *Journal of Personality & Social Psychology, 45,* 492–500.

Gotlib, I.H., & McCann, C.D. (1984). Construct accessibility and depression: An examination of cognitive and affective factors. *Journal of Personality and Social Psychology, 47,* 427–439.

Grady, C.L., & Craik, F.I.M. (2000). Changes in memory processing with age. *Current Opinion in Neurobiology, 10,* 224–231.

Gray, J.R. (2001). Emotional modulation of cognitive control: Approach-withdrawal states double-dissociate spatial from verbal two-back task performance. *Journal of Experimental Psychology: General, 130,* 436–452.

Greicius, M.D., Krasnow, B., Reiss, A.L., & Menon, V. (2003). Functional connectivity in the resting brain: A network analysis of the default mode hypothesis, *Proceedings of the National Academy of Sciences, USA, 100,* 253–258.

Gross, J.J., Carstensen, L.L., Pasupathi, M., Tsai, J., Skorpen, C.G., & Hsu, A.Y.C. (1997). Emotion and aging: Experience, expression, and control. *Psychology and Aging, 12,* 590–599.

Gruhn, D. & Scheibe, S. (2008). Age-related differences in valence and arousal rating of pictures from the International Affective Picture System (APS): Do ratings become more extreme with age. *Behav Res Methods, 40,* 512–21.

Gruhn, D., Smith, J., & Baltes, P.B. (2005). No aging bias favoring memory for positive material: Evidence from a heterogeneity-homogeneity list paradigm using emotionally toned words. *Psychology and Aging, 20,* 579–588.

Gunning-Dixon, F.M., Gur, R.C., Perkins, A.C., Schroder, L., Turner, T., Turetsky, B.I., et al. (2003). Age-related differences in brain activation during emotional face processing. *Neurobiology of Aging, 24,* 285–295.

Gutchess, A.H., Kensinger, E.A., Yoon, C., & Schacter, D.L. (2007). Aging and the self-reference effect in memory. *Memory, 15,* 822–837.

Hadley, C.B., & MacKay, D.G. (2006). Does emotion help or hinder immediate memory? Arousal versus priority-binding mechanisms. *Journal of Experimental Psychology: Learning, Memory, and Cognition, 32,* 79–88.

Hahn, S., Carlson, C., Singer, S., & Gronlund, S.D. (2006). Aging and visual search: Automatic and controlled attentional bias to threat faces. *Acta Psychologia, 123,* 312–336.

Hamann, S. (2001). Cognitive and neural mechanisms of emotional memory. *Trends in Cognitive Sciences, 5,* 394–400.

Hamann, S., Herman, R.A., Nolan, C.L., & Wallen, K. (2004). Men and women differ in amygdala response to visual sexual stimuli. *Nature Neuroscience, 7,* 411–416.

Hamann, S., & Mao, H. (2002). Positive and negative emotional verbal stimuli elicit activity in the left amygdala. *Neuroreport, 13,* 15–19.

Hamann, S., Monarch, E.S., & Goldstein, F.C. (2002). Impaired fear conditioning in Alzheimer's disease. *Neuropsychologia, 40,* 1187–1195.

Hamann, S.B., Cahill, L., McGaugh, J.L., & Squire, L.R. (1997). Intact enhancement of declarative memory for emotional material in amnesia. *Learn Mem.* Sept–Oct., *4*(3), 301–9.

Hamann, S.B., Cahill, L., & Squire, L.R. (1997). Emotional perception and memory in amnesia. *Neuropsychology, 11,* 104–113.

Hamann, S.B., Ely, T.D., Grafton, S.T., & Kilts, C.D. (1999). Amygdala activity related to enhanced memory for pleasant and aversive stimuli. *Nature Neuroscience, 2,* 289–293.

Hamann, S.B., Ely, T.D., Hoffman, J.M., & Kilts, C.D. (2002). Ecstasy and agony: Activation of the human amygdala in positive and negative emotion. *Psychological Science, 13,* 135–141.

Haman, S.B., Monarch, E.S., & Goldstein, F.C. (2000). Memory enhancement for emotional stimuli is impaired in Alzheimer's disease. *Neuropsychology, 14,* 82–92.

Harrison, A.A. (1977). Mere exposure. In L. Berkowitz (Ed.), *Advances in experimental social psychology* (Vol. 10, pp. 39–83). San Diego, CA: Academic Press.

Hartley, A.A. (1989). The cognitive ecology of problem solving. In L.W. Poon, D.C. Rubin, & B.A. Wilson (Eds.), *Everyday cognition in adulthood and late life* (pp. 300–329). New York: Cambridge University Press.

Hasher, L. & Zacks, R.T. (1988). Working memory, comprehension, and aging: A review and a new view. In G.H. Bower (Ed.), *The psychology of learning and motivation: Advances in research and theory* (Vol. 22, pp. 193–225). San Diego, CA: Academic Press.

Hashtroudi, S., Johnson, M.K., & Chrosniak, L.D. (1990). Aging and qualitative characteristics of memories for perceived and imagined complex events. *Psychology and Aging, 5,* 119–126.

Heindel, W.C., Cahn, D.A., & Salmon, D.P. (1997). Non-associative lexical priming is impaired in Alzheimer's disease. *Neuropsychologia, 35,* 1365–1372.

Hermans, D., Vansteenwegen, D., & Eelen, P. (1999). Eye movement registration as a continuous index of attention deployment: Data from a group of spider anxious students. *Cognition and Emotion, 13,* 419–434.

Heuer, F., & Reisberg, D. (1990). Vivid memories of emotional events: The accuracy of remembered minutiae. *Memory and Cognition, 18,* 496–506.

Hikosaka, K., & Watanabe, M. (2000). Delay activity of orbital and lateral prefrontal neurons of the monkey varying with different rewards. *Cerebral Cortex, 10,* 263–271.

Hogan, M.J. (2003). Divided attention in older but not younger adults is impaired by anxiety. *Experimental Aging Research, 29,* 111–136.

Holdstock, J.S., Mayes, A.R., Roberts, N., Cezayirli, E., Isaac, C.L., O'Reilly, R.C., et al. (2002). Under what conditions is recognition spared relative to recall after selective hippocampal damage in humans? *Hippocampus, 12,* 325–340.

Holland, P.C., & Gallagher, M. (2004). Amygdala-frontal interactions and reward expectancy. *Current Opinion in Neurobiology, 14,* 148–155.

Hunt, R.R., & McDaniel, M.A. (1993). The enigma of organization and distinctiveness. *Journal of Memory and Language, 32,* 421–445.

Iidaka, T., Murata, T., Ornori, M., Kosaka, H., Sadato, N., & Yonckura, Y. (2002). Age-related differences in the medial temporal lobe responses to emotional faces as revealed by fMRI. *Hippocampus, 12,* 352–362.

Ikeda, M., Iwanga, N., & Seiwa, H. (1996). 1 Test anxiety and working memory system. *Percept Mot Skills, 82,* 1223–31.

Ikeda, M., Mori, E., Hirono, N., Imamura, T., Shimomura, T., Ikejiri, Y., et al. (1998). Amnestic people with Alzheimer's disease who remembered the Kobe earthquake. *British Journal of Psychiatry, 172,* 425–428.

Ingram, R.E. (1990). Self-focused attention in clinical disorders: Review and a conceptual model. *Psychological Bulletin, 107,* 156–176.

Isen, A.M. (1993). Positive affect and decision making. In M. Lewis & J.M. Haviland (Eds.), *Handbook of emotions* (pp. 261–278). New York: Guilford Press.

Isen, A.M. (1999). Positive affect. In T. Dagleish & M. Powers (Eds.), *The handbook of cognition and emotion* (pp. 75–94). Hillsdale, NJ: Erlbaum.

Isen, A.M., & Daubman, K. (1984). The influence of affect on categorization. *Journal of Personality and Social Psychology, 47,* 1206–1217

Ishai, A., Pessoa, L., Bikle, P.C., & Ungerleider, L.G. (2004). Repetition suppression of faces is modulated by emotion. *Proceedings of the National Academy of Sciences, USA, 101,* 9827–9832.

Izard, C.E. (2007). Basic emotions, natural kinds, emotion schemas, and a new paradigm. *Perspectives on Psychological Science, 2,* 260–280.

Jack, C.R., Petersen, R.C., Xu, Y.C., O'Brien, P.C., Smith, G.E., Ivnik, R.J., et al. (1999). Prediction of Alzheimer's disease with MRI-based hippocampal volume in mild cognitive impairment. *Neurology, 52*, 1397–1403.

Jackson, O., & Schacter, D.L. (2004). Encoding activity in anterior medial temporal lobe supports associative recognition. *NeuroImage, 21*, 456–464.

James, W. (1890). The principles of psychology. Reprinted in R.H. Wozniak (Ed., 1998), *Thoemmes Press—Classics in Psychology*. London: Thoemmes Continuum.

Janet, P. (1889). *L'Automatisme psychologique*. Paris: Alcan.

Johnson, M.K., Hashtroudi, S., & Lindsay, D.S. (1993). Source monitoring. *Psychological Bulletin, 114*, 3–28.

Johnson, M.K., & Raye, C.L. (1981). Reality monitoring. *Psychological Review, 88*, 67–85.

Johnson, M.K., & Raye, C.L. (2000). Cognitive and brain mechanisms of false memories and beliefs. In D.L. Schacter & E. Scarry (Eds.), *Memory, brain, and belief* (pp. 35–86). Cambridge, MA: Harvard University Press

Johnston, J.B. (1923). Further contributions to the study of the evolution of the forebrain. *Journal of Comparative Neurology, 35*, 337–481.

Jonides, J., & Smith, E.E. (1997). The architecture of working memory. In M.D. Rugg (Ed.), *Cognitive neuroscience* (pp. 243–276). Sussex, England: Psychology Press.

Kaada, B.R. (1972). Stimulation and regional ablation of the amygdaloid complex with reference to functional representations. In B.E. Eleftheriou (Ed.), *The neurobiology of the amygdala* (pp. 643–683). New York: Plenum Press.

Kahn, I., Davachi, L., & Wagner, A.D. (2004). Functional-neuroanatomic correlates of recollection: Implications for models of recognition memory. *J Neurosci, 24*, 472–80.

Kalisch, R., Wiech, K., Critchley, H.D., & Dolan, R.J. (2006). Levels of appraisal: A medial prefrontal role in high-level appraisal of emotional material. *NeuroImage, 30*, 1458–1466.

Karama, S., Lecours, A.R., Leroux, J.M., Bourgouin, P., Beaudoin, G., Joubert, S., et al. (2002). Areas of brain activation in males and females during viewing of erotic film excerpts. *Human Brain Mapping, 16*, 1–13.

Kazui, H., Mori, E., Hashimoto, M., Hirono, N., Imamura, T., Tanimukai, S., et al. (2000). Impact of emotion on memory: Controlled study of the influence of emotionally charged material on declarative memory in Alzheimer's disease. *British Journal of Psychiatry, 177*, 343–347.

Keane, M.M., Gabrieli, J.D., Fennema, A.C., Growdon, J.H., & Corkin, S. (1991). Evidence for a dissociation between perceptual and conceptual priming in Alzheimer's disease. *Behavioral Neuroscience, 105*, 326–342.

Keane, M.M., Gabrieli, J.D., Growdon, J.H., & Corkin, S. (1994). Priming in perceptual identification of pseudowords is normal in Alzheimer's disease. *Neuropsychology, 32*, 343–356.

Keane, M.M., Gabrieli, J.D., Mapstone, H.C., Johnson, K.A., & Corkin, S. (1995). Double dissociation of memory capacities after bilateral occipital lobe or medial temporal lobe lesions. *Brain, 118*, 1129–1148.

Keenan, J.M., & Baillet, S.D. (1980). Memory for personally and socially significant events. In R.S. Nickerson (Ed.), *Attention and performance, VIII* (pp. 651–669). Hillsdale, NJ: Erlbaum.

Keil, A., & Ihssen, N. (2004). Identification facilitation for emotionally arousing verbs during the attentional blink. *Emotion, 4*, 23–35.

Kelley, W.M., Miezin, F.M., McDermott, K.B., Buckner, R.L., Raichle, M.E., Cohen, N.J., Ollinger, J.M., Akbudali, E., Conturo, T.E., Snyder, AZ, Peterson, S.E., & Peterson, S.E. (1998, May), Hemispheric specialization in human dorsal frontal cortex and medial temporal lobe for verbal and nonverbal memory encoding. *Neuron., 20*, 927–36.

Kennedy, Q., Mather, M., & Carstensen, L.L. (2004). The role of motivation in the age-related positivity effect in autobiographical memory. *Psychological Science, 15*, 208–214.

Kensinger, E.A. (2004). Remembering emotional experiences: The contribution of valence and arousal. *Reviews in the Neurosciences, 15*, 241–251.

Kensinger, E.A. (2007). How negative emotion affects memory accuracy: Behavioral and neuroimaging evidence. *Current Directions in Psychological Science, 16*, 213–218.

Kensinger, E.A. (2008). Age differences in memory for arousing and nonarousing emotional words. *Journal of Gerontology: Psychological Sciences.*

Kensinger, E.A. (in press). Neuroimaging the formation and retrieval of emotional memories. To appear in *Brain mapping: New research.* Hauppauge, NY: Nova Science Publishers, Inc.

Kensinger, E.A., Anderson, A., Growdon, J.H., & Corkin, S. (2004). Effects of Alzheimer disease on memory for verbal emotional information. *Neuropsychologia, 42*, 791–800.

Kensinger, E.A., Brierley, B., Medford, N., Growdon, J.H., & Corkin, S. (2002). Effects of normal aging and Alzheimer's disease on emotional memory. *Emotion, 2*, 118–134.

Kensinger, E.A., & Corkin, S. (2003a). Alzheimer's disease. In L. Nadel (Ed.), *Encyclopedia of cognitive science.* London: Macmillan Ltd.

Kensinger, E.A., & Corkin, S. (2003b). Effect of negative emotional content on working memory and long-term memory. *Emotion, 3*, 378–393.

Kensinger, E.A., & Corkin, S. (2003c). Memory enhancement for emotional words: Are emotional words more vividly remembered than neutral words? *Memory and Cognition, 31*, 1169–1180.

Kensinger, E.A., & Corkin, S. (2003d). Neural changes in ageing. In L. Nadel (Ed.), *Encyclopedia of cognitive science.* London: Macmillan Ltd.

Kensinger, E.A., & Corkin, S. (2004a). Cognition in aging and age-related disease. In G. Adelman and B.H. Smith (Eds.), *Encyclopedia of neuroscience* (Web, CD-ROM). New York: Elsevier Press.

Kensinger, E.A., & Corkin, S. (2004b). The effects of emotional content and aging on false memories. *Cognitive, Affective, and Behavioral Neuroscience, 4*, 1–9.

Kensinger, E.A., & Corkin, S. (2004c). Two routes to emotional memory: Distinct neural processes for valence and arousal. *Proceedings of the National Academy of Sciences, USA, 101*, 3310–3315.

Kensinger, E.A., & Corkin, S. (2008). Amnesia: Point and counterpoint. In H.L. Roediger, III (Ed.) *Cognitive psychology of memory.* Vol. 1 of *Learning and memory: A comprehensive reference* (J. Byrne, Ed.). Oxford: Elsevier Press.

Kensinger, E.A., Garoff-Eaton, R.J., & Schacter, D.L. (2006). Memory for specific visual details can be enhanced by negative arousing content. *Journal of Memory and Language, 54*, 99–112.

Kensinger, E.A., Garoff-Eaton, R.J., & Schacter, D.L. (2007a). Effects of emotion on memory specificity: Memory trade-offs elicited by negative visually arousing stimuli. *Journal of Memory and Language, 56,* 575–591.

Kensinger, E.A., Garoff-Eaton, R.J., & Schacter, D.L. (2007b). Effects of emotion on memory specificity in young and older adults. *Journal of Gerontology: Psychological Sciences, 62,* 208–215.

Kensinger, E.A., Garoff-Eaton, R.J., & Schacter, D.L. (2007c). How negative emotion enhances the visual specificity of a memory. *Journal of Cognitive Neuroscience, 19,* 1872–1887.

Kensinger, E.A., Gutchess, A.H., & Schacter, D.L. (2007). Effects of aging and encoding instructions on emotion-induced memory trade-offs. *Psychology and Aging, 22,* 781–795.

Kensinger, E.A., Krendl, A.C., & Corkin, S. (2006). Memories of an emotional and a nonemotional event: Effects of aging and delay interval. *Experimental Aging Research, 32,* 23–45.

Kensinger, E.A., & Leclerc, C.M. (in press). Age-related changes in the neural mechanisms supporting emotion processing and emotional memory. *European Journal of Cognitive Psychology.*

Kensinger, E.A., O'Brien, J., Swanberg, K., Garoff-Eaton, R.J., & Schacter, D.L. (2007). The effects of emotional content on reality-monitoring performance in young and older adults. *Psychology and Aging, 22,* 752–764.

Kensinger, E.A., Piguet, O., Krendl, A.C., & Corkin, S. (2005). Memory for contextual details: Effects of emotion and aging. *Psychology and Aging, 20,* 241–250.

Kensinger, E.A., & Schacter, D.L. (2005a). Emotional content and reality-monitoring ability: FMRI evidence for the influence of encoding processes. *Neuropsychologia, 43,* 1429–1443.

Kensinger, E.A., & Schacter, D.L. (2005b). Retrieving accurate and distorted memories: Neuroimaging evidence for effects of emotion. *NeuroImage, 27,* 167–177.

Kensinger, E.A., & Schacter, D.L. (2006a). Amygdala activity is associated with the successful encoding of item, but not source, information for positive and negative stimuli. *Journal of Neuroscience, 26,* 2564–2570.

Kensinger, E.A., & Schacter, D.L. (2006b). Neural processes underlying memory attribution on a reality-monitoring task. *Cerebral Cortex, 16,* 1126–1133.

Kensinger, E.A., & Schacter, D.L. (2006c). Processing emotional pictures and words: Effects of valence and arousal. *Cognitive, Affective, and Behavioral Neuroscience, 6,* 110–126.

Kensinger, E.A., & Schacter, D.L. (2006d). Reality monitoring and memory distortion: Effects of negative, arousing content. *Memory and Cognition, 34,* 251–260.

Kensinger, E.A., & Schacter, D.L. (2006e). When the Red Sox shocked the Yankees: Comparing negative and positive memories. *Psychonomic Bulletin and Review, 13,* 757–763.

Kensinger, E.A., & Schacter, D.L. (2007). Remembering the specific visual details of presented objects: Neuroimaging evidence for effects of emotion. *Neuropsychologia, 45,* 2951–2962.

Kensinger, E.A., & Schacter, D.L. (2008). Neural processes supporting young and older adults' emotional memories. *Journal of Cognitive Neuroscience, 7,* 1–13.

Kern, R.P., Libkuman, T.M., Otani, H., & Holmes, K. (2005). Emotional stimuli, divided attention, and memory. *Emotion, 5,* 408–417.

Kirkpatrick, L., & Cahill, L. (2003). Amygdala modulation of parahippocampal and frontal regions during emotionally influenced memory storage. *Neuroimage, 20,* 2091–2099.

Kim, H., Somerville, L.H., McLean, A.A., Johnstone, T., Shin, L.M., & Whalen, P.J. (2003). Functional MRI responses of the human dorsal amygdala/substantia inominata region to facial expressions of emotion. *Annals of the New York Academy of Sciences, 985,* 533–535.

Kim, S., Goldstein, D., Hasher, L., & Zacks, R.T. (2005). Framing effects in younger and older adults. *Journals of Gerontology: Series B: Psychological Sciences and Social Sciences, 60B,* 215–218.

Kirwan, C.B., & Stark, C.E. (2004). Medial temporal lobe activation during encoding and retrieval of novel face-name pairs. *Hippocampus, 14,* 919–930.

Kityama, S. (1990). Interaction between affect and cognition in word perception. *Journal of Personality and Social Psychology, 58,* 209–217.

Kluver, H., & Bucy, P.C. (1937). "Psychic blindness" and other symptoms following bilateral temporal lobectomy in rhesus monkeys. *American Journal of Physiology, 119,* 352–353.

Knopman, D.S., DeKosky, S.T., Cummings, J.L., Chui, H., Corey-Bloom, J., Relkin, N., et al. (2001). Practice parameter: Diagnosis of dementia (an evidence-based review). *Neurology, 56,* 1143–1153.

Knowlton, B.J., Squire, L.R., & Gluck, M.A. (1994). Probabilistic classification learning in amnesia. *Learning and Memory, 1,* 106–112.

Kober, H., Barrett, L.F., Joseph, J., Bliss-Moreau, E., Lindquist, K., & Wagner, T.D. (2008). Functional groupings and cortical-subcortical interactions in emotion: A meta-analysis of neuroimaging studies. *Neuroimage.*

Kosslyn, S.M., & Thompson, W.L. 2000. Shared mechanisms in visual imagery and visual perception: Insights from cognitive neuroscience. In M.S. Gazzaniga (Ed.), The new cognitive neurosciences (pp. 975–985). Cambridge, MA: MIT Press.

Koutstaal, W., Wagner, A.D., Rotte, M., Maril, A., Buckner, R.L., & Schacter, D.L. (2001). Perceptual specificity in visual object priming: Functional magnetic resonance imaging evidence for a laterality difference in fusiform cortex. *Neuropsychologia, 39,* 184–199.

Krasuski, J.S., Alexander, G.E., Horwitz, B., Daly, E.M., Murphy, D.G., Rapoport, S.I., et al. (1998). Volumes of medial temporal lobe structures in patients with Alzheimer's disease and mild cognitive impairment (and in healthy controls). *Biological Psychiatry, 43,* 60–68.

Kringelbach, M.L. (2005). The human orbitofrontal cortex: Linking reward to hedonic experience. *Nature Reviews Neuroscience, 6,* 691–702.

Kringelbach, M.L., & Rolls, E.T. (2004). The functional neuroanatomy of the human orbitofrontal cortex: Evidence from neuroimaging and neuropsychology. *Progress in Neurobiology, 72,* 341–372.

LaBar, K.S., & Cabeza, R. (2006). Cognitive neuroscience of emotional memory. *Nature Neuroscience Reviews, 7,* 54–56.

LaBar, K.S., Mesulam, M.-M., Gitelman, D.R., & Weintzaub, S. (2000). Emotional curiosity: Modulation of visuospatial attention by arousal is preserved in aging and early-stage Alzheimer's disease. *Neuropsychologia, 38,* 1734–1740.

LaBar, K.S., & Phelps, E.A. (1998). Arousal-mediated memory consolidation: Role of the medial temporal lobe in humans. *Psychological Science, 9,* 490–493.

LaBar, K.S., Torpey, D.C., Cook, C.A., Johnson, S.R., Warren, L.H., Burke, J.R., et al. (2005). Emotional enhancement of perceptual priming is preserved in aging and early-stage Alzheimer's disease. *Neuropsychologia, 43,* 1824–1837

Lachman, M.E., & Bertrand, R.M. (2001). Personality and the self in midlife. In M.E. Lachman (Ed.), *Handbook of midlife development* (pp. 279–309). Hoboken, NJ: John Wiley & Sons.

Lang, P.J. (1985). The cognitive psychophysiology of emotion: Fear and anxiety. In A.H. Tuna & J.D. Masser (Eds.), *Anxiety and the Anxiety Disorders* (pp. 131–170). Hillsdale, NJ: Erlbaum.

Lang, P.J., Bradley, M.M., & Cuthbert, B.N. (1998a). Emotion and motivation: Measuring affective perception. *Journal of Clinical Neurophysiology, 15,* 397–408

Lang, P.J., Bradley, M.M., & Cuthbert, B.N. (1998b). Emotion, motivation, and anxiety: Brain mechanisms and psychophysiology. *Biological Psychiatry, 44,* 1248–1263.

Lang, P.J., Bradley, M.M., & Cuthbert, B.N. (1999). *International affective picture system (IAPS): Technical manual and affective ratings.* Gainesville, FL: The Center for Research in Psychophysiology.

Lang, P.J., Greenwald, M.K., Bradley, M.M., & Hamm, A.O. (1993). Looking at pictures: Affective, facial, visceral, and behavioral reactions. *Psychophysiology, 30,* 261–273.

Lavond, D.G., Kim, J.J., & Thompson, R.F. (1993). Mammalian brain substrates of aversive classical conditioning. *Annual Review of Psychology, 44,* 317–342.

Lazarus, R.S. (1991). *Emotion and adaptation.* New York: Oxford University Press.

Lazarus, R.S., & Folkman, S. (1984). *Stress, appraisal and coping.* New York: Springer.

Leclerc, C.M., & Kensinger, E.A. (2008). Age-related differences in medial prefrontal activation in response to emotional images. *Cognitive, Affective, and Behavioral Neuroscience, 8,* 153–164.

Leclerc, C.M., & Kensinger, E.A. ((2008). Effects of age on detection of emotional information. *Psychology and Aging, 23,* 209–215.

LeDoux, J.E. (1995). Emotion: Clues from the brain. *Annual Review of Psychology, 46,* 209–235.

LeDoux, J.E. (2000). Emotion circuits in the brain. *Annual Review of Neuroscience, 23,* 155–184.

Leigland, L.A., Schulz, L.E., & Janowsky, J.S. (2004). Age-related changes in emotional memory. *Neurobiology of Aging, 25,* 1117–1124.

Levenson, R.W., Carstensen, L.L., & Gottman, J.M. (1994). The influence of age and gender on affect, physiology, and their interrelations: A study of long-term marriages. *Journal of Personality and Social Psychology, 67,* 56–68.

Levenson, R.W., Friesen, W.V., Ekman, P., & Carstensen, L.L. (1991). Emotion, physiology, and expression in old age. *Psychology and Aging, 6,* 28–35.

Levine, L.J., & Bluck, S. (2004). Painting with broad strokes: Happiness and the malleability of event memory. *Cognition and Emotion, 18,* 559–574.

Li, K.Z.H., & Lindenberger, U. (2002). Relations between aging sensory/sensorimotor and cognitive functions. *Neuroscience and Biobehavioral Reviews, 26,* 777–783.

Light, L. (1992). The organization of memory in old age. In F.I.M. Craik & T.A. Salthouse (Eds.), *The handbook of aging and cognition* (pp. 111–165). Hillsdale, NJ: Erlbaum.

Light, L.L. (2000). Memory changes in adulthood. In S.H. Qualls & N. Abeles (Eds.), *Psychology and the aging revolution: How we adapt to longer life.* Washington, DC: American Psychological Association.

Linton, M. (1975). Memory for real-world events. In D.A. Norman & D.E. Rumelhart (Eds.), *Explorations in cognition* (pp. 376–404). San Francisco: Freeman.

Locascio, J.J., Growdon, J.H., & Corkin, S. (1995). Cognitive test performance in detecting, staging, and tracking Alzheimer's disease. *Archives of Neurology, 52,* 1087–1099.

Loftus, E.F. (1979). The malleability of human memory. *American Scientist, 67,* 312–320.

Loftus, E.F., & Burns, T.E. (1982). Mental shock can produce retrograde amnesia. *Memory and Cognition, 10,* 318–323.

Luchies, C.W., Schiffman, J., Richards, L.G., Thompson, M.R., Bazuin, D., & DeYoung, A.J. (2002). Effects of age, step direction, and reaction condition on the ability to step quickly. *The Journals of Gerontology, Series A, 57,* M246.

Luo, Q., Peng, D., Jin, Z., Xu, D., Xiao, L., & Ding, G. (2004). Emotional valence of words modulates the subliminal repetition priming effect in the left fusiform gyrus: An event-related fMRI study. *NeuroImage, 21,* 414–421.

Lupien, S.J., de Leon, M., de Santi, S., Convit, A., Tarshish, C., Nair, N.P.V., Thakur, M., McEwen, B.S., Hauger, R.L., & Meaney, M.J. (1998). Cortisol levels during human aging predict hippocampal atrophy and memory deficits. *Nature Neuroscience, 1,* 69–73.

MacKay, D.G., & Ahmetzanov, M.V. (2005). Emotion, memory and attention in the taboo Stroop paradigm: An experimental analogue of flashbulb memories. *Psychological Science, 16,* 25–32.

MacKay, D.G., Shafto, M., Taylor, J.K., Marian, D.E., Abrams, L., & Dyer, J.R. (2004). Relations between emotion, memory, and attention: Evidence from taboo Stroop, lexical decision, and immediate memory tasks. *Memory and Cognition, 32,* 474–488.

Mackie, D.M., & Worth, L.T. (1989). Processing deficits and the mediation of positive affect in persuasion. *Journal of Personality and Social Psychology, 57,* 27–40.

Mackiewicz, K.L., Sarinopoulos, I., Cleven, K.L., & Nitschke, J.B. (2006). The effect of anticipation and the specificity of sex differences for amygdala and hippocampus function in emotional memory. *Proceedings of the National Academy of Sciences, USA, 103,* 14200–142005.

MacLeod, C., & Mathews, A. (2004). Selective memory effects in anxiety disorders: An overview of research findings and their implications. In D. Reisberg and P. Hertel, (Eds.), *Memory and emotion* (pp. 155–185). New York: Oxford University Press.

MacLeod, C.M. (1991). Half a century of research on the Stroop effect: An integrative review. *Psychological Bulletin, 109,* 163–203.

Malatesta, C.Z., Fiore, M.J., & Messina, J.J. (1987). Affect, personality, and facial expressive characteristics of older people. *Psychology and Aging, 2,* 64–69.

Mandler, G. (1967). Organization and memory. In K.W. Spence & J.T. Spence (Eds.), *The psychology of learning and motivation: Advances in research and theory* (Vol. 1, pp. 328–372). New York: Academic Press.

Mantyla, T. (1993). Knowing but not remembering: Adult age differences in recollective experience. *Memory & Cognition, 21,* 379–388.

Manns, J.R., Hopkins, R.O., & Squire, L.R. (2003). Semantic memory and the human hippocampus. *Neuron, 38,* 127–133.

Maratos, E.J., Dolan, R.J., Morris, J.S., Henson, R.N., & Rugg, M.D. (2001). Neural activity associated with episodic memory for emotional context. *Neuropsychologia, 39,* 910–920.

Maren, S. (2001). Neurobiology of Pavlovian fear conditioning. *Annual Review of Neuroscience, 24,* 897–931.

Markowitsch, H.J., Calabrese, P., Wurker, M., Durwen, H.F., Kessler, J., Babinsky, R., et al. (1994). The amygdala's contribution to memory—a study on two patients with Urbach-Wiethe disease. *Neuroreport, 5,* 1349–1352.

Marsiske, M., & Willis, S.L. (1995). Dimensionality of everyday problem solving in older adults. *Psychology and Aging, 10,* 269–283.

Martin, L.L., & Clore, G.L. (2001). *Theories of mood and cognition: A user's handbook.* Mahwah, NJ: Lawrence Erlbaum Associates.

Martin-Soelch, C., Linthicum, J., & Ernst, M. (2006). Appetitive conditioning: Neural bases and implications for psychopathology. *Neuroscience and Biobehavioral Reviews, 31,* 426–440.

Mather, M. (2006). Why memories may become more positive with age. In B. Uttl, N. Ohta, & A.L. Siegenthaler (Eds.), *Memory and emotion: Interdisciplinary perspectives.* Malden, MA: Blackwell Publishing.

Mather, M. (2007). Emotional arousal and memory binding: An object-based framework. *Perspectives on Psychological Science, 2,* 33–52.

Mather, M., Canli, T., English, T., Whitfield, S., Wais, P., Ochsner, K., et al. (2004). Amygdala responses to emotionally valenced stimuli in older and younger adults. *Psychological Science, 15,* 259–263.

Mather, M. & Carstensen, L.L. (2005). Aging and motivated cognition: The positivity effect in attention and memory. *Trends in Cognitive Sciences, 9,* 296–502.

Mather, M., & Knight, M. (2005). Goal-directed memory: The role of cognitive control in older adults' emotional memory. *Psychology and Aging, 20,* 554–570.

Mather, M., & Knight, M.R. (2006). Angry faces get noticed quickly: Threat detection is not impaired among older adults. *Journals of Gerontology Series B: Psychological Sciences and Social Sciences, 61,* P54–P57.

Mather, M., & Nesmith, K. (in press). Arousal-enhanced location memory for pictures. *Journal of Memory and Language.*

Mathews, A., & Mackintosh, B. (2004). Take a closer look: Emotion modifies the boundary extension effect. *Emotion, 4,* 36–45.

Mathews, A., & MacLeod, C. (1994). Cognitive approaches to emotion and emotional disorders. *Annual Review of Psychology, 45,* 25–50.

Mathews, A., May, J., Mogg, K., & Eysenck, M. (1990). Attentional bias in anxiety: Selective search or defective filtering? *Journal of Abnormal Psychology, 99,* 166–173.

Matt, G.E., Vazquez, C., & Campbell, W.C. (1992). Mood-congruent recall of affectively toned stimuli: A meta-analytic study. *Clinical Psychology Review, 12,* 227–255.

Matthews, G., & Deary, I.J. (1998). *Personality traits.* Cambridge: Cambridge University Press.

May, C.P., Rahhal, T., Berry, E.M., & Leighton, E.A. (2005). Aging, source memory, and emotion. *Psychology of Aging, 20,* 571–578.

Mayberg, H.S., Liotti, M., Brannan, S.K., McGinnis, S., Mahurin, R.K., Jerabek, P.A., et al. (1999). Reciprocal limbic-cortical function and negative mood: Converging PET findings in depression and normal sadness. *American Journal of Psychiatry, 156,* 675–682.

Mayes, A.R., Holdstock, J.S., Issac, C.L., Hunkin, N.M., & Roberts, N. (2002). Relative sparing of item recognition memory in a patient with adult-onset damage limited to the hippocampus. *Hippocampus, 12,* 325–340.

Mayes, A.R., Holdstock., J.S., Issac, C.L., Montaldi, D., Grigor, J., Gummer, A., et al. (2004). Associative recognition in a patient with selective hippocampal lesions and relative normal item recognition. *Hippocampus, 14,* 763–784.

McGaugh, J.L. (2000). Memory—a century of consolidation. *Science, 287,* 248–251.

McGaugh, J.L. (2004). The amygdala modulates the consolidation of memories of emotionally arousing experiences. *Annual Review of Neuroscience, 27,* 1–28.

McIntosh, A.R., & Gonzales-Lima, F. (1994). Network interations among limbic cortics, basal forebrain, and cerebellum differentiate a tone conditioned as a Paulovian excitor or inhibitor: Fluordeoxyglucose mapping and covariance structural modeling. *J Neurophysical 17,* 1717–1733.

McNally, R.J. (1997). Implicit and explicit memory for trauma-related information in PTSD. *Annals of the New York Academy of Sciences, 821,* 219–224.

Michael, T., Ehlers, A., & Halligan, S.L. (2005). Enhanced priming for trauma-related material in posttraumatic stress disorder. *Emotion, 5,* 103–112.

Mickley, K.R., & Kensinger, E.H. (2008). Emotional valence influences the neural correlates associated with remembering and knowing. *Cognitive, Affective, and Behaviorial Neuroscience, 8,* 143–152.

Mikels, J.A., & Reuter-Lorenz, P.A. (in press). Affective working memory: Converging evidence for a new social construct. In S. Voshikawa (Ed.), *Emotional Mind: New Directions in Affective Science.* Tokyo: Springer-Verlag.

Mikels, J.A., Larkin, G.R., Reuter-Lorenz, P.A., & Carstensen, L.L. (2005). Divergent trajectories in the aging mind: Changes in working memory for affective versus visual information with age. *Psychology and Aging, 20,* 542–553.

Miller, E.K., & Cohen, J.D. (2001). An integrative theory of prefrontal cortex function. *Annual Review of Neuroscience, 24,* 167–202.

Mizuno, K., Wakai, M., Takeda, A., & Sobue, G. (2000). Medial temporal atrophy and memory impairment in early stages of Alzheimer's disease: An MRI volumetric and memory assessment study. *Journal of Neurological Sciences, 172,* 18–24.

Moayeri, S.E., Cahill, L., Jin, Y., & Potkin, S.G. (2000). Relative sparing of emotionally influenced memory in Alzheimer's disease. *Neuroreport, 11,* 653–655.

Mogg, K., Millar, N.H., & Bradley, B. (2000). Biases in eye movements to threatening facial expressions in generalized anxiety disorder and depressive disorder. *Journal of Abnormal Psychology, 109,* 695–704.

Moreno, C., Borod, J.C., Welkowitz, J., & Alpert, M. (1993). The perception of facial emotion across the adult life span. *Developmental Neuropsychology, 9,* 305–314.

Mori, E., Ikeda, M., Hirono, N., Kitagaki, H., Imamura, T., & Simomura, T. (1999). Amygdalar volume and emotional memory in Alzheimer's disease. *American Journal of Psychiatry, 156,* 216–222.

Morris, J.S., Friston, K.J., & Dolan, R.J. (1997). Neural responses to salient visual stimuli. *Proceedings of the Royal Society of London. Series B: Biological Sciences, 264*, 769–775.

Mroczek, D.K., & Spiro, A., III. (2003). Modeling intraindividual change in personality traits: Findings from the normative aging study. *Journal of Gerontology Series B: Psychological Sciences and Social Sciences, 58*, P153–165.

Murnen, S.K., & Stockton, M.C. (1997). Gender and self-reported sexual arousal in response to sexual stimuli: A meta-analytic review. *Sex Roles, 37*, 135–153.

Murphy, D.R., Craik, F.I., Li, K.Z., & Schneider, B.A. (2000). Comparing the effects of aging and background noise on short-term memory performance. *Psychology of Aging, 15*, 323–334.

Murphy, N.A., & Isaacowitz, D.M. (2008). Preferences for emotional information in older and younger adults: A meta-analysis of memory and attention tasks. *Psychology and Aging, 23*, 263–286.

Muscatell, K., & Kensinger, E. (2007). *Effect of emotional content on working memory.* Cognitive Neuroscience Society Meeting. New York.

Neisser, U. (1976). *Cognition and reality: Principles and implications of cognitive psychology.* New York: Freeman.

Neisser, U. (1982). Snapshots or benchmarks? In U. Neisser (Ed.), *Memory observed: Remembering in natural contexts.* New York: Freeman.

Neisser, U., & Harsch, N. (1992). Phantom flashbulbs: False recollections of hearing the news about Challenger. In E. Winograd & U. Neisser (Eds.), *Affect and accuracy in recall: Studies of "flashbulb" memories* (pp. 9–31). New York: Cambridge University Press.

Niedenthal, P.M., Halberstadt, J.B., & Setterlund, M.B. (1997). Being happy and seeing "happy": Emotional state mediates visual word recognition. *Cognition and Emotion, 11*, 403–432.

Nitschke, J.B., Heller, W., Palmieri, P.A., & Miller, G.A. (1999). Contrasting patterns of brain activity in anxious apprehension and anxious arousal. *Psychophysiology, 36*, 628–637.

Noesselt, T., Driver, J., Heinze, H.J., & Dolan, R. (2005). Asymmetrical activation in the human brain during processing of fearful faces. *Current Biology, 15*, 424–429.

Norman, D.A., & Shallice, T. (1980). *Attention to action: Willed and automatic control of behaviour.* University of California CHIP Report 99.

Northoff, G., & Bermpohl, F. (2004). Cortical midline structures and the self. *Trends in Cognitive Science, 8*, 102–107.

Northoff, G., Richter, A., Gessner, M., Schlagenhauf, F., Fell, J., Baumgart, F., et al. (2000). Functional dissociation between medial and lateral prefrontal cortical spatiotemporal activation in negative and positive emotions: A combined fMRI/MEG study. *Cerebral Cortex, 10*, 93–107.

O'Doherty, J., Kringelbach, M.L., Rolls, E.T., Hornak, J., & Andrews, C. (2001). Abstract reward and punishment representations in the human orbitiofrontal cortex. *Nature Neuroscience, 4*, 95–102.

Oaksford, M., Morris, F., Grainger, B., Williams, J., & Mark, G. (1996). Mood, reasoning, and central executive processes. *Journal of Experimental Psychology: Learning, Memory, and Cognition, 22*, 476–492.

Ochsner, K.N. (2000). Are affective events richly "remembered" or simply familiar? The experience and process of recognizing feelings past. *Journal of Experimental Psychology: General, 129*, 242–261.

Ochsner, K.N., Bunge, S.A., Gross, J.J., & Gabrieli, J.D. (2002). Rethinking feelings: An fMRI study of the cognitive regulation of emotion. *Journal of Cognitive Neuroscience, 14,* 1215–1229.

Ochsner, K.N., & Gross, J.J. (2005). The cognitive control of emotion. *Trends Cogn Sci, 9,* 242–9.

Ochsner, K.N., Ray, R.D., Cooper, J.C., Robertson, E.R., Chopra, S., Gabrieli, J.D.E., & Gross, J.J. (2004). For better or for worse: Neural systems supporting the cognitive down- and up-regulation of negative emotion. *NeuroImage, 23,* 483–499.

Ohman, A. (1988). Preattention processes in the generation of emotions. In V. Hamilton, G.H. Bower, & N.H. Frijda (Eds.), *Cognitive perspectives on emotion and motivation* (Vol. 44, pp. 127–143). Norwell, MA: Kluwer Academic.

Ohman, A., Flykt, A., & Esteves, F. (2001). Emotion drives attention: Detecting the snake in the grass. *Journal of Experimental Psychology: General, 130,* 466–478.

Ohman, A., & Soares, J.J.F. (1994). Unconscious anxiety: Phobic responses to masked stimuli. *Journal of Abnormal Psychology, 103,* 231–240.

Ohnishi, T., Matsuda, H., Tabira, T., Asada, T., & Uno, M. (2001). Changes in brain morphology in Alzheimer disease and normal aging: Is Alzheimer disease an exaggerated aging process? *American Journal of Neuroradiology, 22,* 1680–1685.

Old, S.R., & Naveh-Benjamin, M. (2008). Differential effects of age on item and associative measures of memory: A meta-analysis. *Psychol Aging, 23,* 104–18.

Ortony, A., Turner, T.J., & Antos, S.J. (1983). A puzzle about affect and recognition memory. *Journal of Experimental Psychology: Learning, Memory, & Cognition, 9,* 725–729.

Packard, M.G., & Cahill, L. (2001). Affective modulation of multiple memory systems. *Current Opinion in Neurobiology, 11,* 752–756.

Packard, M.G., Cahill, L., & McGaugh, J.L. (1994). Amygdala modulation of hippocampal-dependent and caudate nucleus-dependent memory processes. *Proceedings of the National Academy of Sciences, USA, 91,* 8477–8481.

Padovan, C., Versace, R., Thomas-Anterion, C., & Laurent, B. (2002). Evidence for a selective deficit in automatic activation of positive information in patients with Alzheimer's disease in an affective priming paradigm. *Neuropsychologia, 40,* 335–339.

Paller, K.A., & Wagner, A.D. (2002). Observing the transformation of experience into memory. *Trends in Cognitive Sciences, 6,* 93–102.

Panksepp, J. (2007). Neurologizing the psychology of affects: How appraisal-based constructivism and basic emotion theory can coexist. *Perspectives on Psychological Science, 2,* 281–296.

Papez, J.W. (1937). A proposed mechanism of emotion. *Journal of Neuropsychiatry and Clinical Neurosciences, 7,* 103–112.

Papps, B.P., Calder, A.J., Young, A.W., & O'Carroll, R.E. (2003). Dissociation of affective modulation of recollective and perceptual experience following amygdala damage. *Journal of Neurology, Neurosurgery, and Psychiatry, 74,* 243–254.

Paradis, C.M., Solomon, L.Z., Florer, F., & Thompson, T. (2004). Flashbulb memories of personal events of 9/11 and the day after for a sample of New York City residents. *Psychological Reports, 95,* 304–310.

Parent, A. (1996). *Carpenter's human neuroanatomy* (Ninth edition). Media, PA: Williams and Wilkins.

Park, J., & Banaji, M.R. (2000). Mood and heuristics: The influence of happy and sad states on sensitivity and bias in stereotyping. *Journal of Personality and Social Psychology, 78,* 1005–1023.

Payne, J.D., Nadel, L., Allen, J.J.B., Thomas, K.G.F., & Jacobs, W.J. (2002). The effects of experimentally induced stress on false recognition. *Memory, 10,* 1–6.

Perlstein, W.M., Elbert, T., & Stenger, V.A. (2002). Dissociation in human prefrontal cortex of affective influences on working memory-related activity. *Proceedings of the National Academy of Sciences, USA, 99,* 1736–1741.

Pessoa, L. (2005). To what extent are emotional visual stimuli processed without attention and awareness? *Current Opinion in Neurobiology, 15,* 188–196.

Pessoa, L. (2008). On the relationship between emotion and cognition. *Nat Rev Neurosci, 9,* 148–58.

Pessoa, L., Kastner, S., & Underleider, L.G. (2003). Neuroimaging studies of attention: From modulation of sensory processing to top-down control. *Journal of Neuroscience, 23,* 3990–3998.

Pesta, B.J., Murphy, M.D., & Sanders, R.E. (2001). Are emotionally charged lures immune to false memory? *Journal of Experimental Psychology: Learning, Memory, and Cognition, 27,* 328–338.

Peters, E., Hess, T.M., Auman, C., & Vastfjall, D. (2007). Adult age differences in dual information processes and their influence on judgments and decisions: A review. *Perspectives on Psychological Science, 2,* 1–23.

Pezdek, K. (2003). Event memory and autobiographical memory for the events of September 11, 2001. *Applied Cognitive Psychology, 17,* 1033–1045.

Phan, K.L., Wager, T., Taylor, S.F., & Liberzon, I. (2002). Functional neuroanatomy of emotion: A meta-analysis of emotion activation studies in PET and fMRI. *NeuroImage, 16,* 331–348.

Phelps, E.A. (2004). Human emotion and memory: Interactions of the amygdala and hippocampal complex. *Current Opinion in Neurobiology, 14,* 198–202.

Phelps, E.A., LaBar, K.S., Anderson, A.K., O'Connor, K.J., Fulbright, R.J., & Spencer, D.D. (1998). Specifying the contributions of the human amygdala to emotional memory: A case study. *Neurocase, 4,* 527–540.

Phelps, E.A., LaBar, K.S., & Spencer, D.D. (1997). Memory for emotional words following unilateral temporal lobectomy. *Brain and Cognition, 35,* 85–109.

Phelps, E.A., & LeDoux, J.E. (2005). Contributions of the amygdala to emotion processing: From animal models to human behavior. *Neuron, 48,* 175–187.

Phillips, L.H., & Allen, R. (2004). Adult aging and the perceived intensity of emotions in faces and stories. *Aging Clinical and Experimental Research, 16,* 1–10.

Plato. (1992). *Republic.* (G. Grube and C. Reeve, Trans.). Indianapolis: Hackett Publishing Company.

Poldrack, R.A., Selco, S.L., Field, J.E., & Cohen, N.J. (1999). The relationship between skill learning and repetition priming: Experimental and computational analyses. *Journal of Experimental Psychology: Learning, Memory, and Cognition, 25,* 208–235.

Porter, N., & Landfield, P.W. (1998). Stress hormones and brain aging: Adding injury to insult? *Nature Neuroscience, 1,* 3–4.

Pratto, F., & John, O.P. (1991). Automatic vigilance: The attention-grabbing power of negative social information. *Journal of Personality and Social Psychology, 61,* 380–391.

Quirarte, G.L., Roozendaal, B., & McGaugh, J.L. (1997). Glucocorticoid enhancement of memory storage involves noradrenergic activation in the basolateral amygdala. *Proceedings of the National Academy of Sciences, USA, 94,* 14048–14053.

Rahhal, T., May, C.P., & Hasher, L. (2002). Truth and character: Sources that older adults can remember. *Psychological Science, 13,* 101–105.

Randt, C.T., Brown, E.R., & Osborne, D.P. (1981). *Randt memory test.* New York: New York University, Department of Neurology.

Ranganath, C., Johnson, M.K., & D'Esposito, M. (2000). Left anterior prefrontal activation increases with demands to recall specific perceptual information. *Journal of Neuroscience, 20,* RC108.

Ranganath, C., Johnson, M.K., & D'Esposito, M. (2003). Prefrontal activity associated with working memory and episodic long-term memory. *Neuropsychologia, 41,* 378–389.

Ranganath, C., Yonelinas, A.P., Cohen, M.X., Dy, C.J., Tom, S.M., et al. (2004). Dissociable correlates of recollection and familiarity within the medial temporal lobes. *Neuropsychologia, 42,* 2–13.

Ray, R.D., Ochsner, K.N., Cooper, J.C., Robertson, E.R., Gabrieli, J.D., & Gross, J.J. (2005). Individual differences in trait rumination and the neural systems supporting cognitive reappraisal. *Cognitive, Affective, and Behavioral Neuroscience, 5,* 156–168.

Raz, N., Gunning, F.M., Head, D., Dupuis, J.H., McQuain, J., Briggs, S.D., et al. (1997). Selective aging of the human cerebral cortex observed in vivo: Differential vulnerability of the prefrontal gray matter. *Cerebral Cortex, 7,* 268–282.

Reimann, B., & McNally, R.J. (1995). Cognitive processing of personally relevant information. *Cognition and Emotion, 9,* 325–340.

Reisberg, D., & Heuer, F. (2004). Remembering emotional events. In D. Reisberg, and P. Hertel (Eds.), *Memory and emotion* (pp. 3–41). New York: Oxford University Press.

Reisenzein, R. (1994). Pleasure-arousal theory and the intensity of emotions. *Journal of Personality and Social Psychology, 67,* 525–539.

Reuter-Lorenz, P. (2002). New visions of the aging mind and brain. *Trends in Cognitive Sciences, 6,* 394.

Reuter-Lorenz, P.A., Jonides, J., Smith, E.E., Hartley, A., Miller, A., Marshuetz, C., et al. (2000). Age differences in the frontal lateralization of verbal and spatial working memory revealed by PET. *Journal of Cognitive Neuroscience, 212,* 174–187.

Rhodes, G., Halberstadt, J., & Brajkovich, G. (2001). Generalization of mere exposure effects to averaged composite faces. *Social Cognition, 19,* 57–70.

Richards, J.M., & Gross, J.J. (2006). Personality and emotional memory: How regulating emotion impairs memory for emotional events. *Journal of Research in Personality, 40,* 631–651.

Richardson, M.P., Strange, B., & Dolan, R.J. (2004). Encoding of emotional memories depends on the amygdala and hippocampus and their interactions. *Nature Neuroscience, 7,* 278–285.

Robbins, T.W., & Everitt, B.J. (1996). Neurobehavioural mechanisms of reward and motivation. *Current Opinion in Neurobiology, 6,* 228–236.

Roberts, A.C., Robbins, T.W., & Weiskrantz, L. (1998). *The prefrontal cortex: Executive and cognitive functions.* New York: Oxford University Press.

Robinson, M.D. (1998). Running from William James' bear: A review of preattentive mechanisms and their contribution to emotional experience. *Cognition and Emotion, 12,* 667–696.

Roediger, H.L., III, & McDermott, K.B. (1993). Implicit memory in normal human subjects. In H. Spinner & F. Boller (Eds.), *Handbook of neuropsychology* (Vol. 8, pp. 63–131). Amsterdam: Elsevier.

Roediger, H.L., III, Watson, J.M., McDermott, K.B., & Gallo, D.A. (2001). Factors that determine false recall: A multiple regression analysis. *Psychonomic Bulletin & Review, 8,* 385–407.

Rogers, T.B., Kuiper, N.A., & Kirker, W.S. (1977). Self-reference and the encoding of personal information. *Journal of Personality and Social Psychology, 35,* 677–688.

Rolls, E.T. (2000). Memory systems in the brain. *Annual Review of Psychology, 51,* 599–630.

Roudier, M., Marcie, P., Grancher, A-S., Tzortzis, C., Starkstein, S., & Boller, F. (1998). Discrimination of facial identity and of emotions in Alzheimer's disease. *Journal of Neurological Sciences, 154,* 151–158.

Rubin, D.C., & Kozin, M. (1984). Vivid memories. *Cognition, 16,* 63–80.

Rugg, M.D., Fletcher, P.C., Chua, P.M., & Dolan, R.J. (1999). The role of the prefrontal cortex in recognition memory and memory for source: An fMRI study. *NeuroImage, 10,* 520–529.

Rugg, M.D., & Morcom, A.M. (2005). The relationship between brain activity, cognitive performance, and aging: The case of memory. In R. Cabeza, L. Nyberg, & D. Park (Eds.), *Cognitive neuroscience of aging* (pp. 132–156). Oxford, England: Oxford University Press.

Russell, J.A. (1980). A circumplex model of affect. *Journal of Personality and Social Psychology, 39,* 1161–1178.

Russell, J.A., & Barrett, L.F. (1999). Core affect, prototypical emotional episodes, and other things called emotion: Dissecting the elephant. *Journal of Personality and Social Psychology, 76,* 805–819.

Safer, M.A., Christianson, S., Autry, M.W., & Oesterlund, K. (1998). Tunnel memory for traumatic events. *Applied Cognitive Psychology, 12,* 99–117.

Salat, D.H., Kaye, J.A., & Janowsky, J.S. (2001). Selective preservation and degeneration within the prefrontal cortex in aging and Alzheimer's disease. *Archives of Neurology, 58,* 1403–1408.

Salthouse, T.A. (1996). The processing-speed theory of adult age differences in cognition. *Psychological Review, 103,* 403–428.

Satpute, A.B., & Lieberman, M.D. (2006). Integrating automatic and controlled processes into neurocognitive models of social cognition. *Brain Research, 1079,* 86–97.

Schacter, D.L., & Buckner, R.L. (1998). Priming and the brain. *Neuron, 20,* 185–195.

Schacter, D.L., Cooper, L.A., & Delaney, S.M. (1990). Implicit memory for unfamiliar objects depends on access to structural descriptions. *Journal of Experimental Psychology: General, 119,* 5–24.

Schacter, D.L., Dobbins, I.G., & Schnyer, D.M. (2004). Specificity of priming: A cognitive neuroscience perspective. *Nature Reviews Neuroscience, 5,* 853–856.

Schacter, D.L., & Wiseman, A.L. (2006). Reducing memory errors: The distinctiveness heuristic. In R.R. Hunt & J. Worthen (Eds.), *Distinctiveness and memory.* New York: Oxford University Press.

Schaefer, A., & Philippot, P. (2005). Selective effects of emotion on the phenomenal characteristics of autobiographical memories. *Memory, 13,* 148–160.

Schlosberg, H. (1954). Three dimensions of emotion. *Psychological Review, 61,* 81–88.

Schmidt, S.R. (1991). Can we have a distinctive theory of memory? *Memory & Cognition, 19,* 523–542.

Schmidt, S.R. (1994). Effects of humor on sentence memory. *Journal of Experimental Psychology: Learning, Memory, and Cognition, 20,* 953–967.

Schmidt, S.R. (2002). Outstanding memories: The positive and negative effects of nudes on memory. *Journal of Experimental Psychology: Learning, Memory, and Cognition, 28,* 353–361.

Schmidt, S.R. (2004). Autobiographical memories for the September 11th attacks: Reconstructive errors and emotional impairment of memory. *Memory and Cognition, 32,* 443–454.

Schmidt, S.R., & Saari, B. (2007). The emotional memory effect: Differential processing or item distinctiveness? *Memory and Cognition, 35,* 1905–1916.

Schmolck, H., Buffalo, E.A., & Squire, L.R. (2000). Memory distortions develop over time: Recollections of the O.J. Simpson trial verdict after 15 and 32 months. *Psychological Science, 11,* 39–45.

Schmolck, H., & Squire, L.R. (2001). Impaired perception of facial emotions following bilateral damage to the anterior temporal lobe. *Neuropsychology, 15,* 30–38.

Schnyer, D.M., Nicholls, L., & Verfaellie, M. (2005). The role of VMPC in metamemorial judgments of content retrievability. *Journal of Cognitive Neuroscience, 17,* 832–846.

Schultz, W. (2000). Multiple reward systems in the brain. *Nature Reviews Neuroscience, 1,* 199–207.

Scott, S.A. (1993). Dendritic atrophy and remodeling of amygdaloid neurons in Alzheimer's disease. *Dementia, 4,* 264–272.

Scott, S.A., DeKosky, S.T., & Scheff, S.W. (1991). Volumetric atrophy of the amygdala in Alzheimer's disease: Quantitative serial reconstruction. *Neurology, 41,* 351–356.

Scott, S.A., DeKosky, S.T., Sparks, D.C., Knox, C.A., & Scheff, S.W. (1992). Amygdala cell loss and atrophy in Alzheimer's disease. *Annals of Neurology, 32,* 555–563.

Scott, S.K., Young, A.W., Calder, A.J., Hellawell, D.J., Aggleton, J.P., & Johnson, M. (1997). Impaired auditory recognition of fear and anger following bilateral amygdala lesions. *Nature, 385,* 254–257.

Scoville, W.B., & Milner, B. (1957). Loss of recent memory after bilateral hippocampal lesions. *Journal of Neurology, Neurosurgery, & Psychiatry, 20,* 11–21.

Seibert, P.S., & Ellis, H.C. (1991). Irrelevant thoughts, emotional mood states, and cognitive task performance. *Memory and Cognition, 19,* 507–513.

Seidlitz, L., & Diener, E. (1998). Sex differences in the recall of affective experiences. *Journal of Personality and Social Psychology, 74,* 262–271.

Sharot, T., Delgado, M.R., & Phelps, E.A. (2004). How emotion enhances the feeling of remembering. *Nature Neuroscience, 12,* 1376–1380.

Sharot, T., & Phelps, E.A. (2004). How arousal modulates memory: Disentangling the effects of attention and retention. *Cognitive, Affective, and Behavioral Neuroscience, 4,* 294–306.

Shimokawa, A., Yatomi, N., Anamizu, S., Torii, S., Isono, H., & Sugai, Y. (2003). Recognition of facial expressions and emotional situations in patients with dementia of the Alzheimer and vascular types. *Dementia and Geriatric Cognitive Disorders, 15,* 163–168.

Shoqeirat, M.A., & Mayes, A.R. (1991). Disproportionate incidental spatial-memory and recall deficits in amnesia. *Neuropsychologia, 29,* 749–769.

Simon, H.A. (1967). Motivational and emotional controls of cognition. *Psychological Review, 74,* 29–39.

Smith, A.P., Henson, R.N., Dolan, R.J., & Rugg, M.D. (2004). fMRI correlates of the episodic retrieval of emotional contexts. *Neuroimage, 22,* 868–878.

Smith, A.P., Stephan, K.E., Rugg, M.D., & Dolan, R.J. (2006). Task and content modulate amygdala-hippocampal connectivity in emotional retrieval. *Neuron, 49,* 631–638.

Smith, C.D., Malcein, M., Meurer, K., Schmitt, F.A., Markesberv, W.R., & Pettigrew, L.C. (1999). MRI temporal lobe volume measures and neuropsychologic function in Alzheimer's disease. *Journal of Neuroimaging, 9,* 2–9.

Smith, E.E., & Jonides, J. (1999). Storage and executive processes in the frontal lobes. *Science, 283,* 1657–1661.

Smith, M.C., Bibi, U., & Sheard, D.E. (2003). Evidence for the differential impact of time and emotion on personal and event memories for September 11, 2001. *Applied Cognitive Psychology, 17,* 1047–1055.

Spencer, W.D., & Raz, N. (1995). Differential effects of aging on memory for content and context: A meta-analysis. *Psychology and Aging, 10,* 527–539.

Sperling, R., Chua, E., Cocchiarella, A., Rand-Giovannetti, E., Poldrack, R., Schacter, D.L., et al. (2003). Putting names to faces: Successful encoding of associative memories activates the anterior hippocampal formation. *Neuroimage, 20,* 1400–1410.

Sperling, R.A., Bates, J.F., Cocchiarella, A.J., Schacter, D.L., Rosen, B.R., & Albert, M.S. (2001). Encoding novel face-name associations: A functional MRI study. *Human Brain Mapping, 14,* 129–139.

Spies, K., Hesse, F.W., & Hummitzsch, C. (1996). Mood and capacity in Baddeley's model of human memory. *Zeitschrift für Psychologie, 204,* 367–381.

Sprengelmeyer, R., Young, A.W., Schroeder, U., Grossenbacher, P.G., Federlein, J., Buttner, T., et al. (1999). Knowing no fear. *Proceedings of the Biological Sciences, USA, 266,* 2451–2456.

Squire, L.R., Stark, C.E., & Clark, R.E. (2004). The medial temporal lobe. *Annual Review of Neuroscience, 27,* 279–306.

Stark, C.E., & Squire, L.R. (2001). Simple and associative recognition memory in the hippocampal region. *Learning and Memory, 8,* 190–197.

Stefanacci, L., Suzuki, W.A., & Amaral, D.G. (1996). Organization of connections between the amygdaloid complex and the perirhinal and parahippocampal cortices in macaque monkeys. *Journal of Comparative Neurology, 375,* 552–582.

Steidl, S., Mohi-uddin, S., & Anderson, A.K. (2006). Effects of emotional arousal on multiple memory systems: Evidence from declarative and procedural learning. *Learning and Memory, 13,* 650–658.

Storbeck, J., & Clore, G.L. (2005). With sadness comes accuracy; with happiness, false memory: Mood and the false memory effect. *Psychological Science, 16,* 785–791.

Stradler, M.A., Roediger, H.L., III, & McDermott, K.B. (1999). Norms for word lists that create false memories. *Memory and Cognition, 27,* 494–500.

Strange, B.A., Hurlemann, R., & Dolan, R.J. (2003). An emotion-induced retrograde amnesia in humans is amygdala and beta-adrenergic-dependent. *Proc Natl Acad Sci USA, 100,* 13626–31.

Sullivan, E.V., Marsh, L., Mathalon, D.H., Lim, K.O., & Pfefferbaum, A. (1995). Age-related decline in MRI volumes of temporal lobe gray matter but not hippocampus. *Neurobiology of Aging, 16,* 591–606.

Suzuki, W.A., & Amaral, D.G. (2003). Where are the perirhinal and parahippocampal cortices? A historical overview of the nomenclature and boundaries applied to the primate medial temporal lobe. *Neuroscience, 120,* 893–906.

Suzuki, W.A., & Amaral, D.G. (2004). Functional neuroanatomy of the medial temporal lobe memory system. *Cortex, 40,* 220–222.

Swanson, L.W. (2003). The amygdala and its place in the cerebral hemisphere. *Annals of the New York Academy of Science, USA, 985,* 174–184.

Swanson, L.W., & Petrovich, G.D. (1998). What is the amygdala? Trends in *Neuroscience, 21,* 323–331.

Symons, C.S., & Johnson, B.T. (1997). The self-reference effect in memory: A meta-analysis. *Psychological Bulletin, 121,* 371–394.

Symons, D. (1979). *The evolution of human sexuality.* New York: Oxford University Press.

Tabert, M.H., Borod, J.C., Tang, C.Y., Lange, G., Wei, T.C., Johnson, R., et al. (2001). Differential amygdala activation during emotional decision and recognition memory tasks using unpleasant words: An fMRI study. *Neuropsychologia, 39,* 556–573.

Talarico, J.M., & Rubin, D.C. (2003). Confidence, not consistency, characterizes flashbulb memories. *Psychological Science, 14,* 455–461.

Talmi, D., Anderson, A.K., Riggs, L., Caplan, J.B., & Moscovitch, M. (2008). Immediate memory consequences of the effect of emotion on attention to pictures. *Learn Mem, 15*(3), 172–82.

Talmi, D., Luk, B.T.C., McGarry, L.M., & Moscovitch, M. (2007). The contribution of relatedness and distinctiveness to emotionally enhanced memory. *Journal of Memory and Language, 56,* 555–574.

Talmi, D., & Moscovitch, M. (2004). Can semantic relatedness explain the enhancement of memory for emotional words? *Memory and Cognition, 32,* 742–751.

Talmi, D., Schimmack, U., Paterson, T., & Moscovitch, M. (2007). The role of attention in emotional memory enhancement. *Emotion, 7,* 89–102.

Tanapat, P., Hastings, N.B., Reeves, A.J., & Gould, E. (1999). Estrogen stimulates a transient increase in the number of new neurons in the dentate gyrus of the adult female rat. *Journal of Neuroscience, 19,* 5792–5801.

Tay, T., Wang, G., Kifley, A., Lindley, R., Newall, P., & Paul-Mitchell, P. (2006). Sensory and cognitive association in older persons: Findings from an older Australian population. *Gerontology, 52,* 386–39.

Taylor, S.F., Liberzon, I., Fig, L.M., Decker, L.R., Minoshima, S., & Koeppe, R.A. (1998). The effect of emotional content on visual recognition memory: A PET activation study. *Neuroimage, 8,* 188–197.

Tekcan, A.I., Ece, B., Gülgöz, S., & Er, N. (2003). Autobiographical and event memory for 9/11: Changes across one year. *Applied Cognitive Psychology, 17,* 1057–1066.

Tekcan, A.I., & Peynircioglu, Z.F. (2002). Effects of age on flashbulb memories. *Psychology and Aging, 17,* 416–422.

Terracciano, A., McCrae, R.R., Brant, L.J., & Costa, P.T., Jr. (2005). Hierarchical linear modeling analyses of the NEO-PI-R scales in the Baltimore Longitudinal Study of Aging. *Psychology and Aging, 20,* 493–506.

Thomas, L.A., & LaBar, K.S. (2005). Emotional arousal enhances word repetition priming. *Cognition and Emotion, 19,* 1027–1047.

Thomas, R.C., & Hasher, L. (2006). The influence of emotional valence of age differences in early processing and memory. *Psychology and Aging, 21,* 821–825.

Tisserand, D.J., Visser, P.J., van Boxtel, M.P.J., & Jolles, J. (2000). The relation between global and limbic brain volumes on MRI and cognitive performance in healthy individuals across the age range. *Neurobiology of Aging, 21,* 569–576.

Tranel, D., & Hyman, B.T. (1990). Neuropsychological correlates of bilateral amygdala damage. *Archives of Neurology, 47,* 349–355.

Tsai, J.L., Levenson, R.W., & Carstensen, L.L. (2000). Autonomic, subjective, and expressive responses to emotional films in older and younger Chinese Americans and European Americans. *Psychology and Aging, 15,* 684–693.

Tulving, E. (1982). Synergistic ecphory in recall and recognition. *Canadian Journal of Psychology, 36,* 130–147.

Unger, J.W., Lapham, L.W., McNeill, T.H., Eskin, T.A., & Hamill, R.W. (1991). The amygdala in Alzheimer's disease: Neuropathology and Alz 50 immunoreactivity. *Neurobiology of Aging, 12,* 389–399.

Urry, H.L., van Reekum, C.M., Johnstone, T., Kalin, N.H., Thurow, M.E., Schaefer, H.S., Jackson, C.A., Frye, C.J., Greischar, L.L., Alexander, A.L., & Davidson, R.J. (2006). Amygdala and ventromedial prefrontal cortex are inversely coupled during regulation of negative affect and predict the diurnal pattern of cortisol secretion among older adults. *Journal of Neuroscience, 26,* 4415–4425.

Velten, E. (1968). A laboratory task for induction of mood states. *Behavioral Research Therapy, 6,* 473–482.

Vogt, L.J.K., Human, B.T., van Hoesen, G.W., & Damasio, A.R. (1990). Pathological alterations in the amygdala in Alzheimer's disease. *Neuroscience, 37,* 377–385.

Vuilleumier, P., Armony, J.L., Driver, J., & Dolan, R.J. (2001). Effects of attention and emotion on face processing in the human brain: An event-related fMRI study. *Neuron, 30,* 829–841.

Vuilleumier, P., Richardson, M.P., Armony, J.L., Driver, J., & Dolan, R.J. (2004). Distinct influences of amygdala lesion on visual cortical activation during emotional face processing. *Nature Neuroscience, 7,* 1271–1278.

Wagner, A.D., & Koutstaal, W. (2002). Priming. In V.S. Ramachandran (Ed.), *Encyclopedia of the human brain* (Vol. 4, pp. 27–46). San Diego, CA: Academic Press.

Wan, H., Aggleton, J.P., & Brown, M.W. (1999). Different contributions of the hippocampus and perirhinal cortex to recognition memory. *Journal of Neuroscience, 19,* 1142–1148.

Waring, J.D., Payne, J.D., Schacter, D.L., & Kensinger, E.A. (in press). Impact of individual differences upon emotion-induced memory trade-offs. *Cognition and Emotion.*

Watanabe, M. (1996). Reward expectancy in primate prefrontal neurons. *Nature, 382,* 629–632.

Watanabe, M. (1998). Cognitive and motivational operations in primate prefrontal neurons. *Review of Neuroscience, 9,* 225–241.

Watson, D., Clark, L.A., & Tellegen, A. (1988). Development and validation of brief measures of positive and negative affect: The PANAS scales. *Journal of Personality and Social Psychology, 54,* 1063–1070.

Weiskrantz, L.W. & William, A. The effect of ventral rhinencephalic lesions on avoidance thresholds in monkeys. *Journal of Comparative and Physiological Psychology, 51,* 167–171.

Wells, A., & Matthews, G. (1994). *Attention and emotion.* London: Lawrence Erlbaum Associates, Ltd.

White, R.T. (2002). Memory for events after twenty years. *Applied Cognitive Psychology, 16,* 603–612.

Whittington, J.E., & Huppert, F.A. (1998). Neuroticism, psychiatric symptoms and life events. *Personality and Individual Differences, 24,* 97–107.

Whittlesea, B.W.A. (1993). Illusions of familiarity. *Journal of Experimental Psychology: Learning, Memory, and Cognition, 19,* 1235–1253.

Whittlesea, B.W.A., & Williams, L.D. (2000). The source of feelings of familiarity: The discrepancy-attribution hypothesis. *Journal of Experimental Psychology: Learning, Memory, and Cognition, 26,* 547–565.

Wiggs, C.L., & Martin, A. (1998). Properties and mechanisms of perceptual priming. *Current Opinion in Neurobiology, 8,* 227–233.

Williams, J.M.G., Mathews, A., & MacLeod, C. (1996). The emotional Stroop task and psychopathology. *Psychological Bulletin, 120,* 3–24.

Williams, L.M., Brown, K.J., Palmer, D., Liddell, B.J., Kemp, A.H., Olivieri, G., et al. (2006). The mellow years?: Neural basis of improving emotional stability over age. *Journal of Neuroscience, 26,* 6422–6430.

Williams, L.M., Felmingham, K., Kemp, A.H., Rennie, C., Brown, K.J., Bryant, R.A., & Gordon, E. (2007). Mapping frontal-limbic correlates of orienting to change detection. *Neuroreport, 18,* 197–202.

Windmann, S., & Kruger, T. (1998). Subconscious detection of threat as reflected by an enhanced response bias. *Consciousness & Cognition, 7,* 603–633.

Windmann, S., & Kutas, M. (2001). Electrophysiological correlates of emotion-induced recognition bias. *Journal of Cognitive Neuroscience, 13,* 577–592.

Winograd, E., & Killinger, W.A., Jr. (1983). Relating age at encoding in early childhood to adult recall: Development of flashbulb memories. *Journal of Experimental Psychology: General, 112,* 413–422.

Wolters, G., & Goudsmit, J.J. (2005). Flashbulb and event memory of September 11, 2001: Consistency, confidence and age effect. *Psychological Report, 96,* 605–619.

Wright, C.I., Martis, B., Schwartz, C.E., Shin, L.M., Fischer, H.H., McMullin, K., et al. (2003). Novelty responses and differential effects of order in the amygdala, substantia innominata, and inferior temporal cortex. *NeuroImage, 18,* 660–669.

Wright, D.B., Gaskell, G.D., & O'Muircheartaigh, C.A. (1998). Flashbulb memory assumptions: Using national surveys to explore cognitive phenomena. *British Journal of Psychology, 89,* 103–121.

Wurm, L.H., Labouvie-Vief, G., Aycock, J., Rebucal, K.A., & Koch, H. (2004). Performance in auditory and visual emotional Stroop task: A comparison of older and younger adults. *Psychology and Aging, 19,* 523–535.

Yarmey, A.D., & Bull, M.P. (1978). Where were you when President Kennedy was assassinated? *Bulletin of the Psychonomic Society, 11*, 133–135.

Yeung, C.A., Dalgleish, T., Golden, A.M., & Schartau, P. (2006). Reduced specificity of autobiographical memories following a negative mood induction. *Behavioral Research Therapy, 44*, 1481–1490.

Yonelinas, A.P. (2002). The nature of recollection and familiarity: A review of 30 years of research. *Journal of Memory and Language, 46*, 441–517.

Zajonc, R.B. (1984). On the primacy of affect. *American Psychologist, 39*, 117–123.

Zajonc, R.B. (2001). Mere exposure: A gateway to the subliminal. *Current Directions in Psychological Science, 10*, 224–228.

Zald, D.H. (2003). The human amygdala and the emotional evaluation of sensory stimuli. *Brain Research: Brain Research Reviews, 41*, 88–123.

Zolovick, A.J. (1972). Effects of lesions and electrical stimulation of the amygdala on hypothalamic-hypophyseal regulation. In B.E. Eleftheriou (Ed.), *The neurobiology of the amygdala* (pp. 643–683). New York: Plenum Press.

AUTHOR INDEX

SUBJECT INDEX

A

accuracy, of memory 25, 28, 46, 49, 51, 69-71, 73, 75-76, 79, 82, 92, 93, 99, 128, 134-135, 146, 158
adrenal *see also* HPA axis 17, 19
affective state 8-9, 12, 92
affective working memory 130-132
Alzheimer's disease 27-28, 149-155
amnesia 15, 26, 58
amygdala 10, 14, 16-20, 34-36, 37-38, 41, 61-65, 73-76, 81-83, 88-89, 93-95, 97, 105-107, 122
amygdala damage 26-27, 57-60
amygdaloid complex *see* amygdala
anxiety 39-40, 44-45, 102, 124
arousal 6, 10, 14, 18, 35, 37-38, 74, 86, 93-100, 104, 106, 119, 123, 138, 155, 158, 160
associative memory *see* relational memory
atrophy 27, 63, 111, 115-116, 121-122, 141
attention 5-6, 12, 21, 25, 27-28, 39, 43-49, 57, 85-86, 89-90, 92, 94, 96, 101-103, 112, 116, 120, 122, 124, 128, 130, 137, 139, 141, 144, 147, 153, 155, 160
autobiographical memory 103
automatic processing 6, 21, 38, 40, 57, 94-95, 97, 103, 122, 128, 159
axes, of emotion *see also* valence, arousal 6, 10

B

backgrounds *see* scenes
basal ganglia *see also* striatum 41, 122
basolateral amygdala 18-19
Beck Anxiety Inventory 102
bias, in memory 70, 71, 73, 143, 153, 158
bilateral recruitment 116
binding deficit 114
BOLD (blood oxygen level-dependent) *see* functional magnetic resonance imaging
brain imaging *see specific imaging methods*

C

central/peripheral trade-off 85-88, 90-91, 138-140
cingulate gyrus 16, 89, 145

cognition 3-4, 17, 27, 29-30, 58, 63, 70-74, 94, 106, 111, 113, 115-116, 137-138, 146-147, 151-153
cognitive decline 3, 110-111, 149
Columbia shuttle *see also* flashbulb memory 135
compensatory activity 116
conceptual priming 40
confidence 69-71, 74, 99, 158
content 7, 11, 23-26, 35-36, 46-49, 62, 64, 76, 81-84, 87, 114, 127, 131, 137, 144, 146
context, memory for 23, 63, 69, 74-76, 79-84, 87, 110, 113-114, 116, 129, 136-138, 140
controlled processing 6, 23, 48, 52, 70, 95, 112, 122-123, 125, 129, 145, 147, 159-160
correlation 10, 20, 30, 59, 62-64, 69, 81, 111, 122, 138, 155

D

decision making 3, 130
declarative memory 15, 34, 42, 51, 53, 57, 152, 158-160
dementia *see* Alzheimer's disease
detail, memory for 6, 11, 25, 44-45, 48, 57, 63-64, 67-77, 80-89, 91-92, 96, 99-100, 105-106, 114, 116, 127, 133-134, 136-141, 144-147, 152, 156, 158-159
distinctiveness 48, 55-57, 65, 76
distortion 69-70, 76, 81
divided attention 96, 130
domain-general processes 60, 76, 79, 110-112, 160
domain-specific theory of aging 110, 113
dorsal amygdala 106

E

Easterbrook hypothesis *see also* trade-off 85-86
elaboration 22, 45, 49, 56, 97
emotion regulation 103, 121-124, 129
emotion-specific processes 54, 65, 76, 79-80
emotion state *see* affective state
emotional memory enhancement effect 27, 53, 56-58, 61, 95, 97-98, 104, 133, 149-152, 154-155, 158